Things to Come

JOHN PATTEN

Things to Come

The Tories in the 21st Century

SINCLAIR-STEVENSON

First published in Great Britain 1995
by Sinclair-Stevenson
an imprint of Reed Consumer Books Ltd
Michelin House, 81 Fulham Road, London SW3 6RB
and Auckland, Melbourne, Singapore and Toronto

Reprinted 1995

A CIP catalogue record for this book
is available from the British Library
ISBN 1 85619 591 0

Typeset by Dorchester Typesetting Group Ltd
Printed and bound in Great Britain
by Clays Ltd, St Ives plc

For Mary-Claire

Contents

Acknowledgements

My dear wife Louise suggested, in the autumn of 1994, that, having been in the House of Commons since 1979, and a member of some of the administrations since for a number of years, I might write this book. Happily, Christopher Sinclair-Stevenson agreed to publish it, and at a pace. I am most grateful to him for his encouragement and practical help. Miss Rowena Hale prepared the manuscript for the book with speed and accuracy. Mr Simon Heffer suggested its title. He was also good enough to read the final manuscript with a helpfully cruel editorial eye.

I have plundered the ideas and thoughts of a lot of people, as will be evident to them, and have been greatly helped by others. For example, those who have read the books or listened to the speeches of the Chief Rabbi, Dr Jonathan Sachs, and his predecessor, Lord Jacobovitz, will easily recognise that I have been under their spell. The distant Governor of Hong Kong, the best Prime Minister late-twentieth-century Toryism never had the chance to have, gave strictly moral support from afar. The same came, closer to home, from Mr Matthew Carrington, MP, Miss Elizabeth Fleming and Mrs Maureen Varju.

I am particularly indebted, however, to seven people for their practical assistance and inspiring ideas. The Honorary Director of the Royal Institute of Philosophy, Professor Anthony O'Hear, one of the most original contemporary British philosophers, has been selfless in giving his help. So, in exactly the same way, have Dr Sheila Lawlor and Lady O'Hagan. Mr Matthew d'Ancona and Sir Charles Powell have been very kind. The constitutional scholar and authority on Parliament, Professor Philip Norton, gave up much time. So did his one-time pupil at the University of Hull and my special adviser both at the Home Office and at the Department for Education, Mr Cliff Grantham. A paragon amongst that vital but almost wholly unsung Whitehall breed, he has been the greatest of support over five years, including while this book was being prepared. I remain entirely responsible for its contents.

It goes without saying that I gladly acknowledge my individual and collective responsibility for the unhappy as well as the happy events of the years that I served in government, and which will be referred to in these pages.

John Patten, New Year's Day, 1995

Thinking and Governing

The Tories have dominated twentieth-century British politics. Like the West End play *The Mousetrap*, we have run and run. Our running of the country has generally been to the national good. Nowhere else in the Western world has one party had such a grip on a nation's life for so long. The opposition has paid the Tory Party the ultimate political compliment of erecting its total political platform on our foundations. Yet if we are to continue to dominate the politics of the new century, then we must always be the thoughtful party, whether in government or not – and recognise that in the new politics, matters of cultural identity, of feeling secure and feeling right, are going to be just as important as feeling good.

On the eve of the twentieth century it was not then so clear that to stop thinking about what Tories believed in, why we were in the business of politics other than to seek to govern, what the long-term Tory agenda was at any time and how to carry it through, might lead to political decay. On the eve of the twenty-first century it is crystal clear that not to do that thinking means rapid political suicide.

There is nothing particular to the Tory Party in this of course: the same is true for any organisation. But if the Conservative

Party ever stops thinking then our hegemony will be broken. Any government which has held power continuously for sixteen years needs to meet, head on, feelings of boredom by the electorate, their instinct that it may be 'time for a change', the lack of respect that creeps in insidiously due to familiarity with the same faces, rhetoric or political preoccupations. It is hard enough work to govern. To think anew while governing is desperately difficult – but vital. The need is to have a clear agenda both for next year and a sense of where we wish to be in the future, in say the year 2020. If we do not do this, then we will not hold power.

Lord Quinton, that most witty of Tory philosophers, said of the problems of late-nineteenth-century Conservatism that 'the core of the crisis of Conservatism, and Conservative thought, in the late nineteenth century was a loss of faith in the superiority of ancestral collective wisdom – the superior wisdom, found in the constitution as broadly conceived, and the accumulated experience of our predecessors as embodied in traditional institutions, laws and custom.'*

Not many Tories then, on the eve of the twentieth century, probably realised that they were going through an intellectual and thus political crisis. That crisis was founded in the problems presented by generations of inherited wisdom and tradition running into the buffers that were presented by the overwhelming economic, social and educational changes of late-Victorian England. By the same token, if future historians are unhappily given the chance to look back at similar problems in Conservatism, on the eve of the twenty-first century, they would probably point again at some apparently deliberate cessation of thinking. They would describe the decision that the essence of a Conservatism suitable for the times was simply to be there, to run things, to be in government, as at the root of the problem.

The price of political complacency and intellectual stagnation is usually high. In the fairly recent history of Conservatism, we have seen it twice. Under A. J. Balfour complacency and stagnation were by-words; electoral armageddon and Liberal victory followed swiftly. Forty years later some of those same

*Anthony Quinton, *The Politics of Imperfection*, Faber, London, 1978, pp. 89–90.

characteristics were once again by-words under Baldwin and Chamberlain. This approach led inevitably to the post-war electoral assassination of the Tories by Labour. It was a result delayed only by the long years of world conflict. If the Second World War had not happened, then any election of the late 1930s would have produced a result similar in style, if not in magnitude. This is despite the fact that the newly established opinion polls of 1938/9 showed significant Tory leads in issues like the economic recovery.

It is certainly not much in the British character to yearn after blueprints from their politicians. We do not greatly like the abstract, being a pragmatic sort of nation, nor do we care for dogma. In any event, also consistent with the British character, one year's accusations of dogmatism – as over the sale of council houses in the early 1980s – soon becomes another year's accepted and conventional wisdom. But not lusting after dogma must not mean an end of ideas. They are as critical to the Tory Party now and in the future as they were to our past.

If being dogmatic is not particularly British, then visions and visionaries are also alien to our culture: the scepticism which marks the way we view things reinforces the cynicism that most west Europeans have naturally always felt towards their governors bearing big ideas.

In any event big ideas occur only sparingly in any century. The United Kingdom has used up its scant twentieth-century ration with the post-war socialist settlement of welfarism and nationalisation, followed with an almost iron inevitability by the reversion after 1979 to traditional ideas of freedom, personal endeavour and ownership.

The problem for practising politicians is reinforced by the historical impact of these big ideas. Because they are striking and understood, most politicians think they had better have them as well. This is a delusion. More political time has been wasted in the fruitless search for this year's big, or next year's bigger, idea than can be counted.

But, clear ideas and a clearer agenda, underpinned by a sense of history and philosophy, are critical to any party which wishes to do good by holding power. That is why, in the process of winning elections, thought is quite as valuable a commodity as money. Most elections are pretty close. The 1992 election was closer still, and enough of a white-knuckle job for any Conservative. A latter-day diarist might well have recorded of that political battle something similar to Creevy's nineteenth-century account of a relieved but triumphant Duke of Wellington after Waterloo, 'It's been a damned nice thing – the nearest run thing you ever saw in your life . . .' At times of political difficulty – and most months bring some little cloud no bigger than a woman's hand which might just turn into a political horror – all sorts of abilities are necessary in the make-up of the Prime Minister, Ministers, and party managers of the day. They need tactical expertise, managerial ability, and the knack of persuading the media to go this way rather than that. None of these attributes, in the long run at least, will see a government through unless it is firmly founded on an agenda, based on clear thinking, which is understood by both politicians and public alike. Thus, to mix generals, Tories should also remember what Marshal Foch said, 'My centre is giving way, my right is in retreat; situation excellent. I shall attack!' In politics, outside the bearpit of the House of Commons or away from the lamps of the television studio, the best form of attack always is to think. That is what this book is about.

Its sole thesis is that the Tory Party must always be the thoughtful Party. That it must demonstrate that it has a clear view of where Britain should be going, not just next year or at the next general election or after the next general election but well into the next century. Writing in 1976, that great Conservative Party historian, Lord Blake, observed, 'Political parties seldom philosophize when in office. Their leaders are too preoccupied by administrative pressures, too concerned with immediate concerns to have the leisure to reflect on the broad purposes for which their party exists.'* He was correct. But political parties seldom spend seventeen or eighteen consecutive years in office either. In doing so, we must never forget to show the

*Lord Blake and John Patten (eds.), *The Conservative Opportunity*, Macmillan, London, 1976, p. 1.

electorate that we have a very clear map of where we are going next. We have to tell them about the road we are travelling on. We have to explain how this will help make their lives better.

Political gossip is fascinating to many, though political ideas and discourses are barely acceptable in much of polite society. Thus it is vital for the Conservative Party – if it is to go on governing – to escape from the cycle of apparently only philosophising when in opposition, only administering when in office. We failed to break this cycle towards the end of the thirteen years of Tory rule beginning in 1951; we must not repeat it in the 1990s. 'Change is Our Friend' was the title of a Conservative Central Office pamphlet in 1955 – it should stand as an admirable and timeless motif on every Conservative's wall.

Every now and then, it is possible to come across Conservatives beguiled by the notion that it is necessary to have a bit of political convalescence in opposition from time to time. Their siren song runs that, away from the debilitating daily burdens that accompany high office, and out of the penetrating glare of the media spotlight, the Party will be able to recharge its intellectual batteries and think afresh its approach. In other words, only out of office is it possible for Conservatives to 'reflect on the broad purposes of Conservatism' in the way that Lord Blake spoke of some twenty years ago. They believe a (hopefully brief) spell in opposition will be a price worth paying in order to get the Conservative Party back on whatever track they feel it should be on, rediscovering a sense of purpose, and setting out some new agenda for the future.

These siren voices are not only daft but downright dangerous. A period in opposition can be no guaranteed panacea to a party geared, as the Conservative Party is, to governance. Nor would it necessarily be brief. It cannot always be as it was between 1945 and 1951, for example, with a Butler rethinking the Tory script, and a Labour Party in office exhausting itself in six whirlwind years implementing the big ideas of their script.

These dangerous voices also ignore the fact that people tend to vote in general elections on the record of the Party in office and much less on the ideas of their opponents. Myths have grown up about this: for example, that there was a 'golden age' of Tory renewal between 1975 and 1979 based on fresh thinking and the setting of new agendas which swept all before it in the election that year. It certainly was a period of deep thinking, led by Keith Joseph, who helped Margaret Thatcher to distil our new approach, culminating in that splendid little document which was so seminal in the late 1970s, 'The Right Approach'. It did not seem like that at the time, however. I was then a Fellow of a College in Oxford, as well as being Conservative candidate for that city. It was with impatience, but considerable nervousness, that I sat there waiting for Mr Callaghan's announcement in the autumn of 1978 as to whether or not he would call a general election. The bright thinking that we all identify with 20:20 hindsight had barely brushed across my consciousness.

Although I was an assiduous reader of Central Office handouts and pamphlets, the idea of some long-term strategy, let alone the existence of a new 'big idea' about to wash over the country, was not obvious. However, what was clear to me was that the result of an election in that autumn would be very finely balanced, and that it depended entirely on the electorate's view of the record of the Wilson/Callaghan years. So, I recall it was with a sense of enormous relief that I heard Mr Callaghan's serious-jokey announcement that he would not be holding an election, for certainly in the city of Oxford we would not that year have won back the seat from Labour, as we were to do by a whisker in the spring of 1979. It was the disastrous record of the Wilson/ Callaghan years of the mid to late 1970s that was more responsible than any bright new opposition ideas for getting us back into power by a smallish majority in 1979. As much as the general public understood Conservative thinking, they were often fearful of it. It was just a case of being more fed up with all those uncollected bags of rubbish, untreated patients and unburied dead of the winter of discontent.

The cerebration that had begun in the Thatcher/Joseph years went on and developed, in the saddle, throughout the early and mid-1980s. Then was the time that it really hit the national consciousness. It is not only possible, it is imperative, to continue to think just like this in government, or the punishment will be severe. The period in opposition could be permanent, save in a coalition.

For if there were a Labour/Liberal administration following the next general election and the constitution-mongers – in particular the advocates of electoral reform – get their way then a period in opposition for the Tory Party may prove to be an enduring one. Thus, if we want to see off this threat, let alone win a sixth term thereafter (which is quite within our grasp) then it is vital that the government does exactly what Lord Blake doubted any could do: that it philosophises while in office, rejuvenates itself intellectually, and therefore politically, while continuing to run things.

None of this means perpetual political excitement and tumult. It does mean a firm hand on matters, and a continuing search for the Holy Grail of 'good government'. Competent and effective administration, or the perception that this ideal exists, is always going to be crucial to Tory political fortunes. But 'consolidation' will never be a sufficient condition for perpetuating the Tory grip on power. If Conservatives ever leave an intellectual vacuum at the heart of the political debate, then it will soon be filled by others. There is no such thing as 'masterful' inactivity in politics: that reaps its own cruel rewards. If regular in-flight refuelling with fresh thinking is vital for long-distance government, so is a clear flight plan.

The relationship between the Conservative Party in government and the British people should always be like a 'good marriage' – there may be times of stress and difficulty, but always a bed-rock of mutual understanding to carry us through. These days it is getting more and more difficult for politicians to be loved when they are in power. That is particularly difficult for any government when the national or economic situation has not been cheerful. All Western governments have felt the backlash of that during the world recession. The British people may from time to time feel they have fallen out of love with the Conservative Party, or that it is not worth living with them at present – but like that good marriage, provided what brought elector and elected together in the first place is still there, and the elected remain true to it, then breakdowns will be temporary and political flirtation will turn out to be just that.

So I do not believe that the British people should ever fall out of love with what the Conservative Party stands for, with the basic principles and beliefs that combine together to form the bed-rock of modern Conservatism. This is because Conservative instincts are closely calibrated with basic British instincts. If the British electorate, this year or next, appears to be rallying to the cause of the opposition parties, then it is because they no longer see them as posing the same threat to the happy political marriage. The opposition may have moved many of their tents on to Tory ground; we should rejoice a bit at that, and keep moving our own tents forward, not in the pursuit of some brand-new political end, but first in order to get the chance to complete what we began in 1979. We must never forget what we started, and what it is all about. We have to drive home that the Conservative Party is the only rightful heir of the Conservative changes which began in that year. These may take another fifteen years or so to see through to fulfilment. At the same time we must recognise that some of our best friends think that we have moved closer to opposition policies, on welfare and spending, for example.

The task now facing the Conservative Party is thus to demonstrate not just that it is dealing with the fag end of an elderly agenda set in 1979, but rather that it remembers what and why it started and how it intends to build on the changes that followed, as well as introducing new thinking to the needs and changing circumstances of Britain in the twenty-first century.

Therefore, Tories need to complete the agenda as well as think anew. Ideas and the Conservative Party have not always been thought of as obvious bedfellows. John Stuart Mill's description of the Tories in the nineteenth century as 'the stupidest party' was not entirely unwarranted. Certainly Conservatives traditionally show a healthy disdain for abstract, foreign-sounding theorising. It has long been a central tenet of Conservative belief that complex problems in society are not amenable to ultimate solutions, by grand design or government blueprint. I hold to that. Politicians do not and must not try to create things – 'build worlds', 'shape societies', and the rest. It is rather up to the people of the country to do so, if they choose. Thus Conservative politicians must be modest in trying to design and build in some authoritarian way. In their striving to provide opportunities and frameworks, they must be rather determined to steer – not to row

– the nation's life. But a healthy scepticism for political philosophy, or what the Americans will call 'policy wonks' bearing big new ideas, can never exonerate us from taking a view about how we want Britain to look as we approach the twenty-first century.

Since the late 1970s we have occupied the intellectual high political ground in this country. No one disputes that. Other political parties have thrown themselves ineffectually against the rocks that we have built, and now try to pitch their tents amongst the foothills of our ideas. We have raised the level of political discourse to a new paradigm. The 'stupidest party' has turned one hundred and eighty degrees – witness the rampant me-tooism that so marks out opposition political thinking in 1995. Such a seismic shift in Britain's political geology has not come about by accident. The recent Tory times were born of a clear strategy and have rested on the willingness of successive Conservative governments to eschew short-term expediency in favour of the long-term view. Conservative budgets in the early 1980s, deliberately deflating an economy in recession, are some of the best exemplars of just that. If to do that was 'visionary', then it was not necessarily seen as such at the time, rather than as an intensely pragmatic approach. Indeed the word 'vision' is perhaps the most abused and over-used piece of modern political parlance – except, that is, when the word 'initiative' pops up. 'Initiative' should certainly be expunged from the lexicons of all serious politicians, because of its publicity-conscious, here today, gone tomorrow quality, putting ephemera and expediency ahead of long-term strategy. Neither an undergrowth of initiatives nor broad visionary uplands are needed, so much as a clear perception – instantly understandable on any one day – of where we are going as a Party.

'Mid-term manifestos' have sometimes been toyed with as being a good thing for a Conservative government to have, forcing it to think and set down its ideas. The understandable argument against such political artifices is that they are hostages to fortune, and that the only manifesto that matters is on the eve of a general election campaign. In the tough old world of practical politics, alas, that may be true – but it does not exonerate any of us from getting about the business of thinking while running matters.

There are some who doubt the wisdom of this approach even if they think it is desirable. They are part of the hard core of a school of thought within the Conservative Party which argues that it is unnecessary to the Party's electoral fortunes and that people will invariably and inevitably, according to some iron law, cast their vote in the forthcoming election on the basis of just three issues: the economy, the economy, and the economy. For the Conservative Party in government to plunder its intellectual resource banks on other issues, they protest, is merely a distraction from the main objective of reigniting the 'feel-good' factor. Only by getting political and economic cycles back into close synchronisation will electoral rewards come, the argument runs.

Feeling good is an entirely understandable human attribute; and feeling good in a consumer-driven country such as we live in now is often based on pounds in pockets. Thus to understate the importance of the economy to the government's prospects at any election would be sheer folly. Whatever the voters may say to the pollsters during the privacy of a telephone conversation, or when faced with a clip board on a street corner or even when brought together to be questioned in a 'focus group' – to use the unlovely jargon of that unlovely subject psephology – matters nought compared with where they put their cross in the polling booth at the time of an election. And when they come to place those crosses, many will understandably place a high emphasis on what they believe to be the implications of their decision for their own disposable incomes and thus for their families' welfare. In other words, as has been so obvious throughout my political lifetime, people often bemuse pollsters because they wish to punish the government for something it has done or not done or simply because they are bored with it. Being asked how you would vote if there was a general election tomorrow is not the same as having that decision in front of you on the neatly franked ballot paper, with the real implications for you and your family. I always used to think that in a Parliament's mid-term, people told lies to pollsters, and subsequently the truth at general election time; but even that has changed, as general election exit-polls have shown with people coming out and, not to put too fine a point on it, lying to passing pollsters about what they have just done. Indeed the disparity in some general election exit-polls between projection and result can only be explained by Conservative voters not owning up.

Why is this? Perhaps it is the sort of double standards amongst the electorate that they so freely accuse us of having. But maybe this habit, most marked in the last couple of elections, also heralds a new feeling amongst the electorate: that it is not only the economy that should be influencing their voting. I am certain that a demonstrable economic 'feel-good' effect will be one necessary prerequisite to electoral success. But I do not believe that it will always be a sufficient one. Remember George Bush? Even if economic recovery turns into one of those golden economic periods, I do not think that will guarantee that the Conservative Party does more than retain the support of its core electoral base, perhaps thirty-three or thirty-five per cent of the electorate as a whole. Winning the confidence and the votes of the decisive further eight to ten per cent in order to carry us through the winning line is going to be a progressively more and more difficult task. So it is not just the British economy and competitiveness, it is also a matter of the British constitution, the British community, the British family, and the way in which we Britons live now and want to live in the future.

These issues will resonate with increasing loudness from the British people, for in the twenty-first century neither rhetoric nor pocket book will do the trick. But before we can look to the future it is both vital as well as instructive to look to the past. It always has been a central canon of Conservatism that Conservatives look to experience, to what has happened, in order to appreciate what is possible in the future. That is why Conservatives are instinctive builders rather than destroyers. And what we have to build on are the formidable achievements of the Conservative revolution of the 1980s and 1990s. To do that, it is necessary in mid-1995 to assess the state of play after sixteen years of Tory rule.

What does the balance sheet look like? Well, it has been a bravish and pretty successful period. When the Conservative Party was returned to office in 1979 it set about transforming British

politics. The scale of the change was as radical as anything experienced in this country this century: that includes the extraordinary transformation which Labour brought about post-1945.
It is hard to do anything else save admit more than a sneaking
admiration for Labour's vision and energy, even though they
broke themselves on the further shores of the agenda they had. It
was, however, all over in six politically exciting years; we by
comparison have had sixteen so far. 'Revolution' is not a word I
like any more than 'consolidation', yet that is what has happened
in its own very Conservative way. It was 'Conservative revolution' because we are opposed to change for change's sake. We
have, or should have, a deep attachment to things as they
presently exist. We should only seek to fix things when they are
really broken. I do not think anyone would dispute, including
Labour historians, that what we faced in 1979 was a country
badly in need of change. Parts of it quite clearly were 'broke'.
The political and administrative chaos of the winter of 1978–9
was hard to predict, and it is difficult to remember as reality; it
is necessary to pinch yourself to believe that it all was true.
Had Lord Archer written the scenario into one of his novels,
people would have thought such a backcloth for electoral may-
hem simply fanciful.

The theme of the 1951 Conservative manifesto was 'Set the
Country Free'. That is exactly what Conservative governments
since 1979 have set out to achieve. They have set individuals free
to pursue their own ambitions, each doing what she or he wishes
within a framework of law; each able to make the most of life,
free as far as possible of imposition from 'above' or from 'them',
be they central government, local authorities, trade unions, or
restrictive practices, much protected by the law and much loved
by interest groups and the professions.

Even the most minimalist of Conservatives has always recognised some rôle for government, however, not least in protecting
the realm from external attack and maintaining the Queen's
peace at home. Also, and as important for the Conservative, is
the parallel theme that the government must do something to
help those unable to fend for themselves. But these themes have
always been matched by a recognition that government is not

infallible and a large state machine undesirable. Hence the Tory emphasis during recent times on the individual, the family, and ownership, for we believe that they are the best judges of their own needs and those of their loved ones. The same applies to the nation's communities; I draw back from using the all-embracing word 'society', for it has always seemed to me an absurd generalisation to suggest that 'society feels this or that'. Mrs Thatcher was correct when she said 'There is no such thing as society', however much those words later came back to bite her. There is a United Kingdom, and within that, many mansions; individuals, families, extended families, and communities – but all fifty-six million citizens cannot be lumped together under the single heading of 'society'. So since 1979 we have striven hard to ensure that as long as no harm is done to others, individuals should be as free as possible to pursue their own lives. But we also recognise that freedom has its costs. There is also a clear set of duties. The minimum duty is not to harm others; this is policed by the authority of the state. But we also recognise that there is a strong moral responsibility to go beyond that and to think about and care for others in the community. That very responsibility makes a substantial difference to the quality of life and also serves as the ultimate protector of our freedom within the law.

These past sixteen years have seen a formidable set of achievements. Britain is respected within the world; it has strong defences and has behaved with honour in international matters, though hardly with complete success over Europe. Any grown-up Conservative has to admit that for the rest of his or her adult life the European question is going to be the issue likely to cause most dissent and unease. Apart from Europe, the top issues are as always on the home front. They illustrate what we have done and what we can be reasonably boastful about; but at the same time demonstrate how very much further the Tories have to go.

These are making the virtues of diversity understood and accepted; shrinking the state; spreading ownership further; tackling inflation; reducing taxation; reforming trade unions; privatising; persuading people of the benefits of taking responsibility as well as ownership; helping the consumer, the parent, the patient and the tenant; and freeing the professions.

Making a Virtue of Diversity

Central to what we believe in are diversity and choice. But Tories have to recognise that words are not enough. We have tried to put into place more diverse forms of social provision, for example, GP fund-holding practices or National Health Service Trusts or grant-maintained schools. But the absurdity is that having spoken so warmly of diversity we are then accused of introducing inequity or two-tierism.

We have yet to persuade people that our belief in diversity, which is so central to modern Conservative thinking, and which should underpin a thoroughly post-modern Conservatism fit for the twenty-first century, is in their interest. We have only got so far in this process; that is one of the reasons why the next election is so crucial for the Conservative Party, for if the momentum we have gained thus far is lost, the work could be undone. Instead, the British people could find ourselves facing an entirely different interpretation of what community means – and in the case of the modern Labour and Liberal Parties this would amount to giving the maximum responsibility to town halls and reinvented forms of bureaucracy and interest groups, with new and un-British forms of proportional representation.

That is what opposition talk of devolution and regional assemblies is all about – and that is what a reformed House of Lords would end up as: not just the present mixture of hereditary and appointed senatorial figures mixed with the occasional Anglican bishop and the all too occasional ex-Chief Rabbi, but also, it seems, institutionalised positions for everyone from the Association of County Councils and the Police Federation via the Teachers' Unions to the Director of the Institute of Directors and the Director General of the CBI – and please don't forget the Chairmen of each of the new regional assemblies, from Wessex to Severn-Trent and back again.

That is not a form of diversity, but rather a way of institutionalising vested interests, and the increasingly powerful and effective – I take my hat off to them – lobbyists who have so spiritedly made single-issue politics part of the warp and weft of how we live now. There would be no more Tory diversity under that dispensation, no more chance of people running their own schools or perhaps running care in the community as they should – and certainly none of the local pay bargaining that teachers or doctors should, in the real world, be faced with. We have not really done more than clear the brush from the edge of the forest of this agenda.

Shrinking the State

We have been very successful in shrinking the state by disposing of much of what it owned. The government still owns too much, however, everything from the Post Office and the British Waterways Board to the Covent Garden Market Authority and the Scottish Transport Group. We should now dispose of everything that remains by 1999, so the new century can begin with a clean slate. It may not have seemed so at the time, but the business of privatising state industries was relatively easy. Compared to law and order, for example, where many wish us to go faster, we have always run ahead of our membership on privatisation, and need to be constantly persuasive about the benefits. Much more difficult has proved to be the task of shrinking government itself. The state still spends annually more than forty per cent of what the nation produces. Heroic and successful attempts have been made to reduce the size of the civil service, including the highest levels in such Temples of Administration as Her Majesty's Treasury itself. None the less it is imperative that we do not enter the twenty-first century as big-government Conservatives, having gulled ourselves into thinking that well-run, Conservative – but none the less big – government is a good thing.

Some may criticise us for having paused in the task simply because of the political difficulties combined with a feeling that in modern times it is beyond even the most vigorous. It is possible to point at not just the size but the ever growing tentacles of the social security system, which consume more than a third of what government spends, and say that the task is beyond us. Against this background it is also all too easy to just substitute the rhetoric and posturing of what might be thought of as 'social Toryism' – attacking single parents or deploring divorce – for the horrible difficulties of trying to rein in the welfare state and restrain some of its unhappy side effects.

This is painful stuff for Tories. Given that we are the Party of capitalism, and given that a majority of our fellow countrymen either are or, just as important, aspire to be middle class, there is always the danger that future Conservatism will mutate into nothing more than middle-class self-interest. To ensure that this does not happen, this means disobliging vested interests from time to time – not always a politically beneficial thing to do. It also means recognising that being against big bureaucracies does not necessarily mean being against government action. Much of the Tory dilemma in the next century, if we wish to travel through it as small government men and women, is just how to turn such rhetorical generalities as 'you are paying too much tax' into the public spending realities that have to follow. If they do not, and to do so may mean saying no to middle-class constituents, then it is impossible really to lighten the load, and have smaller government.

In other words, rather as over privatisation or selling council houses back in the heroic days of 1979, we have to decide whether or not we really wish to go hard for minimal government. If we decide that this is off-limits or too exhausting, then we will simply rest on our historic laurels. Unhappily, we will thus also have not very much of weight to say to the twenty-first century. We will have decided to concede by stealth a victory to post-war socialism, in as much as we give up on trying to rein in government's instincts to capture wealth and recycle it to the loudest lobbies or to its closest political allies. So, if we decide that working for smaller government is on our agenda, it will mean offending some, being accused of neglecting the interests of others. But to limit government means to benefit families and the community. The lives of our constituents are best served by more liberty, not greater dependency. That liberty can come only from smaller government.

Ownership

Where we have been notably successful is in promoting private ownership. This is not just a matter of doing what is right –

which it is – nor of gaining electoral advantage for a while – which it generally does – for to confer ownership diffuses power. To own their own home is a fundamental desire of most individuals. Indeed every recent public opinion poll reveals that between eighty and ninety per cent of those people questioned want to 'own their own home', and at least for some of them that would be unobtainable. Why do they want this? It gives people a sense of purpose, a private environment in which to live to sleep and eat, to recreate and possibly to bring up a family – or perhaps to house some older member of your own family. Ownership of property however, above all else, is a good thing because it instils a sense of responsibility within the wider community. Since 1979 the idea that home ownership is a good thing has now become the common property of all political parties, and is permanently embedded in our social landscape. The great parliamentary battles to let council tenants buy their own homes, which were fought clause by clause across the face of a number of Bills, now seem the stuff of ancient history. Yet they only happened at the beginning of the 1980s.

Today, more than seven out of ten people own their own homes. To the immense moral profit of families and the social benefit of the nation, we have promoted the home-owning democracy which was once only a dream. But we need to go further, to continue to make it possible for more and more people to get a fingerhold on the sometimes perilous cliff that home ownership represents. There are always risks, some people will muddle their affairs, and not just those at the margins of home ownership either. The rich, too, may over-extend themselves. To that extent home ownership is a bit of a gamble, but we must let people have their own space in which to take their own risks – that is something which is entirely Conservative.

The promotion of ownership should not be confined to the chance of possessing a house or a flat or a farm. The opportunities to share in the prosperity of the nation have expanded enormously through our parallel promotion of share ownership, and the related movement towards personal pension schemes. The number of people owning shares more than trebled after 1979 to over eleven million in 1991. Since then it has fallen quite sharply to nine million. So we are far from an investing country yet; and just as with home ownership, we need to go further. An active Conservative government over the next fifteen years will find ways of promoting as much investment in shares as there is in property, where this is possible consistent with people's income. Share owning should be more than just investing in some ex-public utility. We have not begun to convince enough people that they should be investing in growing companies. That is why it is so important that the City is properly self-regulated, and that financial advice given to individual investors, or those who want to take out a personal pension scheme, is as well founded as possible, to give a sense of reasonable security while taking some risk.

Tackling Inflation

High inflation rates are a curse for industry, for exporters in particular, for those on fixed incomes, and, after a while, even for those in the retail sector or who trade in houses.

For those on fixed incomes, such as pensioners, inflation can be especially pernicious, destroying the capacity to purchase and hence the range of choice available, and making what might be a rather tight old age positively miserable as inflation bites into whatever nest egg has been put aside. The desire to fight inflation was one of the things which brought my generation into politics in the 1970s. It looks as though at long last the beast has been brought to bay. We made a cracking start in the early part of the 1980s, deflating during the world recession. When the good times came in 1987 and 1988 we let it slip the leash, by trying to suppress the market value of the pound sterling through reducing interest rates fast. Inflation roared off again as a result, although not to 1970s socialist levels. The lesson is obvious to us all. I think that it will last a generation, because of all the associated horrors which came with it, like booming house prices that were swiftly followed by the Nemesis of negative equity. Central to the Tory canon has been that a low inflation rate is a *sine qua non* of economic stability. Letting inflation get out of control was a great failure by us all. Getting inflation under control since is one of the greatest achievements of the present government.

Reducing Income Tax

One of the reasons for Conservative victory in 1979 was discontent with high and punitive rates of taxation under a Labour government, exemplified by Denis Healey's promise to induce 'howls of anguish' from the middle classes, and faint echoes of that bullish roar are still to be heard today from Labour's political pygmies who promise to persecute the 'undeserving rich'. Dislike of riches and of endeavour is as prominent in the opposition parties as an instinct not to spend, to cut where possible, and at all costs to reduce taxation is an enduring feature of Conservatism.

Successive Conservative governments have reformed the tax structure, simplified the rates of tax, and reduced income tax – again to levels that few can recall from the past. Throughout, we have felt that the higher the level of personal income the greater degree of individual freedom in deciding on what to spend it, or in what ways to save and invest it. Again, paying the price of both our own economic management in 1987 and 1988, and the world recession, the overall burden of taxation remains too high. Once it is prudent, taxation must resume the downward primrose path.

Trades Union Reform

The power of the trade unions has been reined in. The historic grip they had on the Labour Party has been loosened, and I think that is to the national good. Many in the Labour Party seem to share the same view. The power of a few union leaders to disrupt the economic life of the nation has been broken. So has the capacity of union magnates to dictate policy to their members. In effect, power has been given back to the individual members of trade unions.

The effects have been startling. The number of days lost

through industrial action is lower than at any point since records began in the 1890s – this has been a crucial factor in attracting so much (and greatly needed) inward investment into this country. It has also given self-respect back to management, and good management makes money that pays taxes which pays for welfare. The problems of British industry reside, therefore, no longer so much in matters of labour relations, but in trying to lever up our methods of production to reach those which are so common in the Far East and elsewhere. If industry can do that, the economic advantages will be immense.

Responsibility

Giving people not only the chance to keep and spend more of their own money for the benefit of their own families, but also to take more responsibility, is a huge Tory idea. We are still only scratching the surface of what is a very deep political mine. It offers the same rich possibilities as ownership; and ownership underpins the very taking of responsibility. We should give people greater scope to create a more civic society for themselves, consistent with the fine old Tory principles of ownership and responsibility. The Conservative message, as we open up this second front for a new century, is that the local and mixed are much better that the bureaucratic and uniform. The practical Tory message should be that as much in social as in economic affairs, we will strive to give people a better deal and enhance their opportunities in a new century. The moral component of this message is just as powerful, for it marries the benefits of ownership to the imperatives of responsibility.

Helping Consumer, Parent, Patient and Tenant

The Citizen's Charter, the much derided and laughed at middle-sized idea (and useful movement) has given the individual consumer of public services the right to know precisely what to expect from public bodies. People now understand a bit more about what standards to expect from public servants. It bestows real rather than paper rights and gives information to individuals. This theme of more information is part and parcel of the Tory way of doing things since 1979, for to the surprise of many we have been the most open and accountability-conscious government this century. But with this increasing accountability and openness have come raised expectations, and the new phenomenon of government-appointed bodies sometimes becoming as unpopular as local authorities used to be. A pressing task for Tories as the new century dawns is to redefine accountability. We need to explain how communities are going to be bound together increasingly, how they are going to express their preferences clearly, at a time when central government and local authorities are – or should be – shrinking.

Educational reforms are a helpful case in point. They have been amongst the most extensive ever attempted in this country since state education first began, followed by universal secondary education and then access to all who are qualified in our universities. These have given more power to the parents of school-age children and to their local communities. Parents now have a say in the choice of school for their children. They, along with other members of the community, now also have a real stake in the running of local schools.

The publication of information in the performance tables, once ridiculed but now eagerly awaited, has not only pinpointed the schools that cause concern and highlighted the schools that deserve pats on the back for their performance; it has also exposed how much more needs to be done in the United Kingdom to get a higher performing, more competitive education system. Highly popular moves towards the local management of schools – once viciously attacked by teacher union and self-interested local authority alike – and the still contentious introduction of self-governing status have also made schools and colleges more accountable to the communities they serve. All our universities are now self-governing; all our Further Education Colleges are now self-governing as well; we have been too hesitant, however, in going the whole hog with grant-maintained schools. In education, we have thus become victims of our own democratic instincts, and the pace of progress has contributed to unfair claims of two-tierism in the provision of schools, making easy targets for opposition attacks.

It has been the same with health service reform. General practitioner fund-holding is right. We introduced it because we thought it was better, because it gave power and influence to local GP practices. However, to hold true to ideas of devolution we let it be optional. The benefits were self-evident and clear, with doctors controlling their own budget; this is an innate good. So, we need to move as far and as fast as we can with GP fund-holding, in exactly the same way as with grant-maintained schools.

Performance in the health service is, happily, now also revealed through the publication of much information for hospitals. And again, neither vested interest nor opposition parties have been able to do any more than complain about the introduction, and then come to terms with the reality. Once the cat of information is out of the bag, neither the political consumer nor a watchful media will ever let it be put back in again.

For those who want to rent their own homes we have not done very well. We still have the most atrophied rented sector in the Western world. The right to rent is as important as the right to own property. It encourages people to invest their money in things other than bricks and mortar, like getting a company going; it helps mobility and satisfies the perfectly valid demands of those who don't wish to be tied to ownership. At the pre-election 'Next Step Forward' Bournemouth Conservative Conference of 1986 there was much about the 'right to rent'. We have tried hard since to turn words into reality through successive Housing Acts but we are bogged down. We must take the issue of renting by the scruff of the neck and make it as much common political ground as home ownership has now become.

Freeing the Professions

It has not only been the trade unions who in the past have employed restrictive practices. The professions have too. Some have felt the wind of change over the last sixteen years, notably the legal profession. Most have been successful in resisting change, however, and it is a major stumbling block for any Conservative government that so many of its natural supporters are in exactly those professions where particular and strongly defended vested interests remain. And of course some of these vested interests are not just interested, in a professional sense, in making money, but rather quite as much in controlling the political agenda in their worlds: power over what is happening is the real issue for professions from lawyers to teaching and back again.

Sometimes professionals indeed know best; that is their art or science. But on other occasions the nature and rate of progress is a matter of public and therefore governmental concern. Bringing about necessary change in the interest of citizen and taxpayer – and in the end having control of the agenda – is going to be one of the most pressing tasks for government in the twenty-first century.

What is the overall verdict on the balance sheet so far? So far, not at all bad. It is quite an enviable record. With the concurrence or acceptance of the British people, Conservatism since 1979 has wrought changes few imagined possible and some, like me, did not even foresee in the run-up to that election. So much so, that many who previously opposed these changes now accept them entirely. The Conservatives have set the agenda; led the way; and with a few notable setbacks have completed a lot of tasks. Philosophically others now follow in our wake.

But the agenda has not yet been worked through; some serious mistakes have been made on the way; there are a number of outstanding and pressing matters waiting to be tackled or completed. That is not to take for granted, or as read, the uniqueness of the Conservatives' approach since 1979 set against the political history of the rest of the century. No other party taking office has ever sought to challenge so explicitly so many of the previously held assumptions about the way we live our lives. No party has ever before confronted the entrenched attitudes that build up in all societies, and in the end harm all societies. No party has ever squared up to the nation's alternative power bases – the trade unions, the town halls, the professional associations – and sought to domesticate them. And no party this century has ever consciously sought to transfer so much power and responsibility from the centre, from the hub of the wheel to its rim – taking power from Whitehall and the town hall and giving it to communities and individual citizens.

Not surprisingly, mistakes have been made and not everything has worked wonderfully. We got carried away by our own apparent clarity of thought and then a burst of Party Conference rhetoric to introduce the Community Charge; we suffered from a lack of clarity in deciding that unitary authorities were right for local government in Scotland and Wales, but then let confusion and muddle reign in the way in which we have set about the task in England. We ran into turmoil over school testing. Sometimes we have decided not to face down opposition, or let progress be impeded by it, as in the case of some of the health and education reforms. Joining the ERM became the mother of all mistakes made since 1979. Much of the time, much of the real opposition has come not from the official opposition, which has spent sixteen largely wasted and unthinking years out of office, but rather from the professional pressure groups and Tory backbenches. Their campaigning zeal and excellence has at times left not only the opposition but sometimes the government in the shade.

If it is important to remember mistakes, and even more to memorise their lessons, then it is critical to have on our radar screen the big targets for the future. There are six which this book addresses as the keys to Conservative political discourse and action in the twenty-first century.

Firstly, what are the timeless Tory principles, and how are they going to apply in future? Exactly which of our collected and ancestral experiences and attitudes will help us, like the Greek commander Nestor, to deal with 'The giant mass of things to come'.*

Precisely what is it going to mean to be a Conservative in the new century? We have to be clear about this. It is spitting in the

---

Troilus and Cressida, Act One, Scene iii.

wind to suggest for a moment that we can anticipate everything that we will have to meet. Politics is a sudden and unexpected business, with events crowding in and splendid opportunities presenting themselves. Sometimes they seem to be there only to be stumbled over. Sometimes it is possible to run away with the political swag. So pragmatism, which means acting in the best interests of Britain, is always going to be a guiding light; Conservative principles are there as flames to light us, not chains to bind us. There are certainly some things we can foresee. A number are tangible – like how on earth do we meet the needs of an ageing population? – and these cannot be gainsaid or pushed to one side. Others are more intangible but very much there. What should Conservatives do to meet the aspirations of an increasingly 'rights'-conscious population? Pure political futurology is a mug's game, but planning for a political future is best done rooted in the Conservative past.

Secondly, and against the background of the European drama, we need to articulate much more clearly what it is going to mean to be British in the new century. We will certainly have to restate our identity while recognising that the longer we remain in office the more both the Union and the Conservative Party will come under threat from a dangerous coalition of an alliance of the discontented who believe the only way to break our quasi-permanent hold on office is actually to break up the Union.

All good Tories need to come to the aid of our constitution and argue vigorously in defence of the Union. 'The Union' is one of those seemingly abstract principles which is, so political wise-acres say, not of much interest to the general public – but the campaign fought north of the border in Scotland before the last election, on precisely this issue, was, it is said, enough to save us some seats there. Ulster's future is critical.

Until recently, sheer laziness mixed with a curious indifference has accounted for a lack of Conservative interest in the constitution as a whole. We have not even bothered to get much on to the field, giving a clear run to the constitution-mongers, the charterists, and the carefree importers of foreign legal systems, who collectively would do such damage to our country.

We now need to look not at the framework of our existing

constitution but rather at the particular parts. In other words, the parts of our constitution that could operate more effectively and efficiently. I am conscious of some of the limitations of existing structures and procedures. We need to look afresh at the rights of individual citizens; but we also need to see whether the way in which they are governed can be improved. The rôle of Ministers, Parliament, Europe, all of these have to be consciously examined. Unless the Conservative Party has the political will to put its own imprint on the process of rolling constitutional change and tell the general public what we are about and why, then we could become bogged down in a morass of eventually unwanted and unworkable constitutional changes as part of some grand design sought to cure the nation's ills.

Thirdly, the disestablishing of the state must be a great part of political things to come. In 1979 the Conservative Party came to office and pledged in that much puffed phrase 'to roll back the frontiers of the state': in other words to get government off the backs of the people. As the balance sheet has shown, we have not done badly. We have begun the long and slow process of weaning people off the state, encouraging them to take a greater responsibility for their own lives. But we still have an immensely long way to go. 'Ask not what the state can do for you', but rather 'Ask what you can do for yourselves' should be our clarion call. This means changing the post-war mind-set to fall back on the state as an automatic instinct.

The process of disestablishing the state will not be easy. What has been done so far has taken time, involved rows, needed a new bureaucracy, and, even worse, new regulations, all of which have left some Conservatives feeling anxious. The battle however needs to continue to be joined on the home front. We need to hasten our achievements in health, education and housing. We need to take steps in areas where we haven't even started, for example by devolving much more responsibility to the communities and the private sector and the provision of effective care for the elderly and those in need – if housing associations are a good thing, then 'care associations' should be as effective. We need to shrink the state much further and faster.

Fourthly, families should feel more valued. In recent years the issue of 'the family' has been a political football. And never has a football been kicked around to such unconstructive ends. Political parties feel the need to be seen to be espousing the cause of 'family values' yet very often the rhetoric has outstripped the substance.

There is no more such a thing as a perfect family than there is a perfect government. We certainly cannot legislate to make families happy any more than we can legislate to make individuals good. In any event, it ill behoves any government to tell people how to live. We cannot on the one hand encourage people to take greater responsibility for their own lives and then set down strict parameters within which that responsibility can be exercised. People have a right to make their own choices and they have a right to make their own mistakes. But Conservatives, who do not have a monopoly in wisdom or morality, have always had an abiding belief in the institution of the family. If we believe in it, then when in office we have at least a duty not to undermine it. Some of the drift in recent years of changes in taxation and the legal framework of the family – not least divorce law reform – have, I believe, had a corrosive effect on the institution of the family and, in addition, sent out some damaging signals. So we need to reverse that drift and provide a better framework for the twenty-first-century family.

Fifthly, the ability to meet all these ends is underpinned by what is politically possible; and much of this is determined by the economy. We have seen a century of the Tory domination of British politics, but also a century which opened with nine out of ten people working with their hands to earn their livings, and is closing with nine out of ten people working with their brains to earn their livings. So think to survive, cerebrate to compete, are the themes which will dominate our struggle to greater competitiveness in the twenty-first century.

And if we are to compete, then we have to find ways of matching the competitive spirit that is there in, for example, the economies of the East. That process will involve the classroom as much as the boardroom. We need an even more competitive education system, with learning and relearning across a lifetime, otherwise we will never have the competitive economic system that we need.

Sixthly, all these key strands need to be brought together. The question to be answered is how do we want to live in the early years of the new century? How is good, light-touch government going to help people maintain and improve the quality of their lives? This issue is going to be central to continued electoral success in the next century. Global matters and Britain's place in the world dominate a lot of our public debate and thinking. There is nothing wrong with that. Published minutes of past Cabinet meetings record that the Foreign Secretary of the day is usually the most active contributor to what goes on. Yet it is issues closer to home that dominate most people's thinking. They are much more concerned about their own immediate environment – built and human – and we overlook those concerns at our peril.

The term 'community' has been one of the political buzz-words of the first half of the 1990s. The need to rebuild our communities and instil a greater sense of community spirit has been much debated, but to date the arguments have focused largely on where power and responsibilities lie within local communities. Opposition parties' attitudes to community seem to be concerned with the reinvention of old town hall powers, and the establishment for the first time in British history of a sclerotic system of regional government to deal with so-called 'local issues'. To the Tories, by comparison, a sense of community comes by giving people a direct say in the running of those communities, their schools, their housing estates, the fight against crime.

In 1940, in the midst of one of his most stirring speeches, Winston Churchill called on the British people to redouble their efforts in an attempt to defend what he termed 'the quality of our island life'. In the 1990s, unlike the 1940s, we face not an external threat posed by an invading army, but an internally generated threat posed by the very achievements that successive Conservative governments have striven for – a threat posed by the onward march of what Churchill himself called 'the tide of human progress'.

In other words, we are a small set of islands inhabited by far too many people with too high a standard of living and therefore almost unachievable expectations for the quality of life.

The post-war tide of progress has given us a host of

technological, communication, transportation, housing and other changes. Our island life has been transformed. As a Conservative Party we have therefore to be open and honest about the need for some restraint unless the cracks which are beginning to appear become chasms and themselves strike at the very heart of our urban and rural communities.

We will need more and more to balance convenience with community. As a small and crowded island, we can no longer sustain the pace of change in the way in which we live now that we have witnessed over the post-war period. We need to remember at the same time that in the first part of the twenty-first century our people will not countenance unnecessary sacrifices to their thoroughly modern and convenient late-twentieth-century existence. Nor should they. Great labour will have to be expended in order to preserve what we have left, and to help to revive our sometimes flagging community base. Its very name suggests that the Conservative Party is best placed to capitalise on both the reality and a changing mood of our citizens. In many cases, it is the Party's own natural supporters who are crying out most for action. So we need to rewrite our island's economic and social geography, and set out in clear terms how we want our communities to be both physically and spiritually in the years ahead. These imperatives will be met only if there is an equal understanding of their nature by British Tories, now and then.

The British Tories

What do the Tories stand for? More importantly, where exactly should they stand in the new century?

It is very easy to analyse or to eviscerate recent political history. There is nothing wrong with good political commentary, of course, when thoughtful and well written or given. Much wood pulp is transformed nightly in pursuit of this task, and camera crews scud here and there shooting thousands of feet of film to get those critical seconds that will see the light of the TV news bulletin. What most commentators write is often quite forgettable, as it is meant to be, for their art is in the observation of the passing scene. A few are of sterner and more lasting stuff. These great men can help to mould events. Occasionally collective and collected wisdom is distilled into a book of considerable weight and insight, but usually their observations are as short-lived as the daily newspaper and the nightly news bulletin in which they ply their trade.

So there is little point in looking to them for deep wisdom about where the Conservative Party goes next. In any event, newspaper headlines are rarely a good basis for determining the agenda of a mature Party; political stuntism usually results from such a habit. If it is vital for Conservatives to say where we see ourselves going in the years ahead, showing the country the political road-map that we intend to try to follow, that has to come from within. We have to be securely based in our past, but also make the intellectual, philosophical and political effort to look beyond this week's headlines, the following week's big debate, and even next year's general election. We need therefore to show that we have at least a fifteen-year view that will enable us to match the better achievements of the last fifteen Tory years. So, long after the fireworks and the hullabaloo that greet the new millennium have died away, we have to demonstrate that our eyes are fixed firmly on a strategy for Britain towards 2020.

To do this, we must think first about our past and how it should underpin us; second about our distinctive values and how they should guide us; and third where we actually want to be, the shape of the nation and therefore the Party well into the next century.

As we look at this trio in turn, we need to be certain about one thing – the electorate is now better educated and better informed than ever. All those news programmes and comment columns which so persecute innocent or self-important politicians alike ensure that this is the case. Electors no longer seem to have the traditional party loyalties that used to be there, as psephologists never forget to tell us. Since the post-Second World War peak in party membership in this country, the numbers of hard-core Tories and Labourites and Liberals have diminished year on year. People simply do not join political organisations, or churches for that matter, in the way they did in hundreds of thousands in the post-war years, with their half-crown subscriptions or shillings into the collection plate. This is because for the politically minded there are many alternatives to party membership; 'single-issue' groups have mushroomed, cohering around the needs of the disabled, the aspirations of women, plans about the environment and a multitude of other opportunities for campaigning energies. For the socially minded, the 1990s present many more outlets than there were in the 1940s or 1950s, when the Tory branch or Labour Club were potent players in the local recreational round. Now membership of book clubs or the National Trust attract more loyalty and affection. British people seem increasingly cynical about all politicians, even though 'throw the rascals out' is an ancient and popular cry, as old as the political hills. Electors are much more questioning than when I first went into politics in the 1970s.

Old loyalties have substantially gone; information by the yard has arrived, and people simply think more about what they want from their politicians. That is a good thing. We have, as Conservatives, to respond to the ever more sophisticated consumers of our political products.

As we ponder those responses, and mould them for a new century, our continuing development as the natural party of British government must be based securely in our past. There is a lot to be proud of about the Conservative contribution to the nation, often matching the experiences of the United Kingdom, step by step, for more than two centuries. We have flourished as a Party for longer than any other in the known world. That fact itself is remarkable, and too little-celebrated.

Some have suggested that this can only be explained by an almost magical – or at least instinctive – symbiosis between one political party and a good slice of the British people. This history is all the more remarkable for there is no bible of Tory beliefs, there are no tablets of Tory stone given to guide us. There is certainly no set text nor any little blue book that Tories can hold aloft as representing a clear and enduring distillation of our beliefs.

This is because to be a Conservative is, in the end, to hold a particular view of human nature and of society, rather than to cleave to a doctrinal theory; that has always been what makes up either the instinctive or the thoughtful Tory – or Tory convert.

Looking back at Tory writers and thinkers as the tradition cascades from Hooker and Clarendon through Bolingbroke and Hume via Burke and then Disraeli to the late lamented Oakeshott, the reader finds that the real and the knowable are always preferred to the abstract. This is a continuing view that binds one Tory generation with the next.

All this has been chronicled in the excellent row of books which should be on the shelves of any practising Tory or those interested in our ways. These include volumes* by Lord Hugh Cecil; the then Mr Quintin Hogg; the then Mr Ian Gilmour; The Right Honourable Christopher Patten; Professor Roger Scruton; and Mr David Willetts. For the very cerebral there is one by the Right Honourable William Waldegrave.

These are the best narratives of our traditions. They are all written by practitioners, with the exception of the remarkable Professor Scruton. He manages now to combine being both a thinking Conservative and an ardent fox-hunter. This was something that Quintin Hogg thought impossible in 1947, when he wrote in his book that no sensible Tory put politics first; the more intelligent, according to him, preferred religion, the less so the pursuit of the fox.

Indeed, few practising Conservatives would ever dream of describing themselves as intellectuals. If part of this instinctive diffidence about theory, philosophy and writing it all down can be attributed to the Tory cast of mind, a substantial part, too, can be attributed to the long periods that Conservatives have just been getting on with things in government. In Oakeshott's words, 'The ship has stayed afloat.' Thus oceans of time have been spent running things to this admirable end, during the thirteen years between 1951 and 1964, and then the show that opened in 1979 and is still running sixteen years later. This extraordinary electoral success, combined with an apparent lack of over-explicit philosophy, has looked sometimes as if we exist for nothing more than to be in government. So some ask, does this mean the Conservatives see little need to locate the body of principles which make up our creed? Or perhaps, is there nothing there at all? That is a perfectly proper pair of questions.

The answer is, there is a very great deal there. It lies in the unique complexity of values that link and underpin us. Our

*Lord Hugh Cecil, *Conservatism*, Williams and Northgate, London, 1912; Quintin Hogg, *The Case for Conservatism*, Penguin, London, 1947; Ian Gilmour, *Inside Right*, Hutchinson, London, 1977; Christopher Patten, *The Tory Case*, Longman, London, 1983; Roger Scruton, *The Meaning of Conservatism*, Penguin, London, 1990; David Willetts, *Modern Conservatism*, Penguin, London, 1992; William Waldegrave, *The Binding of Leviathan*, Hamish Hamilton, London, 1978.

principles are not Ruskin's 'vile concatenation of straight lines' but rather much more interwoven. Three themes in our values are dominant. Firstly, the instinct for traditionalism, liking established institutions and customs; secondly, thinking that we are all, as subjects – or citizens as we are now called – in it together, organically knitted with each other; and thirdly, a tradition of being deeply sceptical about philosophical grand designs or political big ideas as well as deeply suspicious about the theoretical speculations of individual clever fellows.

This last line of thought accepts that there may well be philosophical Conservatism to be laboured over by philosophers, but prefers to ponder its political twin, practical Conservatism. Generally we recognise that different social arrangements are appropriate to different times therefore. We do not have some timeless ideal of a perpetual civilised order – which underlay, for example, pure socialism or pure communism and which was sometimes imposed on people and communities whose historical experiences had not led them to it. Thus we are not a special breed of spaniels, like Lord Melbourne's whigs. Deliberately cross-bred (rather than mongrel), this has made us appealing to all sorts and classes in our country. Neither an uneasy coalition nor some unpractical and illusory 'Broad Church', we eschew hatred of any part of our nation. Equally, we should eschew xenophobia, while remaining openly proud of our country. Victoria Glendinning, in her masterful view of Trollope, sums it up, 'Party allegiance, in Anthony's vision, was a state of mind rather than a belief system . . .'*

Realism rather than dreaming, then, is the key Tory trait. That is there in seers old and new. The pungently anti-liberal Sir James Fitzjames-Stephen, who had a brutal directness of mind entirely in keeping with having been a robust judge in nineteenth-century India, felt that if we were to have liberty, that implied the right to acquire property. And the right to acquire property automatically entails inequality. So we are not all equal, save before our God. Law and property preserve our liberty. So, if we want to be free, we must all be capitalists too. For it is just as Enoch Powell, a

*Victoria Glendinning, *Trollope*, Hutchinson, London, 1992, p. 384.

34

century later, said, 'We are a capitalist party. We uphold the capitalist free economy', going on more fully, in case the slower reader had not quite grasped the point, 'Whatever else the Conservative Party stands for, unless it is the party of free choice, free competition, free enterprise, unless it is the party of capitalism then it has no function in the contemporary world, then it has nothing to say to modern Britain.'* This is both trenchant and true; it is also at least one timeless current running through Toryism.

So ownership is a good thing for the Tory. Some laud it simply as a bastion against an overmighty state, as it diffuses power and ensures independence from government in a way that can never be achieved by people who have to rely on the state entirely for shelter, food, welfare and income. One factor which encouraged me in the 1970s to do that now rather antique-sounding thing, join in 'the fight against socialism', was the Community Land Bill. 'Stop the land grab', I campaigned as a trainee prospective Parliamentary candidate, helping to cover Oxford and its voters with little round stickers proclaiming that message. Trite, but right; for to allow council officials to identify and then alienate private property at will for supposed 'community' purposes (above and beyond the compulsory purchase arrangements enshrined in law which are happily more constrained than in a country like France) would have been an absolute evil. Thanks to the 1979 election, the Act never had the chance.

Ownership is, however, more than a bastion against 'them', interfering Ministers or demented local authority officials. For ownership is an extension of personality. It should therefore be a stimulus to further and future personal and community development. It should ensure a sense of belonging. It must inculcate a sense of duty as well as a sense of rights. This is central to Toryism.

The same goes for the Tory belief in market forces; happily we are all market forces men and women now, right across the political spectrum, Tories from conviction, the opposition apparently more from recent political expediency. Allowing the free interplay of market forces is a guarantee of individual freedom, matching and marching hand in hand with the right to own

*Enoch Powell, *Freedom and Reality*, Batsford, London, 1969, p. 10.

property. It is also an essential dynamic of personal, community and national welfare – or, as I prefer, good old prosperity. Government intervention in anything more than maintaining the legal framework for and social discipline of the market leads to inefficiency, a decline in the ability to compete, and eventual misery up and down the land, as we saw in some dreadful days under Labour during the 1970s.

Equally lasting as an integral part of the Tory way is the desire for strong but limited government. The two are not incompatible. Strong government is not the same as comprehensive government. Indeed the most austere sort of Conservative would wish to restrict government to its traditional tasks, just the maintenance of law and order within, and the defence of the country from aggression without. There is a lot more to strong government now, in everything from looking after the weak to protecting the environment. But government should never be all embracing; thus Tories in government must guard against that great temptation of power, to over-govern, over-interfere, to do things simply because it is there. That kind of government can end up as interfering despotism by default, and turn the citizen into the servant of the state.

Listen to de Tocqueville speaking at length down the years as a Frenchman in revolutionary America with words that are as relevant today.*

Thus I think that the price of oppression which threatens democracies is different from anything there has ever been in the world before. Our contemporaries will find no prototype of it in their memories. I have myself vainly searched for a word which exactly expresses the whole of the conception I have formed. Such old words as 'desperatism' and 'tyranny' do not fit. This thing is new, and as I cannot find a word for it, I must try to define it.

I am trying to imagine under what novel features the desperatism may appear in the world. In the first place I see an innumerable multitude of men, alike and equal, constantly

*Alexis de Tocqueville, *Democracy in America*, translated by George Lawrence, ed. J. P. Mayer, Fontana Press, 1994, pp. 691–2.

circling around in pursuit of the petty and banal pleasures with which they glut their souls. Each one of them, who is drawn into himself, is almost unaware of the fate of the rest. Mankind, before him, consists in his children and his personal friends. As for the rest of his fellow citizens, they are near enough, but he does not notice them. He touches them but feels nothing. He exists in and for himself. And though he may have a family, one can at least say he has not got a fatherland.

*Over this kind of men stands an immense, protective power which is alone responsible for procuring their enjoyment and watching over their fate. That power is absolute, thoughtful of detail, orderly, provident and gentle.** It would resemble parental authority if, father-like, it tried to prepare its charges for a man's life, but on the contrary it only tries to keep them in perpetual childhood. It likes to see the citizens enjoying themselves, providing they think of nothing but enjoyment. It gladly works for their happiness but wants to be sole agent in judge of it. It provides for their security, foresees and supplies their necessities, facilitates their pleasures, manages their principal concerns, directs their industry, makes rules for their testaments, and divides their inheritances. Why should it not entirely relieve them from the trouble of thinking and all the cares of living? Thus it daily makes the exercise of free choice less useful and rarer, restricts the activity of free will within a narrower compass, then little by little robs each citizen of the proper use of his own faculties . . .

This telling text should be in the first red box of every new Minister, for there is an imperative for governments not to crowd out the space in which we need to live freely. Even the most benevolent Conservatism must avoid interference. It must allow not just for economic activity between consenting adults, but also for the exercise of basic responsibility. It must let people take their own risks; and, as private citizens, exercise public virtue.

*Author's italics.

This means both the giving of money, and, as importantly, time. Together these make up the public duty of charity, however much derided that word is by some in the chattering classes, and all on the left. Conservatism needs to ensure that there is adequate and proper 'democratic space', the destroyer of which is over-government; Conservatives must be the deadly enemy of that seductive political vice.

Conservatism is, however, not just about capitalism and difference and liberty and freedom from over-prescription and the rest of our Party mantra. It is also about even deeper matters. Conservatives certainly do not claim absolute wisdom or the possession of some magic lore written down in a Party constitution. We have never as a Party, very wisely, had one of those, in any detailed political sense. Just look at the problems the poor Labour Party has been caused by the one it has dating back to 1918. Values rather are central to Toryism, which is against relativism, the idea that there are no absolute values. This attitude helps to define our position. Relativism, much more than the political correctness which feeds off it, has been one of the most damaging of post-war political and social phenomena. It has been swallowed whole by the chattering classes, by some in the churches, and by much of academic life. Most recent British philosophy has encouraged this.

Philosophy generally, and moral philosophy in particular, has become so utterly reductive that the received wisdom seems reduced to the view that all moral philosophy can do is to find inconsistencies in the other chap's arguments, and then point out where they are on a slippery slope. For example, if abortion is permissible at twenty-eight weeks, why not infanticide as so many babies are viable at twenty-eight weeks? If moral philosophy itself has now become so arid and fastidiously inhuman, it is not surprising that academic institutions generally shy away from promoting values – except an unargued and often irritable insistence on the fashionable liberal positions. It is a pity that British moral philosophy has become so scientific, pedantic, and cliquish in its attitudes.

Better than that sort of thing is to listen to the Chief Rabbi, Dr Jonathan Sachs, writing in 1994, 'We have abandoned the task of teaching our children a clear sense of right and wrong because we are not sure there is such a thing, and, when they need us, we are not there. We have given our children videos but not our time. We have given them condoms, but not an ethic of self-restraint. Who can blame them if they translate the relativities of our ethics into the proposition that what is right is what I feel like and can get away with?'

Now that is wisdom on stilts. It should be appreciated whole by all relativist moral philosophers, sometimes relativist church-men, and also by the most relaxed and liberal of Tories, them-selves representing a most honourable tradition in our Party. So, while Tories should recognise (as I have pointed out) that differ-ent social arrangements are appropriate to different times, that there is not some theoretical and timeless Tory masterplan, they must also know that things are not relative and that values are central.

In their private lives and community activities this should be a constant theme for Tories. But if it is right for the ordinary goose, it should be sauce for the government gander. Thus Tory-ism looks to the governing classes not for didactic sermonising but, rather, proper humility and firmness of purpose mixed with a spot of ethical leadership by example. Any set of policies should be informed by this continuing and strenuous attempt at political high-mindedness. In other words, the very process of government must, for a Tory, have a moral content – or if Tories are uneasy with the word morality because of its supposed churchy or preachy overtones, then the phrase 'principled' gov-ernment will do just as well.

Any code for government might begin with keeping to the rules. What this means is that the rules for the conduct of Ministers now publicly available, and which govern the conduct of Ministerial life, should always be closely observed. That is a pretty easy process. With the help of the Civil Service it gives us one of the most incorrupt forms of government anywhere on the planet. These rules are austere. Quite properly British Ministerial life, not itself particularly well paid, has fewer perks than those of other Western administrations. Our Civil Servants – who in my experi-ence are punctilious in dealing with their own proprietorial concerns – are rightly hawk-like in the oversight of what Ministers do in their use of public funds. If those rules, straddling everything from entertainment to declarations of personal interest, are observed to the letter, then there is a framework of conduct clear for all to see.

However, the issues of the good conduct of government go much deeper than the formal public face of properly constrained and guided Ministerial conduct. For government must take a moral or principled view of what it does, so that it may imbue all its actions with them. This sort of thing may not have been fashionable since the time of Carlyle; if so, it is time it came back into fashion. Rather than waiting for rumours of sleaze to emerge, the penetrating media finding out something, or one of the general public's periodic fits of morality to bring the issue back on to the agenda, Tories must always take the lead in ensuring a continuous moral or principled thread to the actions of government. We should say so publicly and proudly. To display to the electorate that we do keep these things at the front of our minds is neither pious nor prim – nor does it fly in the face of Tory pragmatism and the inevitable compromises or judgments of Solomon that political circumstance demands. Truth is central, and of recurring concern to each generation. As of the city swindlers he was excoriating, so we can agree with Trollope's New Zealander on governments past, present and future, 'It is not of swindlers and liars that we need to live in fear, but of the fact that swindling and lying are gradually becoming not abhorrent to our minds . . .'

Thus it is right that the government will say that it will not do immoral things. For example, it will refuse needlessly to spend taxpayers' money in the pursuit of sectional interests or the buying off of a lobbyist. It is not, or at least not to a Tory, the business of government to do that sort of thing. Equally wrong, in a moral as well as economic sense, is to spend fecklessly in a way that has to be funded by debt, so saddling our children's children with the results of public expenditure binges.

The most difficult moral issue of all, rarely addressed by any Tory writer on Toryism – entirely understandable perhaps – is that of sexual conduct and how this obtrudes on to public life. This is not just about government avoiding the promotion of tax laws which undermine marriage or promoting contraception for underage children but rather that the Tory Party has to expect a lot from its MPs and Ministers in this respect, just as it relies on their financial probity. After all, the family is, every Party Conference hears, a 'fundamental Conservative value'. Even left-wing sociologists now point out the devastating effects of its erosion, thirty or forty years after they helped initiate that process. The family is also the fount of moral education and the bastion of many of our freedoms. If we feel like this and really mean it, rather than just mouthing it, we cannot rely as public men and women on the comforting but imaginary prop apparently provided by the alleged – but false – distinction between 'public life' and 'private life'. Because we may think that government has no right to pronounce on or interfere in private matters, this does not mean that it need not worry about the standards of private conduct of its Ministers. The point is not just that everything we do, even in private, affects those around us in some way; it is more that society depends on morality as its social glue. Thus a change in the nature of the glue and those who uphold it affects everyone. Hard. though this may be, the elector is bound to draw conclusions about his governors from what he knows of their private conduct, even where it does not strictly affect their government duties. This public–private distinction, as invoked by the liberal consensus, is not really politically neutral either. It is a weapon used by those who wish to see a more secular and value-free society. It is a goal which in a sense disenfranchises the often inarticulate voice of traditional morality or principle, so often intimidated by the garrulousness of the liberal consensus. We should rather as Tories give more voice to this principled approach. After all, Conservative Chancellors of the Exchequer in their budget speeches sometimes talk about raising taxes for social ends. For example, they purport to promote a healthier nation by hitting the smoker's pocket. How good it would be to hear a tax change announced in some future budget speech to bring extra help for families with children 'to promote a healthier family', putting flesh on the rhetoric about being 'the Party of the family'.

As the proud party of capitalism as well, Conservative governments must continuously have exactly that same moral or principled sense towards the workings of capitalism and the market mechanism that underpins it. The market always needs a framework of personal and corporate morality, in exactly the same way as government Ministers and government Departments need them. If it does not have them, capitalism will be weakened. Thus, everyone in business has a duty to behave ethically. That sense of ethics should imbue decision taking and business operations alike.

If business people start from a standpoint of common morality, as the majority most certainly do, that is always to the public good. Respect for the law must be there, honesty and fairness are paramount – neither building up false expectation nor deliberately misleading people; these are not bad rules of thumb for politicians as well! But while we want businesses and business people to be responsible, large- or small-scale 'social responsibility' is the province of government, local authorities and personal community charity, not of business. The false veneer of morality sometimes tacked on to the public face of companies is summed up in the most extreme theories of 'stake holding' – in other words, the view that the workforce, customers, suppliers, the community, and its environment matter just as much as the shareholder. If it is right for businesses to become involved in their local, regional or national economies for the purposes of performing better as a business, that is all very well; but 'social-responsibility programmes' dealing with urban decay or educating youngsters or preventing them offending are odd activities for business, unless they are supported because they improve markets, labour supply or profitability. Indeed, using the assets of companies to benefit people other than shareholders could be regarded as misappropriation. Individuals, local authorities, and central government should not seek to persuade business to perform tasks that more properly belong to them.

We should also remember that will-o'-the-wisp quality of 'tone' in our political stance. This also has a public virtue, and one that can be turned not only to political advantage but to that of the fabric of the kingdom itself. This sort of behaviour used to be called 'gentlemanly conduct'. It has been derided by most since the 1960s. It was suspected a hundred years earlier in the 1860s of being a plot by the aristocracy to keep the middle classes in their place. To some then it was a matter of treating their women as kindly as their horses, but happily, gentlemanly conduct lurks there, unsung, in every stratum of our community today. It is found in the Civil Servant, letting slip some of his income on a monthly basis to different charities via payroll giving. It is in the disabled pensioner in some decrepit edge-of-town council estate doing that little kindness to someone who is even more physically debilitated than he is.

Of course 'gentlemanly conduct' may fall foul of the accusation of 'genderism', and all the rest of the politically correct claptrap which so damages the richness of our language and inhibits creative thought. The essence of its meaning is, however, right, good, timeless, and – helpfully – instinctively Tory. We are often told in a post-Auschwitz age, when artists, of all people, like a Bacon or a Freud, have often insisted on portraying the human form as, if not absolutely degraded then essentially ugly, animalised and base, that nothing else is possible or true to how things are. This is not so, certainly as far as personal conduct is concerned. What is possible is determined by the attitudes we choose to take up and more importantly to encourage. This is all the more important when we have seen the horrors that men and women are capable of. We do need to present other visions of what is possible. A Conservative would wish his Ministers to embody this, his children's teachers to instil it in their charges, to live like this himself – and to wish others in civil society of all political views to have it as part of their instinctive conduct.

So what exactly is this instinct which should be central to Toryism? The Romans had a word for it – *nobilitas*. The medieval French called it *gentillesse*. Richardson gives us *Grandisonian* from the hero of his novel, and that naturally appealed to Carlyle.* There is not an easy contemporary equivalent. It is certainly the opposite of resentment, that understandable instinct that has been one of the engines of both theoretical communism and formalised state socialism. Whatever word is chosen, it is

---

*Sir C. G. Duffy, *Conversations with Carlyle*, London, 1892, p. 203, where Carlyle talks of 'A man of scrupulous veracity, correctness and integrity, a kind of Grandisonian style of magnanimity . . .'

grounded in an overriding sense of duty to their fellow men and women that every Conservative should feel, and emphasises our national potentialities for graciousness, courage, magnanimity and honour.

Does all this require a religious context? For a lot of people this helps; though not necessarily in a dogmatic way. It is certainly not vital. In saying that human beings can and should be 'noble', displaying *nobilitas* or whatever, I am simply suggesting that they should adopt some goals which are binding. So, I think it is a positive duty of thinking and instinctive Tories alike to adhere to the general view that a life influenced by noble ideals and a sense of honour is a better form of life than one without a sense of shame. This is surely one of the main aims of education. Without preaching, and by example, this is a quality which Toryism should always attempt to promote. It is the other and more human side of the coin from the more formal issues of public morality and principle that should guide Ministers and governments alike.

Government, both visible and invisible, must not overflow its banks either. The levees which are raised up to contain the Whitehall river need to be kept constantly in a state of good repair – by government itself, by tough opposition, and a watchful media. That is not to say that change is anathema to Conservatism. The political river can meander. Acceptance of change follows from a Conservative view of society as something which is evolutionary and not static as a principle. Indeed, in terms of political advantage and the gathering of votes, change is very often our friend. Conservative change is not always cautious change. Sometimes it must be brave. But it should always go with the grain. Change for the sake of it is bad to the Conservative, even if politics (in government or opposition) has to be a business of apparent perpetual motion in order to meet the demands of the times and an over-excitable, inquisitive, and plot-hungry media who have an ever-present need to fill page or screen. Equally bad is wholesale change which threatens the existing fabric of society.

So the purpose of change should always be to try to improve the lot of men and women, attempting to cure ills, trying to strengthen what is there already; there is also nothing wrong with complete innovation, if it fits within the template of the British experience. Privatisation since 1979 is a good and obvious example of that, taking us back to where we were, to a state which we should never have left. The problem with change is in determining not only where to start but when to stop. It is not even a theoretical weakness in the Tory armoury to say that there can be no hard and fast rules in determining at which point change is necessary. What is clear is that the need must be apparent and the way of getting there mapped out. For example it has seemed obvious in the worlds of local authorities both in Scotland and in Wales that they were not working well as to the interests of local people. So change commenced to a clear plan, the plans were well sold, and single-tier local government introduced. These are very different experiences from that in England of course where the need was not so clear, and the plans more opaque, with depressing results both for local democracy in some places and for the reputation of good central government everywhere. Tories need to be certain that change is necessary, and then carry through those changes with certainty and conviction.

These Conservative approaches to matters both public and private can, when taken together, lead to a first charge, that Conservatives are all too often more likely to know what they are against rather than what they are for. It can also lead to a second charge, that simply because the Conservatives are not dominated by some philosophy, some ancient political straitjacket made up of Clause Fours and other elderly provisions appropriate to some past political epoch, they are simply there because they are there. Of course, flexibility is in-built into Conservatism and that flexibility, therefore, has helped the sometimes everlasting-seeming success. Some have felt that the Conservatives possess a sort of political alchemy in the voting booth. And to prove it between 1881 and 1992 we have won seventeen of the twenty-nine general elections held. The first of these charges can continue to be refuted as firmly as ever, for knowing what is not liked helps to define what a Party is. On the second charge, the jury is out as an ever-better-educated, informed political consumer will want to know what we really stand for in the new century. It is these politically footloose and fancy free whom we must persuade to grant us the privilege of continuing to govern. We must not allow the myth that we are politically infallible, and generally rule as of right, to delude us. For while change may well be our ally, chance may equally well not always be so. It is time that we more than sketched out the ways in which we wish to be seen, and our goals for what Conservatism should mean in the next century, even though beyond its early years stretches political infinity and *terra incognita*, peopled by a shadowy generation of political dragons still in the delivery suite. This exercise must be rooted in our past, and guided by our view of things.

What is to be done? Firstly, by the end of the first decade of the new century we must have persuaded an electorate brought up on a diet of rationalism and materialism in an era of White-hall knowing best, to realise that every problem will not be solved by more government and taxpayers' money. This is an historic task for us. The truth is that government is of its very nature fallible, necessarily ignorant. It cannot know all. Thus it should not spend all. The suggestion that it can leads to the nonsense of Ministers pretending that they do have, or should have, policies for everything. This can lead them, because they assume omniscience and omnipresence, to instruct Civil Servants to invade the places where they are hitherto uninvolved, to invent new schemes, or – by spending new sums of taxpayers' money – to buy off the lobbyists who are campaigning for government to 'do something' about the latest 'crisis'.

Secondly, and flowing directly from the overriding imperative to set out our stall, there is a parallel need to encourage the reinvention of 'democratic space'. This, while certainly an inelegant phrase, is a rather more positive way of expressing what that much overworked phrase 'small government' means. In other words, rather than thinking the task is just to ask government to stay within the narrow confines of its own banks, this approach puts the boot back on the individual's foot. We need to ensure that our fellow citizens enjoy much more of what might be thought of as *democratic space*. This is to be found not only in free economic activity but also in exercising basic responsibility – citizens *taking their own risks* and, in the parallel exercise of civic virtue, *giving money and taking the time to be charitable.*

In many ways, as we have seen, the long-run Conservative changes since 1979 have completed much of the easy part of the agenda. This has been helped by communism self-destructing and socialism shifting more in the direction of market capitalism. Doing the easy bits first and making them stick was the political right approach. Nationalisation is now off the agenda; ownership is on it. There are about seventy per cent of our people who own their own homes in whole or part, with another fifteen per cent queuing up to get the chance; then there are nine and a half million share owners; eight and a quarter million personal pension owners as well. The ratchet effect of capitalism has worked well, so far. However, it will be much more difficult to persuade those same individuals, and the communities in which they live, to make the Tory concept of democratic space come alive through people getting on with running their own lives, taking responsibility, helping to care in the community, run their hospitals, govern their schools.

It is up to us to persuade particularly the young that the powers and duties of government are limited – or should be – in order to encourage private and community initiative as opposed to the knee-jerk appeals for government resources and government money to solve every problem. This is certainly not to say that everyone should be standing on his or her own feet by some target date like 2020. Helping many of those who cannot is not necessarily best done by bureaucracy. It may be better done by individuals, families, churches, charitable institutions or voluntary organisations. The flourishing of such institutions is a better sign of a flourishing community than any number of offices spreading across the landscape. There needs to be a proper humility regarding what cannot be done by government, plus a proper respect for what can be done by others.

We must redouble our efforts in the new century to make sure that we do not let de Tocqueville's all-embracing 'tutelary' power become the post-modern Tory norm, just to be efficiently implemented by big government Tories. We need to turn the concept of the active citizen into a twenty-first-century reality.

Thirdly, we have to make absolutely clear that power in any

area of government policy is to be centralised only if that is the best way of then quickly devolving it. That is exactly what some education legislation in the late 1980s and early 1990s did, taking power to the centre, but only so that it could then be rapidly diffused to the rim of the wheel, to parents and schools. Taking power to the centre is generally a bad thing unless this is done specifically so that it can be diffused to the citizen and the community. Then it is a public virtue, as we see in the National Health Service.

Fourthly, we must speak without embarrassment of our pride and achievements in being British. The reinvention of unembarrassed patriotism is vital for quickening the spirit of the nation, invigorating community and economy alike. This means pride in our rule of law; in our social tolerance (remarkable not only in itself but for being so unremarked upon); our institutions, particularly the monarchy; our heritage, built and natural, historical and artistic. This last task is no mean one, either, to achieve in an island which often seems just too small to contain the wealth and aspirations of the people who live within its shores, where nimbyism (not in my backyard) too often now meets the plasticated theme park. George Orwell faced up to this even as Britain faced her Nazi and then Japanese enemies in the last great war when he derided '. . . the sniggering of the intellectuals at patriotism and physical courage, the persistent effort to chip away English morale and speed a hedonistic what-do-I-get-out-of-it attitude to life . . .'*

In French schools today, the children are taught to love their country and their *pays*; in Japan, their country as well as their village. These are contemporary and politically incorrect vices for too many in modern Britain which need to be turned again into the civic virtues that they are; not xenophobic, just natural and indigenous. They are quite understandable to most foreigners – for they feel exactly the same about their nations.

Fifthly, we must ensure a style and substance of criminal justice which is respected by law-abiding and law-breaking alike.

---

*George Orwell, *The Penguin Essays of George Orwell*, London, 1984, pp. 145 and 189.

This is one of the most difficult tasks of all. It demands effective policing and punishment which is not soft. Neither successive Home Secretaries nor generations of Chief and other Constables can easily be hauled into the dock for failing in these tasks. For evil, temptation, weakness of will are always present; there is a lot to steal; people may even be a spot careless with their property, not that that ever excuses the light-fingeredness of others. Everyone knows these things in their heart of hearts. They do not expect their complete eradication; they know the practical difficulties. But most put the provision of security for people and property as one of the prime *raisons d'être* of the very existence of government. Woe betide any party that is perceived as not trying to provide this. They also want security from fraud, from savers' and pensioners' money being expropriated; they certainly do not believe in the existence of 'victimless city crime' and they want these fraudsters and their doings not just regulated out of existence but punished as well – they feel this just as strongly as they believe in the market and its benefits. We need to catch our breath on law and order, not just moving on with tougher punishments and tougher conditions for criminals as we should, but starting on the process of stamping out the very roots of crime in the youngest in our country as part of a long-term approach. We should have done this years ago. We need to ensure that children being born this year are taught to grow straight, rather than crooked. A wise gentleman, Mr A. W. Morris, ninety years of age when he wrote to me out of the blue in September 1994 from Stroud in Gloucestershire, summed up the task so well, 'The government is capable of organising a powerful group of able men to create, say, a more advanced and less overcrowded transport system by the end of the next decade. It is even more vital to have an effective consensus of moral power created in the same period to remove barriers for the good people in every walk of life, to exercise their benevolence and honesty.' The practical responses to crime have to be consolidated, and Conservative governments will need to take much more of a lead in promoting just that 'effective consensus' with all the risks attached of being accused of preaching.

Sixthly, all this must be underpinned by a much more

competitive educational system, ensuring parental choice and a diversity of types of schools and curricula taught by people unafraid to emphasise what is true and worthwhile. This is as vital for the moral and social fabric of our country (see chapters four and five) as it is for our economic health (see chapter six); education is the key ingredient in international competitiveness, and the Education Ministry is, or should be, in part a powerful economic Ministry.

Seventhly, the drum beat of low taxes and low inflation to encourage individual initiative and responsibility must boom louder and louder. But financial rectitude must resonate too, a critical aspect of morality in government. It is immoral gratu-itously to bequeath debts to our children. Our aim must be not only to reduce taxation and permanently steady inflation, but also to repay the cost of past recessions – and past public expen-diture binges. All of this is hard to do, but simple to grasp; I think the general public is grasping it and will not forgive a gov-ernment which does not also do just that.

Eighthly, we have to win the argument about the virtues of common law and precedent over written constitutions, charters, and all the rest of the artificial constructs of the 'constitution-mongers'. The Britishness of our ever-evolving constitutional arrangements are the best protection of our liberties, deeply rooted in our political culture.

Ninthly, security from threats abroad must be assured. This is the same as the traditional demands for peace and security at home. It must be clear that our foreign policy is driven by our interests and what relates to them, whether in Europe, within any broader alliances that may follow, or the world at large. Helping to keep the world peace is no bad thing, provided that the burden is shared. And, by the same token, it must be our rule that for-eign entanglements whose aim and scope are unclear are very bad things, and that these should play no part in the Tory view of foreign policy.

These are nine sturdy pillars that should sustain Tory philos-ophy and practice in the first decades of the new century. They are also a programme that can guide action. Together they define how our rulers should be lessening the business of government.

They are in tune with our history and our instinctive recognition of the nature of things which makes us favour limited government, autonomous institutions like the family, imperatives such as individual freedom. They can also help us refocus on the traditional Tory hesitation about human and hence government perfectibility. They should reinforce our sense of the corrupting dangers of power and government's need to concentrate on the basic task of providing the framework within which individual decisions and transactions can freely be made, life privately lived.

All of this depends on the protection of the law and the framework of our constitution, to which we need urgently to turn as a party, with a vigour we have never shown so far this century.

3

The British Constitution

The undermining of institutions in the United Kingdom seems in the mid-1990s to be endemic. Almost all the players in our constitutional arrangements are under attack, and their standing diminished, with the sole exception of the armed forces. It is an urgent task for the whole of the country, and not just a political party, to rekindle respect for our institutions. If they are undermined then so are the very building blocks of our country. This vital reassertion of respect can come only from within the culture of the country itself. The disease will certainly not magically be put right overnight by constitutional changes. Documents and judgements are meaningless, and incapable of binding up any country's wounds or improving its way of life, unless that selfsame country has a political culture and social cohesion which renders them viable.

What all constitutions, whether written or uncodified, should try to do is to resolve de Tocqueville's 'conflicting passions', for all citizens naturally, '. . . Feel the need of guidance, and they long to stay free'.*

*Alexis de Tocqueville, *Democracy in America*, translated by George Lawrence, ed. J. P. Mayer, Fontana Press, London, 1994, p. 693.

We have traditionally tried to resolve this dilemma through our partly written but not wholly codified constitutional settlement. It dates back to a period way before there was any written constitution in any other country. The British constitution works at least as well as any written constitution. The guarantees, or checks and balances, in our arrangements are, naturally, particular to the British. These are made up of the Queen, the two Houses of Parliament, the courts, and the media (surprised though some of these would be to know that they are thought of as part of our constitutional settlement!). In their way, they can be quite as important as the courts. Perhaps the media do deserve to be dignified in the procession in front of the Monarch at the State Opening of Parliament, possibly some figure in an ermine-trimmed raincoat, carrying the Great Notebook of State.

Resistance to the codification of our constitutional arrangements in some great *omnium gatherum* written text is practical and honourable. It is not reactionary. The Conservative instinct is to recognise that no constitutional settlement, whether written or unwritten, can be perfect. It also feels that rolling constitutional change, as appropriate, is the best way of promoting those steady improvements in the way in which we run ourselves. This is done simply by reconciling the very reconcilable, contained in the two historic dictums of Edmund Burke and Lord Falkland. It was Burke, who has been more passingly and thoughtlessly prayed in aid by Conservative writers than is decent, who laid down that, 'A state without the means of some change is without the means of its own conservation.' This is right. It is also entirely compatible with Falkland's timeless thought when he wrote, 'When it is not necessary to change, it is necessary not to change.'

So, sometimes the Tory attitude is 'leave it alone', and on other occasions it is 'let's have a spot of improvement here'. This approach contrasts very strongly with the serious root-and-branch, knock-it-all-down-and-start-again approach of the constitution-mongers. This is a harmless enough subject of debate for the chattering classes, in the cosiness of a seminar room, or around the table of some think-tank. It is immensely damaging in practice.

We British have the knack of not trying to fix what is not broken. Large-scale constitutional reform usually comes along after a war or a revolution in foreign countries. It has generally happened here in the past when the ruling classes of the day were in a serious spot of bother, as during the civil unease which led to the Reform Acts of 1832 and 1867.

Sensible, mature, and relaxed countries like the UK in the 1990s, not facing these varied foreign or domestic plagues, therefore do not need constitutional demolition gangs to move in with some new, written edifice.

It is very important for us to be realistic and eschew romanticism, however, as we try to keep our constitution in good condition. It is easy to pour retrospective scorn on George III, who, in his pithy and Hanoverian way, believed that our informal constitution was 'The most perfect of human formations'. The Duke of Wellington, on the same subject, told the House of Lords that, 'I am fully convinced that the country possesses at the present moment a legislature which answers all the good purposes of legislation and this to a greater degree than any legislature has ever answered in any country whatsoever.' Charming and dated though these may be, I suspect that it is in the gut instinct of the British to side with this sort of approach, rather than with all those extremely wise jurists, academics and commentators. These, at the drop of a chat show invitation or the rising up of some self-styled charter/convention/commission, are used to producing, overnight, over-arching written settlements. They, it is promised, will immediately abolish evil and lead the country to broad, sunlit uplands all according to some new and 'fair' electoral formula. Real life is not like that, but as Conservatives on the eve of a new century we must keep our constitutional tackle in order, for fear that these arguments might take hold.

In post-war Britain, discussion of constitutional issues has generally followed two separate cycles, one long-term and one short-term. The short-term cycle produces concerned debate at two critical phases: the first during mid-term losses in by-elections such as have plagued governments of all political colours since the early 1960s, and secondly, in the run-up to a general election. If the outcome of the coming election appears tight, then the dangers of the Sovereign being drawn into controversy in the event of a hung Parliament are endlessly pondered. If, on the other hand, the outcome appears certain, the implications of yet more 'single-party government' become rather the focus of concern.

When the two cycles coincide, television and radio stations dust off Professor A, Doctor B, or Constitutional Reform Movement Leader C, to comment on what should be done. Their opinions and plans are advanced further and further until they explode in the face of an economic up-turn or unexpected election victory. They are all then put back into their constitutional boxes again until the next time they are needed.

The long-term cycle has usually followed concerns about economic performance or patterns of government. Lengthy economic down-turns generate discussions about the relationship between economic performance and the structures of government. Not so long ago, the Electoral Reform Society decided to go into the whole issue. They commissioned a professor to investigate it all, particularly the links between political systems and economic performance. His unequivocal answer – and to the credit of the Electoral Reform Society, they promptly published his findings – was that there was absolutely no link at all. 'Differences in economic performance,' the professor concluded, 'cannot be explained by differences in electoral systems.'* By contrast, a period in which one party occupied office for any great length of time raises questions about the relationship between the electoral system and political, as well as economic, stability. Naturally enough, sustained periods in office by any one party encourage the opposition to question the utility of the existing arrangements. If you cannot win, it is always best to try to change the rules.

Set against all of this, it is self-serving nonsense to suggest, as some constitution-mongers have done, that the battle lines are drawn between 'necessary change' *versus* 'no change'. Rather, it is a debate between a collectivist philosophy, which believes in the wisdom of the all-embracing written word and that of jurists to decide what is best for the individual, and a philosophy that emphasises common sense and continuity.

*Professor R. Rose, *What are the Economic Consequences of PR?*, Electoral Reform Society, London, 1992.

The collectivist's constitutional philosophy is usually elitist, and dictates grand schemes of reform, to be imposed from above. In this approach there will be a written document, about which unelected judges or some unelected 'constitutional body' will decide. The essentially Conservative philosophy (which has seen us through the last two hundred and fifty years, and so should certainly see us through to 2020 and beyond) dictates a very different approach. This is one of balance. The state thus has a rôle in providing a framework within which individuals can enjoy freedom. What this means is protecting the rights of individuals, and where rights are recognised but not protected, of ensuring their embodiment in law. Conservatives set their face against prejudice, which is as wrong morally as it is politically. Prejudice inclines citizens to be alienated from the rest of society. That is not healthy for our communities, and becomes a cancer within the body politic. The Conservative approach must therefore be one of vigilance to ensure that all citizens enjoy the equal protection of law. If they do not, then the short answer is that that law must be changed or improved. Critical to this approach is that Tories view the state as the servant of the citizen, providing the legal framework within which the citizen can operate as a free individual, and not the reverse. Tories are also careful not to *use* the word 'discrimination' loosely in this respect. To discriminate between the competent and incompetent, the liars and the honest, is quite right: it is not at all unconstitutional or unfair.

'Let's have a new constitution' is one of those appealingly simple slogans that sounds good. It purports to offer remedies for all known ills in a way which the very skilful purveyors of patent medicine so successfully used to beguile innocent purchasers in Victorian England, or from the tail of a cart on the fast westward-moving frontier of the western United States. They offer more than they can deliver. Why? It is because there is a good deal more to constitutions than the wording of formal documents.

Some think that this is a shellbacked approach. Written constitutions must be powerful documents, by definition, runs the argument. It looks conclusive, after all, for do they not codify core provisions; generally enjoy the status of higher law; and are they not normally amendable only by extraordinary procedures, because they are so entrenched?

The reality, however, can be very different. To assume that such single codified documents automatically protect the civil rights of citizens is a demonstrable – if continuing – fallacy. Lately, the Bill of Rights in a country like Brazil has offered no protection for young, homeless children being murdered by death squads. In some older democracies such devices, although purporting to protect citizens equally, have failed to deliver what they promise in exactly the same way. Just look at the way in which one provision of the United States' written constitution to 'protect the rights of the individual', which is the right to bear arms, actually seems to make it easier for lots of those individuals to be shot by each other.

The demands for an entrenched Bill of Rights, in this country, appear to be based on two entirely false premises. The first is that such Bills are necessary to protect the liberties of the individual. They are not. The necessary protection comes from the political culture of a nation. Judge Hand, described once as the 'greatest living American jurist', argued that men should not put their faith in constitutions, laws or the courts. 'Liberty,' he declared, 'lies in the hearts of men and women.' When it dies, he went on, 'no constitution, no law, no court' could do much to help it. The political culture of Britain is well entrenched, and that provides a much more powerful constraint on government than any Bill of Rights could ever manage. It is bizarre to suggest that the rights which our citizens have taken for themselves over the years should be handed over to judges. For an entrenched Bill of Rights invariably involves the resolution of political questions by judicial means. To take two examples, whether or not abortion and capital punishment should be permitted is a political issue, and it must be resolved by elected representatives answerable to their people, not by an unelected body of judges struggling to interpret just what that phrase 'to enjoy the right to life' in some new codified British constitution might mean.

The second false premise which underpins demands for an entrenched Bill of Rights is that they are automatically a protector of 'liberal' values. In fact, Bills of Rights are what the judges make of them. The broader the terms in which they are drawn, the greater the capacity of judges to mould them in ways that they want; and for a very long time. Just as an entrenched Bill of Rights embodies the values of a particular generation and may continue to protect those values long after their moral validity has been first doubted and then destroyed, so the Wisdom of Solomon exercised by one generation of judges may become entrenched in a way which profoundly disturbs later decades. Judges operating a written constitution may interpret provisions, as they undoubtedly did in the United States in the 1930s, in the way that favours organised and local interests – in those days, rather rich ones as well. Such interests won the day because they had the money to pursue the cases in courts. Judges may, in addition, interpret constitutional provisions in a way which favours the state. This also happened in the United States. During the Second World War, the Supreme Court upheld as lawful the internment of a number of unfortunate Japanese-Americans living on the west coast of America. It took a long time for the Court to admit that it got it wrong.

Rights and freedoms in any country always best come from an unspoken and shared assumption about how people should live, what things are acceptable, and what are intolerable. With this sort of historic culture, a Bill of Rights is unnecessary. Without it, it won't help. Look at the old USSR for a good case study. It had one of the most liberal constitutions ever, but this served only as a pretext for the Communist Party to circumvent it, producing a contempt for law and freedom in a people unversed in such things under Tsar and Commissar alike.

What the British have to date wisely recognised is that human affairs are too complex to be absolutely codified. Explicit principles are abridgements of practice. Often these may then mislead, and in any case produce a great (and essentially illiberal) increase in litigation. The rich are always better at this. Legal aid will always be limited. So, real interest in freedom and rights should lead any political culture to cultivate the wisdom and judgement on which such things rest, and not by comparison to cultivate the illusion that they can exist without them. We can see the effects of this in some of the worst manifestations of United States life

– some rancorous, litigious, and rather disunited people forever appealing to 'Rights' through the courts.

In our country, Westminster is where constitutional changes have best been designed. These changes have often come from the Conservatives. Tory governments have done more than just think about the constitution, they have acted over the centuries. They extended the franchise in 1867, and gave the vote progressively to more and more women in the coalition of 1918, and again in government in 1928. Then it was a Conservative government that made it possible for more people to enter the peerage for life in 1958. It was a Conservative government which made it possible, albeit grudgingly, for hereditary peers to leave the peerage for life in 1963. In the lifetime of the present Conservative administration since 1979, the constitutional innovations have rolled on. A good example is found in the introduction of the select committees in the early 1980s. They have been afforced by the useful administrative devices of the Citizens' Charters of the early 1990s. This has helped to confer more real – not paper – rights on ordinary people. Thus our citizens have the right to information about the performance of services nationally or the right to treatment by the NHS within a clearly defined period.

The Conservative approach to the constitution, one of introducing new ways of running things better on a step-by-step basis, is best summed up by the low-key sounding 'rolling constitutional change'. Constitutional measures, when they come, are not always dramatic, are useful, and tend to go with the grain. When we have tried the big bang approach in the past, we have not generally got it right. Conservatives have sometimes variously indulged in the reworking of formal documents or in the bold redrawing of maps. This process has not always been successful, as we can see with the reforms of local government and of the NHS in the early 1970s. Why did they go wrong? It was because they were grand designs, meant to be bold and single strokes answering problems, but actually lacked subtlety and a sensitivity to needs and realities. They were simply much too theoretical, and, in the local government reforms, showed historical ignorance. Despite such setbacks, each time a Conservative government tries to depoliticise an area or unravel a bureaucracy, then it is also busy at changing our constitutional settlement. The way in which matters are evolving, for example through transferring the opportunity to run schools away from bureaucrats and directly to parents who take over control of grant-maintained schools, is in itself a constitutional innovation of some significance. This process confers rights, and responsibilities, if citizens wish to take them back from the state which, since the middle of the last century, has been taking them away.

If a new form of individual constitutional empowerment is introduced in this way, it cannot easily be reversed. That has been a characteristic feature of the development of rights in the United Kingdom. For, once embodied in statute, a civil right is rarely reversed. The result is a growing body of clearly defined rights, each meeting particular and recognisable needs. The combination of a body of 'rights', with their nature clearly defined in statute law, renders civil rights less liable to sudden change or collapse than is the case that may derive from the provisions of a written document. There, one particular interpretation by a few jurists could nullify much at a stroke.

Similarly, largely unsung changes have also been happening in the way in which government runs itself. These have profound constitutional implications in practice. This is because of the way in which Britain is now so far ahead of most of our international partners in building new systems for the provision of services to the public, through a process of what is correctly thought of as 'government by contract'. We now have a growing number of service-providing agencies which are increasingly separated from the Whitehall Departments that used, in a sometimes muddled sort of way, to exercise their functions. There were often hopeless and irresolvable conflicts of interest caused by the rôles of specifying what should be provided, providing it, and then checking on the quality control of what was provided all being hopelessly jumbled together. It was entirely characteristic of old-style big government before 1979 that entitlements, service and the standards to which these were delivered were improvised and muddled. There are now more ways that people can get remedies and redress. These also represent important constitutional innovations.

Parliament is central to our way of doing constitutional things.

It is, and must remain, our main mechanism for introducing and then protecting rights, supported by the courts. When it is perceived that rights are being infringed, there is no resort to grand abstract principles or detached constitutional structures, but instead rather a reliance on people themselves to make their voices heard. Parliament is the body through which grievances should and can be channelled most effectively. It is certainly used increasingly for that purpose. Constituents make far greater use of their Member of Parliament now, as any MP's secretary groaning under the weekly post bag would attest. Citizens are now organised much more in single issue groups. They lobby Parliament on an unprecedented scale compared even to 1979. Lobbyists get the result they seek. Different bodies, charitable, professional or consumer, often succeed with a lot of what they want to achieve in the legislative process. Lobbying is part of democracy; it is good to see it flourishing, even though it may be tiring for the legislators who are its butts. It is good to live in a late-twentieth-century Britain which is reasonably rights-conscious. Citizens in the twenty-first century will be more and more active in protecting and defending – but also advancing – their interests. Perhaps half of the pressure groups today have only sprung into existence in the last twenty years or so. These are not always the big battalions, but also members of the myriad of the smaller campaigning platoons. As a result of their activities, the statute book looks different from what it would have been without their work. They have proved an effective part of the British political process. They have also carved their own niche in our constitutional arrangements.

Would their position, and more importantly that of individual citizens, be helped by the incorporation of the European Convention of Human Rights, for example? Only some of its proponents suggest that all of its provisions should be embodied in British law. Yet if we start from scratch, what would we include? The right to life? What are the implications for capital punishment and abortion? Do we include a right to education? Does that, then, give legal protection to private education? The rights for which widespread popular support exists are usually rights already both widely recognised and protected in statute. Yet the idea of incorporation is a serious one and some very serious people have been amongst its advocates. They deserve to be taken equally seriously. It is, after all, more than forty years since we ratified the European Convention on Human Rights, and almost thirty years since we granted an individual the right to petition to the European Commission and thence to the court. Clearly, we should now go the whole European hog, runs their argument. There are two flaws. The first is that the United Kingdom has a history and a culture that sets it apart to a recognisable degree. All other European countries have distinctive histories and cultures too, with their use of Roman rather than common law, though Scottish law follows the former to a degree.

The second flaw is in the assumption that there is some 'European path'. The constitutions, and procedures for protecting rights, differ remarkably country from country, even though they may have formally incorporated the European Convention. In France, despite its written constitution, the individual has no right of access to the Constitutional Council, for example; matters can only be referred via the National Assembly. By comparison, in the south of Europe, the Greek constitution confers on Greek citizens the right to participate in social and political affairs in so far as they do not 'violate the constitution and moral values'. To say that the United Kingdom should follow thus the 'rest of Europe' is meaningless – there is no rest of Europe to follow in this respect. The countries of Europe have been under different influences, different religious pressures – including in the past the ultramontane claims of the Roman Catholic Church – and different external threats.

The United Kingdom should continue to accept and apply the principles of the convention; it would fly in the face of history not to do that, for we played a major rôle in the drafting of those principles. But to incorporate the broad provisions into UK domestic law would be an unnecessary and meaningless diversion. This is because our common and statute law already accurately secures the freedom and rights set out in the convention itself.

One of the major problems with the convention is that it is drafted in very general terms. This can make interpretation

highly unpredictable. Worse, it would confer upon hitherto independent judges for the first time the responsibility of developing
public policy in this country. To introduce the European convention would upset the clear and historic British balance of powers
which exists between executive, legislature, and judiciary. Adju-
dicating on matters raised on the convention would therefore
necessarily involve unelected judges in policy decisions for which
they are totally unfitted. What should happen is that judges
should continue to interpret the laws which Parliament has made.
The United Kingdom would lose from incorporation, firstly,
because we would politicise the judiciary, and secondly, because
we would introduce the fantasy into UK domestic law that its
appearance here would magically extend freedom and rights.

In the middle of the last decade, the then barrister and now
great clearing banker, the Lord Alexander QC, none the less
wrote* in his forceful argument in favour of incorporation in *The
Listener*, 'In the end, incorporation would involve an act of faith.
No one can tell – just as the founders of the American constitution could not tell – what effects judicial decisions would have on
the development of society.' There seems little point in introducing some new 'act of faith' into an already strong and balanced
political culture which is nicely poised on the cusp between
effectiveness (the capacity of government to govern) and consent
(maintaining popular support for the political system). To
incorporate would mean a substantial blow to Parliamentary
sovereignty and that the courts could strike down legislation at
will if it conflicted with the provisions of the convention *as they
interpreted it.*

It is far better that rights are determined and protected through
the activities of elected representatives in the House of Commons. MPs are elected by and accountable to the citizens of
their constituencies. These are relatively small by international
standards. They have to relate to the people they pass in the
street or meet at the farm gate, or they will not be re-elected.
Parliamentary life in Westminster is equally intimate. Anyone
who has seen a Chamber able to seat four hundred and fifty

*Robert Alexander QC, *The Listener*, 5 February 1987, p. 4.

when six hundred and fifty try to get in, when a Budget is to be presented or a Queen's speech debated, will know that. The intimacy is compounded as anyone who has had the chance to look behind the green baize door of Parliamentary life must appreciate. And even deeper in the Palace of Westminster, where strangers cannot stray, that closeness is further compounded. In the Tea Room, crammed with sleeping, gossiping, reading, arguing, plotting Members, rank with the smell of humanity, bacon sandwiches and cocoa during a late-night sitting, there is an extraordinary sense of businesslike proximity. It is the same when the discreet doors in the linenfold panelling are penetrated to the still surprisingly neo-Victorian plumbing of the place. There much effective Parliamentary and government business is transacted while hands are washed.

That odd mixture of grandeur and formality is reflected in the lives of Parliamentarians in their own constituencies. They are likely to be treated with great respect during some dignified occasion at the local cenotaph on Remembrance Sunday or while attending the Annual Civic Reception. In the next breath they will find themselves abused face-to-face in market square or shopping centre, where they are wise to walk from time to time. Like the Roman, it is good for a Parliamentarian to walk across the forum and have his or her sleeve plucked. That link between electors and elected, which is much buttressed by the splendid old UK system of the regular MP's surgery or advice centre, is lost at our peril. It helps to reinforce our rights. There is no other Parliamentary democracy in the world where it is as easy for the electors to have their fifteen minutes' worth at a weekly or fortnightly surgery with even the Prime Minister or the greatest Cabinet Minister in the land, available to their own electors in their own constituency. Electoral reform would destroy this.

There is no state of electoral grace to which we in the UK can aspire. This is because there is no perfectly fair electoral system, and never can be. The horrors are there aplenty, depending on the electoral system opted for. Our own Liberal Democrats, with staggering intellectual dishonesty, talk as if a 'proportional system' was a system of election on offer as an alternative to our existing system. It is not. They also speak of 'fair votes' and 'proportional representation' as if the two were synonymous. They are not, either. Proportional representation, rather, is a generic term for a large number of electoral systems, very few of which are strictly proportional and some of which are positively crackpot. Liberal Democrats tend to favour one rather Irish system, called 'single transferable vote', while Labour supporters of electoral reform tend to favour the Germanic 'additional members system'. Both systems clearly demonstrate that what reformers want is far from fair, proportional, let alone problem-free. The uses of the former in Ireland, and of the latter in Germany reveal the extent to which both systems allow third parties to wield disproportionate political power, and to do so without reference to the people. In 1982, for example, the Free Democrats in Germany simply switched allegiance overnight from the one major party of that country to the other, thus creating a new government shaped somewhat in its image, but without consulting the electors. The government was not made by the German people. The government was made by a Party that often struggled to get more than the five per cent of votes necessary to be represented in the Bundestag itself. It is alien to the British spirit to look to a system which has, as an inbuilt characteristic, the chance that it might produce a government cobbled together in this way. This can lead to coalitions for which not one elector has definitively voted. Disproportionate political power can be wielded not by the largest single party, as under our present system, but one of the smallest parties. Where, it can be wondered, is the splendid integrity in all of that? The practical manifestations of purely theoretical fairness or proportionality would do little to maintain faith in our political system.

The real dangers presented by the constitution-mongers and chartists are that their activities raise expectations which can never be met, and which elsewhere have not been met. They are dangerous because they are distractions from, not solutions to, the problems of individuals in the end. By comparison, the great benefit of our present electoral system, which, like *all* alternatives, is unfair to a point, is twofold. It produces a close and intimate relationship between the Member and those who voted for that Member. It generally produces a clear-cut majority for one party or another.

This Parliamentary system which has evolved over the last thousand years is underpinned by a close-knit system of local councils. They derive their powers from Parliament in our system, and, as it is not federal, they are best referred to as local authorities, not as 'local government'. Half or less of our people bother to vote for them usually, but none the less they are a very important part of our way of life. Thousand upon thousand of active citizens run those Parish Councils, Districts Councils, County or Metropolitan Councils. Britain is one of the most densely populated countries on earth. It is also one of the most intensely governed countries on earth. Some wish to make it more closely governed yet. The Labour Party want to introduce an extra and expensive tier of regional government in England in order to throw a cloak of 'fairness' over their plans for devolution in Wales and Scotland. They, and the Liberals as well, want to impose a new layer of government that no citizen is calling for south of Scotch Corner or east of Offa's Dyke.

If this happened, at best there would be extra bureaucracy, more interference and additional cost; at worst, there would be the very Balkanisation of Britain. If such plans were realised, they would guarantee us the title of the most over-administered, over-governed, and over-burdened nation on earth. It is important for Tories to expose and then win these arguments in the national good and at considerable political profit, too. Electors must realise that their lives would be more interfered with, and that they would have to pay heartily for the pleasure.

Walk into the streets or lanes of England, where there is two-tier local government, and ask a passing Council Taxpayer who runs education or street cleaning? You will get the responsibility laid indiscriminately at the door of County or District Council. Many local electors not only have that sense of confusion, but do not feel particularly close to the local authorities that are meant to serve them. This would be much worse if there was an extra tier inserted between local authorities and central government as Labour plan.

An extra new layer of regional government as Labour and Liberals wish would not be any closer to the people. Regional assemblies would lead to greater confusion and new tensions within the region. They would certainly lead to conflict between regions and the central Parliament. Why did the Orkney and Shetland Islands vote 'no' in the 1979 devolution referendum in Scotland? It seems because they were distrustful of 'rule from Edinburgh'. Experience and the creation of new counties in England after 1974 is also instructive. Why was the county of Humberside never popular with its inhabitants? Not just because of local attachment to the historical counties of Lincolnshire and East Riding but also because south-bank towns like Scunthorpe or Grimsby are wary of being dominated by the much larger Hull on the north bank of the River Humber.

No one has satisfactorily answered what the functions of such regional authorities would be, why they should be brought into existence in the first place, let alone what they would cost. Their geography in England would be problematic. Usually when politicians draw lines on maps they make a muddle. Just look at our experiences with local government reform in the early 1970s, some of which have been recently put right by once more re-splitting asunder what should never have been joined in the case of, for example, a bastardised authority like 'Hereford and Worcester', or 'Avon'. It is true that in some parts of the country, there is some sense of regional place. The eastern counties of Norfolk, Suffolk, and part of Essex have a coherence – but then exactly where Essex becomes part of the Home Counties or London is another matter. Certainly Yorkshire has a strong sense of identity. But go to a place like Oxfordshire in the middle of England and the picture is different. Talk to a Cowley car worker and he and his family feel they belong to the industrial midlands. Address a London-bound commuter and they feel part of the Home Counties. Someone living locally and working in one of the new high-tech university and science-related industrial parks probably feels detached from both and rather part of the Thames golden triangle. But some on Boars Hill, let alone the ex-Berkshire Downs now in the county, certainly feel part of Wessex.

The views of many local people, as expressed in recent years to the Local Government Commissioners, have been (with the exception of notoriously unpopular local government rearrangements like Cleveland or Avon) to leave things much as they are.

That same instinct would surely be reignited should regional government become a reality. The circumstances of Northern Ireland within the union are different and special: brave attempts to silence the gun there continue, though with considerable implications for our national sovereignty and causing unease to unionists like me. In Scotland and Wales, the government had the courage of its convictions and imposed single-tier local authorities. It is here their flirtation is turning into full-scale romance with Regional Assemblies for Labour and Liberals alike.

There would be no economic benefit in these for Wales or Scotland. Rather, these additional assemblies would present burdens on those regions which are at present net beneficiaries of support from the rest of the Kingdom. In Scotland for example, which some think is spoilt rotten by the southern taxpayer, *per capita* spending is nearly a quarter higher than in England. With devolved tax-raising powers, the burden of taxation on the people of Scotland would be greater than on the people of the rest of the United Kingdom, and that would have damaging economic and political implications for Scotland. The same would go for Wales.

Equally, there would be no political benefit, for the devolving of tax raising and some legislative powers could threaten the unity of the United Kingdom. It is clear that in equity, Scotland and Wales would have to lose a significant number of their seats in the Westminster Parliament in order to bring their electoral quotas into line with those south of the border. The underlying reason why the Labour and Liberal Parties dishonestly plan for Regional Assemblies in England is to justify keeping that disproportionate number of Scottish and Welsh MPs in the Westminster Parliament, dominated in particular by Labour Members. Hundreds of millions of pounds a year would be spent on just the administrative costs of the unwanted and ramshackle new regional councils in England, let alone the money that they would seek to spend in order to justify their existence. And all of this would be to provide an excuse for keeping the Scottish *status quo* in Westminster. There would be a rabbit-like breeding of assemblies across the land simply to justify as little change as possible at Westminster. These plans represent the most extreme form known to man of trying to have a constitutional cake, and eat it, at the same time.

To say that either the British government or our local authorities were perfect in their arrangements would, however, be a nonsense. We need to continue to develop our constitutional arrangements. But our instinctive Tory suspicion of politicising the judiciary or introducing strange and unknowable new electoral systems, let alone Balkanising Britain by the introduction of regional government, should continue to inform our reactions to change of this sort. However, it is not contradictory to say that some change must characterise how we arrange things.

This is quite right for there are still some parts of our political system that would be strengthened by modest and well-honed change. In considering this, we should start at the centre, where we always have in British life, with government and Parliament. There we have generations and centuries of experience and attitude to draw upon in moulding the shape of that change and its direction. This can sometimes indeed be what Civil Servants call, with characteristic understatement, 'a challenge'. By comparison, seeking the correct form of change at the supra-national level of the European Union and our relations within it seems sometimes a task-impossible. This is partly because we have precious little past to call upon in understanding our relations with a body of which we have been a fully fledged member for only a few years. There is no Tory past to guide us in our relations with a grouping which itself is growing and mutating at a pace entirely unfamiliar to the nation state, as well as expanding in size all the while.

The emphasis of changes introduced both at home and within the European Union in the new century must be informed by three imperatives. The first is improving the quality of government. The second is to make government more responsive to the needs of the people. The third is to ensure that people can identify with their government. Our approach should be always to have power cascading downwards, and democracy ascending upwards.

British government is too big. Just because bigger government is well run by Conservatives, it does not mean that it is *ipso facto* good government. Making it smaller is an intensely demanding as well as practical task. Part of this involves some changes with a constitutional flavour. There are too many Ministers. There are too many Government Departments as well. Most Government Departments remain too large, with too many Civil Servants, good though these often are.

Most Ministers have enormous power to do good conferred on them – even though the biggest danger of long Ministerial life is not becoming a power-junkie, but rather a polished administrator. All over the Western world, in particular, pressures on the executive have grown enormously in recent decades. They reach a pitch in the United Kingdom because of the very nature of our Parliamentary democracy, with Ministers being responsible to their own constituencies as well as for their own Ministerial decisions. Times have certainly changed since Baldwin spent hours on the front bench of the House of Commons listening to debates, albeit often buried in his copy of Dod's Parliamentary Companion, learning the biographical details of Members. Only just over thirty years ago Macmillan could still go occasionally in the afternoons to the library of the House or to his club, to read Trollope. Even as late as those years, one politician accepted office only on condition that he could continue to hunt two days a week. By the time the late Nicholas Ridley was telling his junior Ministers at the Department of the Environment in the late 1980s, 'Not to bother to come in on Monday mornings if they wanted to stay on past the weekend to fish a bit', that was no more than a romantic and stylish suggestion. The pressure on Ministerial time is enormous. Ministers, with their apparent willingness to become involved in everything from what we eat to how we travel, inventing all those 'cones hotlines' in order to help to make it easier, have enormously increased the pressures on themselves. They prey on and are prey in their turn to the twenty-four-hour, seven-days-a-week media operations that characterise national life now. It is a rare junior Minister these days who can accept office on the condition that he still does something else. That made the dentist Sir Paul Beresford MP all the more remarkable when he said in 1994 that he would accept office as a junior Environment Minister on the condition that he could still draw teeth at the weekend. Sir Paul is a throwback, and a very laudable one, to past days, for he said that he did not expect to remain in politics for ever. This was a very Tory statement in the era of the career politician.

It would be foolish to imagine that we can return to the lost world of Trollope-reading, fox-hunting and fishing on a grand scale amongst Ministers – at least until and unless the state is much reduced in size. In the meantime, Ministers need all the will power and all the help they can get in order to be the steersmen and not oarsmen of our national life. This would be helped by a conscious effort to reduce the numbers of Ministers overall. The number of junior Ministers has grown enormously over the past forty years, partly as an immediate reaction to the apparent pressures of ever more minute involvement by government in the lives of the country, and partly as an expression of the desire of successive Prime Ministers and Chief Whips to have as many people as possible on the government payroll. This practice ensures majorities in votes at the dead of night – but also at considerable cost to the taxpayer – where persuasion or loyalty might fail to make up the numbers.

The tendency to grow government can be seen most sharply in the population explosion of Parliamentary Private Secretaries. Some are necessary. To be one is a privilege whether an MP reaches Ministerial office or not at a later stage. It gives instant, albeit unpaid, insight into the workings of government. It provides an invaluable service to their ministerial masters, keeping them in touch with Parliamentary opinion, plots, and the prospects of political tantrums. But during the last time that there was a long stretch of Tory government, in the 1950s and 1960s, only Cabinet Ministers tended to have them. Parliament was managed none the worse. In the early 1980s at the Home Office, for example, the Home Secretary of the day had his PPS, and the Ministers of State shared one between them. That was a recent innovation. Now every Minister of State has his own PPS, as do some Ministers of State in the House of Lords as well. Harmless? Only up to a point, for the mushrooming of Parliamentary Private Secretaries is a symptom of big government and of an administrative rather than strategic and political attitude to life – as well as a desire to make party management easier.

If Secretaries of State and Ministers in charge of Departments are to be steersmen, rather than oarsmen forgetfully pulling on the oars of administration, then they need help. They get splendid help from the Civil Service. These highly trained and intelligent men and women are themselves one of the checks on any abuse of power, yet will always do as they are told, and produce policy papers, options and balance sheets to order. There are no bad Civil Servants, only bad Ministers. Critically, they should, as one head of the Civil Service said, always withhold that last ounce of commitment from the government of the day. Under our constitutional conventions that is quite right too. Equally right, therefore, is the need for the political heads of Government Departments to have their own small team of advisers to give that commitment.

The hard-working special adviser that each Secretary of State has is not, and cannot, be enough. Often quite young, most of these unsung heroes and heroines of Whitehall work longer hours not only than Civil Servants but, in some cases, their Ministerial masters. They labour nightly, trying to mind their Secretary of State's political back, write their speeches, and advise what on earth is going on within the Department that may affect policy development. So paralleling some reduction in the number of junior Ministers – who too often are reduced to carrying out public relations functions, consuming substantial resources in the private offices and support-staff and drivers and cars – should be the introduction of a proper Ministerial policy unit. The members should be recruited in the same way as special advisers are today, and be subject to the same Civil Service contracts and conditions for the time that they are serving their Secretary of State. There should be three or four full-time policy advisers in each team. Some would be drawn from the same pool of talent whence come present-day special advisers. Others would be seconded in from business, academic life, and doubtless – should the times alter – the trade unions. They would be devoted to supporting the strategic needs of the government exercised through the vision and will of the Secretary of State. Their rôle would be ring-fenced, if those new teams were to avoid the problems that have so obviously beset the No. 10 policy unit in times past, due to becoming much too involved in administration or micro-political matters. They would need to stand clearly apart from day-to-day administration, but rather ensure that long-term strategic thinking took place, and that the Minister was given the mechanisms to control the direction of his Department. With will power no Secretary of State now, even without such help, need be the prisoner in the tower of his or her Department. But their efficiency would be greatly enhanced, while still being properly subject to the constitutional disciplines of Parliament and the constitutional checks of the Civil Service. None of this is to decry the Civil Service.

There is always idle argument about whether there are too many Government Departments, whether they should be amalgamated, and whether things would be improved if shotgun marriages between some took place. For example, it is probably right that in due course and at the appropriate moment – which means when unemployment is going down fast and, even more importantly, uncertainty about job security is not high in people's concerns – the Department of Employment might well be abolished. Part of its function could go to the already large Department of Social Security. Others, like responsibility for training and retraining, could go to the Department of Education, ending that damaging division between 'training' and 'education' in the UK which is unique in the Western world.

Other ideas jostle each other in the corridors of government. For example, slimming down a Department of Trade and Industry which is already pretty thin thanks to the efforts of the President of the Board of Trade, and making it more an office of free trade. Others would say that the functions of the Office of Science and Technology and those of the Department of Trade and Industry as far as research should be merged as quickly as possible – six to eight billion pounds a year can be spent from both sources. They argue that the fragmentation that exists is not necessarily to the good. Most applaud the drive already begun by the Chancellor of the Exchequer to make Her Majesty's Treasury fitter for its modern purposes. Lots of distinguished Treasury Civil Servants are leaving, as the 'down-sizing' which they have observed from afar in British industry suddenly becomes part of their life, too. If it is important to keep up that momentum it is also vital to ensure that the right people come into the Treasury. Who are these paragons? Whitehall's brightest and best young-sters seem to get sown there like dragon's teeth. A healthy leaven of outsiders, both from across the rest of Whitehall (which it gen-erally terrorises) and from business, commerce and industry (who often think that it does not always understand them), would help to benefit the Treasury culture. Its intellectual fire power and fis-cal prudence are some of the Treasury's greatest virtues; but not even those who have loved the Treasury most would call it the most creative of places, even under the most creative of Chancel-lors. Without ditching proper prudence over the expenditure of taxpayers' funds, such changes would help to alter the cast of mind that has made the Treasury seem populated entirely by the abominable no-men and no-women of Whitehall.

These sorts of changes are, however, in reality nothing more than continuing administrative and executive improvements. If well done, they will lead to cost savings and greater efficiences. Any undertaking needs to bring these about on a rolling basis to meet changing circumstances. So tinkering with the numbers of Ministries and Ministers, or the style of their activities, should not be mistaken for being of supreme constitutional import.

The Civil Service itself is, however, an important part of our constitutional arrangements. In it resides the constitutional wis-dom of generations. But it needs to be reduced further in size. There should be further government by contract, with many more agencies. This would leave the core of Civil Service activity where it always should be, clearly within the circle of Whitehall wagons. Much constitutional lore is distilled and resides in the mind of the Cabinet Secretary of the day. Occasionally, at Cabi-net, he is called on to rule over the constitutional propriety of an issue. To sense the cogs and wheels whirring and then to hear the grave advice being given is, in a way, to see the British consti-tution being made flesh. Each new entrant has the key to the Cabinet Secretary's splendid but hidden panelled rooms in his briefcase.

So while the Civil Service needs to be refined, reformed and slim-med, it is vital that its values (which underpin our constitutional settlement) are maintained. The Northcote–Trevelyan report of the mid-1850s propagated a lot of values which are as proper for the Civil Service now as then. This cocktail was made up of objectivity, impartiality and integrity, properly linked to promotional merit, and all shielded behind the concept of confidentiality. This last has led to the 'I brief, they leak' attitude of Ministers towards what they say, and what their Civil Servants might inadvisedly make public without authority. Civil Servants are not bloodless creatures, as anyone who has worked with them even for the briefest of times as a Minister will sense. Max Weber, that greatest of sociologists, said that '. . . the ideal official conducts his office in a spirit of formalistic impersonality, without hatred or passion, and hence without affection or enthusiasm'. Being made of flesh and blood, the hatreds and passions are sometimes there, however much submerged behind the exquisite deference with which the Civil Service handles Ministerial figures, however high or low. Strong Ministerial oversight of these public-spirited creatures is thus vital. This is not just to ensure that government policies are properly followed, but also that Civil Servants in Departments (in whom reside enormous power of an unseen sort, to hinder government, or to irritate the public) are properly controlled. When politicians go off the rails, it is generally in public. Much more hidden are the vices of Civil Servants. There is certainly a time when the public administrator can become, if not absolutely drunk with power, then unfit to be in charge of such as they have been delegated or obtained.

Most Civil Servants do avoid going on the Whitehall bottle like this. They do pick up the Civil Service ethos. There are some codes for them to cleave to. The self-consciously titled 'First Division Association', to which belong many of the senior Civil Servants in Whitehall, has its own self-regulating code of practice. The then head of the Civil Service, Sir Robert Armstrong, thought it about time back in 1985 that the 'duties and responsibilities of Civil Servants in relation to Ministers' should be formally promulgated. A new, thirteen-point code was introduced by Ministers in 1995. But of the systematic inculcation of ethics, there is none. A careful search of the Civil Service College Prospectus for 1994/1995 shows a myriad of management-oriented courses. But there is absolutely nothing on ethics anywhere, whether in the standard training for newcomers, in the development of fast streamers, or for those at the top of the tree, again delightfully known as the 'one, two, three programme' (this echoes the grading structure of the Civil Service with its grades one, two, three and below). One senior and talented Civil Servant wrote in a private letter on 14 October 1994 in response to a question which ran, 'Where do you get your values as a Civil Servant?', in the following vein, '. . . We pick them up by accident, and randomly, if at all. There is certainly no formal effort to induct Civil Servants in it [i.e. ethics] at any point in their careers.' If that is the case, osmosis seems to work pretty well, and as a result there is only the odd rotten apple in any one Whitehall barrel.

Change there needs to be, however. To question the need for the present uniform and traditional Civil Service is hardly radical and is not unconstitutional. There is no need to place the Civil Service on a statutory basis, for example, to protect its values. It is possible to continue to transmit essential ethical and constitutional values while changing the Civil Service. And that change is coming fast with the devolution of functions, the introduction of agencies, pay delegation and open competition for recruitment. Of course, some of the self-proclaimed values of the Civil Service like impartiality, integrity and objectivity are not at all alien to the private sector. It would be impertinent for any Civil Servant to suggest that the private sector's management approaches or techniques automatically mean low ethical standards.

To say that Britain in the new century will no longer need to be administered by a post-Northcote–Trevelyan hierarchical Civil Service is not to promote some radical constitutional outrage. The Britain which the Tory Party will be part of then should be one where the state is smaller, where private provision, private ownership and private responsibility are encouraged, and market rigidities continue to break down. These changes and flexibilities will need to be reflected in the Civil Service itself. An understanding of these new needs and the challenges of the new century will be greatly helped by the introduction of fixed-term contracts within the Civil Service. That means they would be just like employees in any of the world-beating business concerns in our country. Of course, to some extent the British Civil Service is of itself a world-beating concern, admired and echoed around the globe as it is. If both national and international respect is to be maintained in the twenty-first century, so the pace of change has to be maintained too. The concept of 'jobs for life' is on its death-bed throughout late-twentieth-century England; a number of job changes, and fixed-term contracts will be part of the life of the vast majority in twenty-first-century Britain. So the Civil Service must move with the sometimes painful times. It is vital to get the right candidates in the mid-1990s; that can only be done by open advertisement and open competition for all appointments at all levels. And it would probably be to the common Civil Service good if the recruitment of 'fast streamers' quickly came to an end too. The Whitehall world, like the world outside, is changing so fast that the perceived high-flyer of today may have skills which turn out not to be entirely appropriate for 2020. This near-apostolic succession of high fliers is no longer proper; those best suited to tasks are best recruited and trained nearer the time. The leadership qualities needed within the Civil Service are not and should not be seen as somehow unique.*

These changes are critical to the better running of the country. Equally critical in the twenty-first century is the task of ensuring that while losing neither its ethical sense nor its ability to act on the constitutional stage, the Civil Service should be recrafted so it is much smaller, much more fit for the old purpose of giving policy guidance to Ministers, and the new one of overseeing the work of agencies and others in the brave new world of 'government by contract'.

Civil Servants, like their ministerial masters, are, or should be, in proper fear of Parliament. If they are not, then there is something wrong with Parliament itself. Parliament has variously reformed itself over the years, and for the better. The most significant, but by no means the only reform of recent decades, was the creation of the Departmental Select Committees in 1979 by that latter-day

*Barry Legg MP has much to say on this in his *Civil Service Reform*, European Policy Forum, November 1994.

Bagehot, the then Leader of the House of Commons Norman St John Stevas MP. These have been a rip-roaring success, and it is difficult to imagine Parliamentary life without them. Their detailed questioning is an excellent discipline on Minister and Civil Servant alike. They have not by themselves answered all of the problems encountered by the House of Commons, however.

Certainly select committees are an important part of making sure that Parliament is effective. An effective Parliament, engaging in the task not only of law making but of subjecting the executive and its measures to sustained scrutiny, is not only good for the political system as a whole but for government in particular. An effective Parliament keeps government on its toes, forces government to think through the case for its measures and allows them to be improved in the light of debate and advice channelled through both Houses. Simply by being seen to be doing its job both reasonably and rationally, Parliament enhances support for the political system. By the very virtue of doing this, it facilitates a much greater willingness on the part of citizens to accept and comply with the results of divisions of public policy.

Despite recent experimental changes introduced in early 1995 the House of Commons sits for longer than any other legislative Chamber in the world. (It is an odd reflection on the way we do things that the runner-up should be the House of Lords!) Time may be of the essence sometimes in Parliamentary life, but such vast expenditure of time is not necessarily nor closely correlated with Parliamentary efficiency. Little purpose is served by pointless debates late at night dragging on for hour after hour, long after media deadlines have passed and public interest has expired. Parliament should never dance to the media's tunes, but the public should be given the best opportunities possible to understand what is going on in its debating chambers. This can only be done through the media. So all those traditional and traditionally poorly attended middle-of-the-early-morning debates get neither front benches nor back benches on both sides of the House anywhere much at all. If current experiments with earlier finishing times in the evening and some morning sittings to free Fridays for MPs, including Ministers, to guarantee to be in their constituencies are a success, permanent change should urgently follow.

Equally, legislation is too often barely properly scrutinised despite all the hours debating it. This is a great constitutional scandal and one in which all who have been Ministers in post-war years have conspired to a degree. Far too often, large swathes of material in Parliamentary Bills are not considered properly by a standing committee. The bizarre fact is that for reasons of Parliamentary tradition and bloody-mindedness, enormous amounts of time are expended on debating the early clauses of a Bill in committee, and then suddenly a guillotine is imposed in order to get a measure through and down to the House of Lords. There it goes in a partly undigested mass, and is often greatly improved by the Upper House. The time has come when there should be the automatic time-tabling of Bills. This would allow all parts of a Bill to be properly considered. The historical rights of the Opposition in Parliament would not be affected in any material sense by this. Virtually no Bill has ever been substantially changed just as a consequence of an opposition party delaying it for hours, night after night, through use of a standing committee's dilatory procedures.

Two other major procedural changes must come in by the new century. The first is the regular use of special standing committees. These allow Bill committees to take evidence from outside bodies, all those agitated lobbies and lobbyists, before getting down to looking at the details of the Bill, clause by clause. A bare handful of such Bills have ever been referred to a committee so far. It should now be exceptional that a Bill does not go to such a committee. Legislating well, with the exception of understandable emergency measures, takes time and care. That imperative should lead on to a second, linked reform. At present a Bill not passed in a session falls when the House is prorogued at the end of the Parliamentary year. Much better if there were also a two-year legislative cycle for some Bills, which would allow for a much more rational process. Some of them could then be introduced on a staggered basis. This will avoid the rush to get Bills ready for introduction at the start of the session. It will also prevent several Standing Committees having to meet all at the same time. Time could be carved out for evidence taking, using the procedures for special Standing Committees. With the time-tabling which must accompany these reforms, government would as now know when the measure would complete its Parliamentary stages, properly scrutinised.

In this way, by the new century, government would continue to get its business, the Opposition would get the opportunity properly to oppose and scrutinise, lobbyists would be heard, the House of Lords would no longer be force-fed to the point of legislative indigestion – and the country would likely get better-made laws. None of these changes would take the focus of national interest away from the enjoyable and sometimes illuminating bear-pit that is the House of Commons Chamber at its best. If a Bill cannot gain assent then of course it will fall at the second prorogation, which protects against an elective dictatorship. Much public interest would also be restored if there were fewer late-night sittings, with the earlier drawing of Parliamentary stumps, and more concentrated debate when the rest of the country was awake. Better laws; much greater interest in and understanding of Parliament by those for whom the laws are made.

Down at the other end of the Palace of Westminster is the House of Lords, the other vital Parliamentary part of our constitutional arrangements. It is a curious body. Unique in the Parliamentary world, it is if not an anachronism then an oddity which, by the very nature of its hereditary basis, battled through the nineteenth century and the early part of the twentieth century at its very own Thermopylae. It was defending a civilisation which it felt was identical with its own interests. Prime Ministers earlier in this century, like Asquith, thus had a congenital enmity to the Upper House. These days any Prime Minister would be forgiven for having sometimes such a congenital enmity to the House of Lords. But rather than defending a civilisation which is anachronistic as it did at the beginning of the century, now at the end of the century it has become one of the main foci for organised resistence to the government of the day. Its traditional revising rôle has been joined by a certain amount of institutionalised guerrilla warfare over legislation. Because of the poor look-in that they get during the committee stages of Bills that start their career in the House of Commons, many lobbyists reserve their major efforts for the Lords. There they get listened to. There also, because of the lack of time government has left, up against the end-of-session deadlines, they can get results too, in the compromises and bargains struck in order to get a Bill to Royal Assent.

It is conventional wisdom – and true – that the House of Lords is good at revising legislation. It does a remarkable job as scrutinising Chamber. In many ways it is a much more efficient Chamber than the House of Commons at the other end of the Palace. The House of Lords offers the nation considerable value for money, doing a most worthwhile job at very little cost. The work there in the scrutiny of draft legislation from the European Community is, for example, outstanding. A similar accolade is deserved by its committee on Science and Technology. The Upper House should be encouraged to develop and make great use of committees for scrutinising other sectors of public policy. In short, it should be encouraged to play to its strengths.

At the moment it is, as it often has been in the past, the plaything of those who wish to reform it. Yet many proposals for the reform of the House of Lords are in reality cooked up for other ends, say to get to devolution, or reform of the electoral system, but by another route. This is both intellectually dishonest and unpractical. If reforms are to come to our voting system, or to the way in which we are run at a regional level (with full devolution to some parts of the Kingdom), then these need to be sorted out first, and certainly before there is any decision on the composition, shape, and place of the Upper House. Such reform of the revising Chamber logically should only come if at all after the big issues have been sorted out.

All countries with bicameral systems strive to find ways of selecting their Upper Chambers in a way different from its lower home. Few are without problems. Large-scale reform of the House of Lords has in the past, and will in the future, be the Gallipoli of any government unless, remarkably, it has the wholehearted support of all sides of the House of Commons. The unholy, or to some holy, coalition of interests between left and right in the House of Commons, which joined up like those opposed to Robespierre, to murder by slow strangulation the last attempts to reform the House of Lords in 1968 and 1969, have heirs-in-waiting on the green benches today. On the left of them are those who would wish to abolish the Lords altogether. On the right of them and indeed in much of the middle ground of the Tory Party, there are those who object to reform on historical and constitutional grounds. Few at present want an elected second Chamber. It should be resisted in the twenty-first century too, for it would thus simply replicate the first Chamber. If on the other hand the second Chamber were to be appointed by Prime Minister or Party, then the surfeit of patronage would be overwhelming. 'Removing hereditary peerages' might seem the easiest task for a new and self-consciously modern century. But in a completely unplanned, and rather barmy way, the House of Lords in its present mix seems to work well. Sometimes the descendent genes of the hereditary holders of seats can produce formidable legislators and Ministers, sometimes a more random element.

The life peerages the Tory government introduced in 1958 allow patronage for the deserving and the reflection of national interest and concerns. It is trite but true to observe that while no one would have designed it this way, it does seem to work. The challenge for the new-constitution-mongers is to produce something which is guaranteed to work better.

That is not to say that the House of Lords, like the House of Commons, could not itself work better. The House of Lords needs to be taken as seriously as possible by government. The Labour Party, which has hard-working and effective 'working peers', has also presently committed itself to not having Ministers in the Lords. By contrast, in the twenty-first century, more senior and high-quality Ministers should be in the House of Lords as part of Conservative governments. There should be more Cabinet Ministers there too, over and above the two presently 'statutory' appointments of Lord Chancellor and Leader of the House of Lords.

Why will questions of reform always seemingly fall foul of lack of any agreement on what should be done? We should work with what we have. What we have is a working Chamber that is at its best complementary to, rather than in competition with, the first Chamber. It is not unusual worldwide to have an appointed second Chamber. It is unusual indeed to have one based even partly on the hereditary principle, but creations are now almost always of life peerages. What the now-appointed second Chamber does is more than worthwhile. The House of Lords should be more rather than less important as a reviser of legislation, a home for penetrating select committees and a forensic scrutineer of European proposals – as well as a world-class court of appeal – in the twenty-first century. The purposes of conservation, rolling constitutional change – and Conservatism as well – will be served if the House of Lords is encouraged to play to its present strengths in the new century, in a characteristically British way. This includes the creation of new hereditary peers in cases of suitable distinction and public service.

The challenges of constitutional and Parliamentary reform on the home front all pale into insignificance compared with that presented by Europe both to the country, and to the Conservative Party. That challenge is likely to change in nature and style. To have any clear view of how to handle European Constitutional issues means taking many giant steps back and doing what as a country we rarely do, speculating on what our nationalism means, on what exactly it is to be British in the late twentieth century. To do this, we need to ask what sort of people we are. This is very difficult. It goes against the British grain to beat our chests and talk about the glory of our country, in the way in which the French or citizens of the United States do so easily. Winston Churchill asked in the wartime years of our enemies, 'What sort of people do they think we are?' Yet by the mid-1960s Enoch Powell thought he was still havering over the answer as we are a 'nation of ditherers who refuse to make up our minds'.

We have already drunk deeply from the European cup. A myriad of advantages, practical problems and appalling decisions face us as a result. In facing up to them, however, the very fact that we are going through all that turmoil means not only that we have the chance to think our way through some problems, but we are forced to recraft our nationalism within a new framework. This has to be soundly based to make it suitable for the future. Orwell got it right in the dark times of 1941. 'What has kept England on its feet during the past year? In part, no doubt, some vague idea about a better future, but chiefly the atavistic emotion of patriotism, the in-growing feeling of the English-speaking peoples that they are superior to foreigners . . .'* These may be splendidly politically incorrect words for some today, but they give a clue of how to proceed. We depend on foreign countries for our economic future, much of our recent excellent recovery has been export led, and more of it underpinned by massive foreign inward investment. Then again, most of us like it when we get the chance to go abroad, are amused by, as we are infuriated by, the foreigners we meet in their countries and ours. In this we only echo those same instincts we might have to many of our different fellow citizens within our islands. Most of us are happy to co-operate in a myriad of European and world organisations, the European Unions, NATOs, and United Nations of the world as presently cast. But in the end not just the best but the most of us feel glad to be British simply because this is where we happen to have been born. We have a sense of place and a sense of history which makes us glad, above all else, to be British citizens – it is rare to find anyone, of however liberal a view, who in the end would prefer to substitute European or some form of world citizenship for simply being British. Perhaps George Orwell's use of the word 'superior' was not so extraordinary after all, understandable though its usage was in the wartime years. It means rejoicing in being different, taking pride in being part of a nation state. Those feelings, underwritten as they are by the additional emotions, often beat in the heart or inform the minds of the Scottish, the Welsh, or those who come from Ulster. They do not and should not ever stop us from making alliances which are informed by British interests. We should be happy to make coalitions and join groups – but only where this makes the British people cheerful and better off. That should be our starting point in refining our relations with a European Union that is growing fast. Most people want to be part of Europe (there is an economic advantage to it; do not miss out) yet at the same time are strongly nationalistic (this is not in *Britain's* interest). Other countries feel exactly the same. There is nothing odd in having a sense of place, nothing shameful in patriotism.

There are two hard questions that we have to ask first, and they have unpleasant answers to them for Conservatives. The

*George Orwell, *The Penguin Essays of George Orwell*, London, 1984, p. 194.

first question is, 'Is Britain content with its current relationships within the European Union?' As is clear, the answer to that is no. The second question is, 'Is the Conservative Party making a success of the European issue at home and abroad, both as a government and as a Party?' The answer again is no. It is unlikely that these answers can be turned to a couple of triumphant 'yeses' in just a year or two. It is extremely unlikely they will be solved in the crucibles of the 1996 Inter-Governmental Conferences. Rather, it is likely to take some difficult years both to get the relationship right, and to ensure the disarming of what historians will judge as the single most explosive challenge facing the Tory Party in the whole course of the twentieth century.

The correct and necessarily long-term approach to this should rest on two assumptions. The first is that the promotion of individual rights and the national interest should remain a defining characteristic of the Conservative Party. Secondly, that examination of issues on their merits is likely to yield much higher dividends in the long run than second-guessing public preferences or trading on long-held prejudices.

Politics is all too often just about making difficult matters bearable, and compromising to achieve satisfactory ends. That is exactly the same in foreign as it is in domestic policy. Governments of both Parties since the 1970s have, for entirely understandable reasons, suffered from bouts of schizophrenia over Europe. The focus has not always been clear.

Sometimes, during negotiations with our European partners at everything from six to twelve in number, we have been a proud and forceful nation state. We have been 'battling for Britain', and successive Prime Ministers have come back 'with triumphs'. It is fascinating for anyone who has the energy, as well as the linguistic skills, to read the press of each of the twelve members of the European Union to see how, after each great council or summit, most countries have their own 'triumphs' – but equally just how unremarked they are in the media of the different nations.

On other occasions, we have gone through the European glass darkly, sallying forth into complex and fundamental negotiations with an approach of 'Let's see what happens, then let's get the best deal we can.' Almost worse, sometimes this attitude dissolves into that of a policy magical-mystery tour. Worst of all has been the fact that sometimes we have not read the big print, let alone the fine print; or if we did, amnesia about it has overwhelmed us later.

Our starting point in our European future should be that of a nation state. Is this some reactionary manifestation of mid-1990s Orwellian patriotism? No, it is simply because that is the new reality of world, let alone European, politics. So much of the mind-set of the founding fathers of Europe in the 1940s and 1950s, and of the treaty-mongers of the 1980s, was formed against a background of world power blocks and superpowers; hence the 'super-state'. Suddenly, the super-state has become old-cheese. Nationalism, sometimes almost meeting regionalism, is and will be the world driving force in the next few decades. Just look at what is happening in central and eastern Europe, let alone in the wider world. Why is this? Sometimes it may indeed be because of old enmities, ethnic urges, or mad-cap patriotism. But for the most sensible of those who support the nation state as the core form of government, it is because this reflects the history and heritage of the country on the one hand, and because it meets the instinctive wish of most citizens to be in charge of their own affairs on the other.

It is not therefore impolite, in European terms, to say that the idea of a 'European super-state' is yesterday's big, but today's outdated, idea. It is certainly tomorrow's unneeded concept. It is hard to envisage the circumstances in which the British people would accept, if things go badly wrong, a British government saying, 'It is not our fault, it is Europe's.' People in the United Kingdom want to be able to blame their own government if things go wrong, they want to know who to point the finger at. They certainly also want to have the chance to put someone else into government who can do better, if they think the alternative more appealing. None of this flies in the face of European co-operation, rather it goes with the grain of a Europe of nation states, rather than a dated super-state. Super-statism is past its sell-by date. Attitudes of this sort to Europe are showing their age, as indeed are the treaties on which Europe itself is founded.

It is vital that the European Union does not enter the next

century looking like a forty-something wallflower at a tea dance, the results of all that habitual over-indulgence in attempted big-European government becoming all too apparent. Just as C. P. Snow once identified two cultures in the Britain of the 1960s, so it is clear that there are two in the Europe of the 1990s. One is rather corporatist, regulatory and therefore inward and federal leaning. The other is deregulatory, in favour of small government in Europe as much as at home, and is outward looking by comparison. It is only through the nation states of a widening Europe that all those problems and different attitudes to European affairs can be reconciled, and the two cultures that endlessly clash and collide within Europe can be lived with. They will never be wholly reconcilable. Some of this is due to our different legal traditions. The common law tradition of the United Kingdom, except Scotland, is largely enabling. Subjects can do what they want until they are told they cannot. The Roman law tradition of most of the rest of Europe means that subjects cannot do things unless within a carefully regulated code. This means that the instinct in many other European nation states is more towards regulation and 'order' and harmonisation. There is nothing wrong with that, for that is a matter for those nation states. The problem comes when that regulatory culture attempts to drive too much of the European process.

These problems are reflected again in different countries' attitudes to European Commission and Parliamentary matters. In recent years there has been a major shift of political power upwards to the institutions of the Community and now the Union, which has not been matched by any parallel increase in accountability, either to the European Parliament on the one hand, or to the national Parliaments of the different nation states on the other. The attitudes of the Dutch, for example, to Parliamentary control are very different from those that inform a Conservative view of Europe. It is generally the Dutch instinct that democratic control on European governance should be strengthened by, in its turn, a process of strengthening the European rather than its own national Parliament. Our instincts are surely and rightly in the other direction. We do not wish to see further power passing to the institutions of the European Union. We will know if this approach carries the day when a few at least of the more than five thousand lobbyists who pack Brussels decide they need to have at least branch offices in Westminster and the Parliaments of other nation states.

It is this mixture of different attitudes, visions and politics which has brought about a Europe of at least two cultures. One, which needless to say Tories identify as old-fashioned and reflecting the thinking of the 1940s and 1950s, is essentially corporatist and much driven by dated trade unionism. Europeans who cleave to this view look to tight control and clear frameworks for how we are to live in the future. A British – essentially Tory – view, which is increasingly shared by some of the postulant nation states seeking or about to achieve membership, is more relaxed and open. This sees the European rationale remaining largely economic, and realises the terrifying threats of world competition that could overwhelm Europe if it goes down the dated, over-regulated, and highly inward-looking super-state road. A 1960s and 1970s closed-shop-style Europe at the turn of the century would be a bad thing. A twenty-first-century enabling Europe would be a very good thing indeed. We need to proceed towards this not only in the interests of Britain, but also in the interests of Europe. And we need to seek to shape the Union in a way that favours Britain's interests and Europe's interests, for the two are often highly compatible. Conservatives have always taken a view that British interests should dictate foreign policy. We have always eschewed universal brotherhood and decried grand schemes based on abstract principles. This will always be stronger when Britain approaches European debate on its own clearly thought-out agenda, and not – as lamentably sometimes has been the case – when it merely reacts to the proposals of others.

In contemplating how we proceed, we have to remember two things. The first is John Stuart Mill's good old dictum that 'the people for whom the form of government is intended must be willing to accept it; or at least not so unwilling as to oppose an insurmountable obstacle to its establishment'.* But we also have to remember what we have signed up to, for statesmanship is not

---

* J. S. Mill, *Considerations on Representative Government* (1861), as quoted by M. Horsmann and A. Marshal in *After the Nation State*, HarperCollins, 1994, p. 249.

best aided by forgetfulness. It is uncomfortable for many in the Conservative Party to look the words to which we have signed up full in the face. It is wrong in the interests of point scoring at home to erect a fence between membership and withdrawal in order to sit on it, refusing to recognise what successive Conservative governments have led us into. It is perfectly intellectually acceptable, on the other hand, to recognise all those binding commitments, to say that they are no longer appropriate, and to campaign for withdrawal, however inappropriate that might be in the long-term interests of the United Kingdom. Post-modern politics will, with its much better informed electorate, always have to be honest politics. All of us who have been involved in trudging through the voting lobbies at various stages since the early 1970s must recognise what we have done and avoid the ultimate political inelegance of pretending that we haven't. For example, it is silly to suggest that the European Union is anything other than a supra-national system even if it is not and should not be a superstate. That Europe is a supra-national system has twofold significance. Firstly, rights and duties are created for individuals (rather than states alone). Secondly, that in these respects European law prevails over national law in the event of a conflict. Lord Denning was all too right when he said that European law was coming up the estuaries and rivers of the United Kingdom. It is not easy to erect legal Thames-barrier lookalikes against them now.

Conservative governments were quite explicit about this process right back at the beginning of the 1970s. The then Sir Keith Joseph was questioned by a backbench Member of Parliament who asked whether, if negotiations could successfully be concluded on other terms, the government would be prepared to accept articles 117 and 118 of the Treaty of Rome which aimed to co-ordinate social policies with other member countries with a view to the harmonisation of the living and working conditions in the member states in an upward (*sic*) direction. Sir Keith's answer was unequivocal. It was that, 'Her Majesty's government are prepared to accept the articles 117 and 118 of the Treaty of Rome.'* We cannot say that we were not warned nearly a

---

*Written answer, 6 April 1971, *Hansard*, Volume 815, column 61.

quarter of a century ago. For those who did not then closely scrutinise *Hansard*, the European White Paper of 1971 was and is
there for all to see. It is unequivocal in what it said, 'If the political implications of joining Europe are at present clearest in the
economic field, it is because the Community is primarily concerned with economic policy.' Critically the White Paper went on
to say, 'The six have firmly and repeatedly made clear they reject
the concept that European unity should be limited to the formation of a free trade area.'* We were certainly warned.

The way, if not the pace, in which Europe was travelling was
thus clear from the outset of our decision to apply again for
membership in the earlier 1970s. These were not just vague aspirations expressed in the broad-brush; they were there in stark
black and white in the not-so-fine print of papers that we later
signed up to as well. A lot of innocent fun can be had in politics
when we find that the fine print has not been read. There is certainly reason to doubt that the late John Smith, himself a talented
lawyer, fully understood the European Socialist Manifesto for the
1994 European elections before signing up to it. Yet we have
done the same sort of thing. No one could doubt Lady Thatcher's
passionate commitment to being British and defending our sovereignty. She was, however, reported recently as saying in response
to a question about the signing of the Single European Act, 'It
was a mistake. We didn't read the small print.'** Then others
have recoiled, as I would do, from the idea of Britain becoming
part of a Europe in which the members are subject to the further
authority of federal institutions – as if this would be something
new and terrible to behold. While, however, we should not wish
for more federalism in a Europe of nation states, we must recognise that we joined the European Community, which included a
court charged with the rôle of enforcing the binding treaties,
more than twenty years ago. We must never pretend that federal
institutions, long in existence, whose authority we have signed up
to somehow do not exist. It is critical into a new century that we
seek greater clarity in European agreements – we must also both

---

*White Paper, July 1971, Cmnd 4715, p. 10.
**Report in the *Daily Mail*, 4 October 1994.

read them and understand their implications.

We should thus be the fine print men and women of Europe. This will be vital both in the Inter-Governmental Conferences in 1996, and those others that will follow in future decades. We should ensure that Europe asks itself not detailed and unhealthily self-obsessed or sometimes plain irrelevant questions about our internal mechanisms, but rather ponders the big strategic issues of how we can flourish. The debate about a single currency is a good example of one of these. It has to be seen against the fact that we now have in Europe the highest labour costs on earth. The European Union has the shortest working hours, the longest holidays and the best benefits anywhere. We also have more than twenty-five million unemployed people and the number is still rising in many countries in Europe, though happily not in the UK. Part of the reason for this, in addition to the increasing competitiveness in British business, is that we have opted out of some of the measures which load those non-wage labour costs on similar businesses amongst our European partners.

The Employment Secretary battles against them. We have forced Europe to begin to recognise that the Far East, and the countries of the North American Free Trade Area, are a terrible threat. Set against those threats, internal arguments about the harmonisation of this or that over the next twenty or thirty years should be seen in world terms as an economic – if not a political – mouse compared with the competitive lions over the Eastern horizon. Countries there are bent on not allowing themselves to be put into a harmonisation arm-lock. The reality is that the idea of a single currency is much more of a political or constitutional than an economic construct, born of the laudable instinct to 'bind Europe together'. It already seems a tired approach. What appears right to a man shaped by the German Chancellor Kohl's formative experiences – coming as he does from the Rhineland Palatinate in the middle of Europe – will be questioned by the new generation of Europeans, as well as by the new members of the wider European Union. The economic problems of a single currency are enormous. The constitutional implications are plain. If we have a single currency, then we have to have a single central bank. That will mean that the European Central Bank would have, eventually, a rôle not just in monetary policy via the setting of interest rates, but also of necessity and flowing from that, in fiscal policy. Practically that would mean less and less control over our own economic management. Constitutionally it would mean that we would probably eventually have only the same sort of margin of economic freedom left, for example, to a state within the federal United States. Thus it is critically important we do not let Europe in the late 1990s reproduce the sort of closed-shop economic conditions that brought so many of my generation into practical politics as we campaigned against them at home in the mid and late 1970s. Politicians should now listen carefully to why the likes of Lord Hanson and other great global business-men argue so strongly against a single currency. The pragmatic Tory response to the idea should simply be to pour practical cold water all over it, while being perfectly open-minded about the possible development of parallel or common currencies *if* that is what is wanted. If so, let them be market driven – because they meet economic needs and the *desiderata* of trade. They will flour-ish if they are both used and useful. We must not let Europe be preoccupied by the task of recreating the past through constitu-tional devices, even though the left in this country will be all too happy with a single currency becoming the 'Clause Four' of a corporatist's Europe. 'Never say never' is not a bad political maxim, but it seems inconceivable that a British Parliament would accept a single currency unless our economy had suffered from repeated competitive devaluations elsewhere in Europe or if it saw inward and British investment being directed elsewhere within a European monetary zone with thousands of British jobs being lost as a result.

Strong British government should always know where it is going in Europe and elsewhere. It should make up its own mind. It should not fall back on referenda to get it out of holes, nor to patch up internal party problems. If matters which are both prac-tical, and also affect our sovereignty, are to come up in IGCs over the decades, then it can never be right to strike an attitude which is waiting to see what happens, then having a referendum on it. The single currency idea is just one example of this.

This pragmatic and sensible Tory approach should inform our

attitude to all future 'constitutional' matters in Europe. As the years roll on, other issues will doubtless pop up and be as contentious as the single currency concept. 'Age-old rivalries' must be held in check. War must be prevented. New ways of 'promoting social harmony' will doubtless be dreamt up. The Union must be persuaded to have the courage to reassess the means by which these ends are achieved in the light of new developments. This must not be allowed to remain a matter for the Court, but should be one for the member states. We must not permit the imposition of one-sided solutions through the manipulation of the Community's institutional framework. And the pounding must be very long on the economic realities. Policy makers on the right must not confine our arguments about competitiveness to labour costs alone. The social, and thus political, cost of closing the gap between a more competitive Far East or NAFTA by lowering labour costs alone is too high to contemplate for European countries. Yet low-wage economies producing high-quality goods and services present formidable competition. The problem is that, in the Far East in particular, their wages are so much lower than those both in the UK or Europe at large that we cannot hope to compete with them by driving down our wage levels to theirs. The other side of the coin is that those in Europe who so misguidedly seek to protect the European labour force by the imposition of legal strait-jackets must realise that even a World Trade Organisation with the widest possible remit will never raise Far Eastern production costs to ours in a month of European Sundays. In the next century, the social policy arguments currently raging within Europe will become more global. That is an inevitable consequence of economic development and personal expectations in rapidly developing countries.

In this process of reform, Europe must face up to worldwide economic realities, and to responsibilities that come with a widening Union. We also, on our part, have to face up to the realities of what we signed up to, however much we might regret it now. Believing in Parliamentary democracy, there can be no substitute for Parliament's help in this. Those in the House of Commons who argue most fiercely that it is to national Parliaments that Europe's aggrieved citizens should first look, must therefore themselves devote more time to European issues. It is indeed remarkable that it is our second, unelected Chamber which has established a Europe-wide reputation for scrutinising new developments in the European Community. The House of Commons thus needs to be much more effective in scrutinising European matters itself.

The House of Commons has, of course, developed its procedures, especially in response to the Single European Act with the creation of the Standing Committees on European Documents. However, a good deal needs to be done to allow the House the opportunity to take a broader perspective of the developments within the Community. One way of doing this would be to create a separate 'European Affairs Committee'; another would be through encouraging the present and generally effective Departmental Select Committees to take a much more regular interest in European Union issues affecting their remit.

This must be reinforced by much greater understanding of how decisions are taken at the highest levels in Europe itself. The lack of transparency that is there at the moment derives from the secretive nature of decision making. The Council of Ministers meets behind closed doors and no one, including national Parliaments, has any idea what goes on until after the fighting is over. There is clearly a case for these meetings being opened up, and for decision making to be much more visible to the citizens of the member states. The centralisation of decision making in Brussels has also caused many problems, for it leaves citizens of the different nation states fearful of too much being decided 'in Brussels' rather than by their own national institutions. This fear was obvious during the various national debates over the ratification of the Maastricht Treaty. The Treaty had a go at recognising this problem through recognition in its turn of the need for 'subsidiarity' – for decisions to be taken at the lowest level of government possible, with only decisions that cannot be taken at lower levels going to Brussels. We now need to turn this into reality. Recognition of the need for subsidiarity is not of itself sufficient to ensure the implementation of the principle. There is no mechanism written into the Treaty that stipulates who is to decide at what level decisions are taken. Thus there is the danger that institutions of the Community will rule that some matters can only be decided at the level of Brussels while national governments take a contrary view. Resolving such conflicts through the European Court of Justice is a long and unwieldy process, to put it mildly. It is essential therefore that the 1996 Inter-Governmental Conferences agree a specific mechanism for determining what issues are to be decided at Brussels level, and then put a barrier around those issues. As the existing treaties are drawn, there is far too much scope for the Community to encroach on areas that should be left to national institutions to decide. The treaties at present have far too many of the undesirable characteristics of written constitutions, with their provisions too broadly drawn, allowing for interpretation this way and that by judges. The European Court of Justice certainly comprises highly competent jurists. By its very nature, however, it is far too geared towards an interpretation of the treaties that naturally is Brussels-centric.

Above all else, Britain must determine in future to carry more clout in Europe. Britain has punched well below its weight from the outset, quite unlike in any other field of UK diplomatic endeavour. It is not possible to punch at a country's weight if that same country simultaneously uses an institution to which it belongs as a punchbag. Not enough people in Europe have minded about the UK reaction to proposals in the past. Ideas which aim at the heart of the interests of a Germany or a France and unlikely to produce strong resistance in those countries have rarely seen the light of day. The institutions of the Union are now so accustomed to UK resistance that our reaction is given much less weight than it deserves. All this means throwing ourselves into the warp and weft of Europe, accepting those matters which are acceptable. If some are not, this means joining with the inevitable number of others who feel the same sort of way in order to go, within the overall framework, in different ways or in different directions or at different speeds. It is a European inevitability that this pattern will emerge when a Slovakia's voice joins Britain's at the table. Such an approach recognises the reality of the nation state. To do this is neither jingoistic nor anti-European. Recognising the much stronger centralist European instincts of a Holland or a Belgium, none the less it seems inconceivable that the next century will see some great devotion by the peoples of those nation states to 'Europe' as an institution. The Community has for years tried to offset the corporatist bias in the treaties with the idea of a so-called 'people's Europe'. But the solutions put forward have rarely been illuminating or effective. By giving the Community and then the European Union the iconography of a state with its flags, anthems, passports, postage stamps and the rest, European policy makers have not produced a groundswell of loyalty to the institution, rather they have applied leeches to an anaemic patient.

Back to Orwell. In every country of the magnified Europe to be of twenty nation states or more, you can find in their languages and their ways exactly what he expressed about being a member of a particular nationality: 'England has got to be true to herself . . . the heirs of Nelson and Cromwell are not in the House of Lords. They are in the fields and the streets, in the factories and the armed forces, in the four-ale bar and the suburban back garden; and at present they are still kept under by a generation of ghosts . . . we must add to our heritage or lose it.'* Yet Europe has also entered our bloodstream in a way that would have been inconceivable when Orwell was writing in wartime England. It is there now in our law in a way that surprises many and that many do not care for. It is there in physical European links, all those trips through the Channel Tunnel, or those booze cruises over to Channel ports, which do give us a bit more of a taste of Europe. But to recognise that is not also to accept the inevitability of federalism. Such dated super-statism would be damaging not just to British interests but to the interests of most other European nation states. It certainly would be deadly to our constitution. It would also devastate for ever our attempts to have smaller government in the United Kingdom.

*Orwell, *op. cit.*, p. 194.

4

The British Government

Conservatives regard the British constitution as a decent old house to be kept in good repair. It has lasted and flourished like that of no other European democracy. Our constitution is matched for effective and working permanence only by that of the USA. We are instinctively in favour also of a strong state – provided only that it is as small as possible. But Tories do not therefore think that the state is automatically a moral and practical good in itself. Rather, we think only that it should be turned to good moral and practical ends. That is our instinctive view of civic life and of the state's strictly limited rôle in it, as the servant of the people. The root of our present discontent is that, because of the best of intentions and following fashion, we became fellow travellers of an over-mighty state between the late 1940s and the late 1970s. We were collaborators with the process that led to an explosion of government. This was some thirty years of historic aberration, treading otherwise than on our usual primrose path. The brave and now self-exiled David Selbourne, once ejected from that desolate home of lost causes at Ruskin College, Oxford, has later fired back from amongst the hilltop towers of medieval Urbino that there is now a 'narcotic habit' which compounds every civic problem.* This is the ubiquitous and instinctive transfer of moral – and thus actual – responsibility to 'them', the state and its servants. The opposition parties, in particular Labour, will never face this down. It is not only part of their addiction, it is a large part of their very reason for being. The Labour Party is thus inexorably hooked on the big-state habit. Put another way, in the end they feel that public expenditure is a telling index of compassion. And if it is, then of course the big state is a good thing and must follow as a result.

The problem for us as Conservatives is that a lot British people, reared on this approach, instinctively feel the same way too. This is not something that can easily be changed by a speech here, or a policy there. For just as a teenager might be described as having an attitude problem, so the attitude issue for the British in the late twentieth century is that the big-statism post-1945 has been all too seductive stuff for too many of our citizens. Successive post-war generations have been brought up instinctively to ask 'them', blame 'them', believe in 'them', and their ability to solve problems – or at least that they, and not we, should try to do so. More than one generation has now been brought up to think that someone else is always responsible.

The Tory task is not now to reinvent a mythical and state-free past. For the England, and then the United Kingdom, of the historical record has always had a state doing things, taxing and taking responsibility. The existence of the state is properly the mark of a civilised society. For example, there has for centuries been a welfare system, legislated for nationally and applied locally, even if for some sturdy beggars at the tail of a cart in Tudor England the application may not have seemed all that benevolent at the time. We need to ensure that a new equilibrium between subject and state is reached in the twenty-first century which is beneficial, and based on a much smaller rôle for the state. This is the new political frontier. We thus need a reshaped style of government paralleled by a greater freedom for the individual; more active citizens being drawn in, not just living in, but playing their

*David Selbourne, *The Principle of Duty*, Sinclair-Stevenson, London, 1994, *passim*.

part in making communities tick better. This drive should be one which can pull together all varieties of Conservatism.

There are many strands of thought which twine and twist together to form the viscera of Conservatism. There always have been. A belief in the need to keep government in its box is however a theme which all Tories share. Since 1979 we have been busy at the business of reinventing the way that we conduct government to this end. We have been trying to recast government as something which is there only when necessary, with some but not yet real success. The state in its idealised form should be seen as strong, benign, not interfering, leaving our citizens to get on with their lives. With British government, just as with Schumacher and Third World development, small surely should be beautiful.

The problem in bringing about this desirable state of affairs is found in human nature itself. If we had lived amidst the blighted fields of nineteenth-century Londonderry with blackened potatoes foretelling an even bleaker future, or in the sinks of mid-Victorian east London in a dark courtyard dwelling redolent of rats and sewers, then the thought of some all-providing state would have had an understandable charm. Increasing affluence and increasing understanding of the needs of others did indeed do their work over the following one hundred and fifty years. This did not save all of those who suffered in country and town alike, but it did help their descendants live longer and happier lives. The trouble is, several bridges too far were crossed in the process. The territory on the other side that was reached, after the engulfing waves of state-welfarism post-1945 had washed across the land, has ended up peopled by some who in the end find it easier to let 'them' do it. Ideas of individual endeavour, of democratic space in which to live your own life and exercise your own charity as well as take your own risks all seem fine in principle but rather daunting in practice.

There are two vital ingredients if we are to bring back small government permanently. We need to remove ownership and to remove responsibility from the state as much as possible and give them back to individuals, family and community alike. Persuading the individual (those eagerly snapped-up council houses) or the private investor (those privatised utilities and the shares in them) to take attractive options on offer is pretty easy. Persuading the individual or the community to take more responsibilities (run your own GP fund-holding practice, control your own grant-maintained school) is tougher by comparison. In the middle of it all is the Whitehall spider. This is a necessary bureaucracy staffed by good men and women who, given the chance, will however naturally spin a bigger web, naturally unable to resist the urge when given the power to do so, just as the serial chicken-killing fox or badger cannot forswear another couple of heads once safely inside the coop. Their power depends on those enemies of smaller government, which are higher levels of taxation. These not only stunt economic growth, they encourage nepotistic bureaucracy and the dependency which feeds off it. Conservatives must not rob people of the moral choice to help others, and must not crowd out personal responsibility with overwhelming intervention.

To bring the necessary changes about means another period of what might be thought of as 'social emigration', matching what our people have already gone through since 1945 with the coming of welfarism, and since the 1960s with the shape of new attitudes. People who were alive and alert before those fundamental changes that began at the end of the Second World War must feel they have ended up living in another country having travelled across the five intervening decades. To live through these enormous social upheavals is to have undergone a certain loss of identity, exactly equivalent to the experiences following emigration. Britain before the coming of the National Health Service, the welfare state, public ownership, mass education and mass communications with its added instant mass entertainment, the huge rise in post-war crime and the huge decline in church attendance and social conformity, is indeed a very different country from the Britain of 1995.

The last half century has seen the great energies and good motives of government overflow too much their old retaining banks. We need to rebuild them, returning the land on either side below the levees to become lightly governed once again. We began that task in 1979, but it will take many more years to complete. It will involve trying to return to private ownership those things that should be owned privately, and to give back to private endeavour those parts of life which are better conducted privately. These are difficult enough tasks in themselves. But it also means constantly ensuring that we do not add new excrescences on to the surface of government, or let the waters of centralisation overtop their banks once again. Indeed government has little business, for example, telling people as it did in 1994 to eat three small potatoes a day or consume a portion of mackerel, salmon or herring once a week – 'Oily fish are good for you' – any more than it has to let exist a measure in its present form* which allows the banning of simple eye-catching roadside signs for local businesses. Some tea shops and pubs have in the mid-1990s closed as a result; the inhabitants of one Teddy Bear Museum might have had, as recently as 1994, to tea party elsewhere because the signs telling of their existence on the roads leading to the town had to be removed. Stopping these nonsenses emerging is an eternal task – even for Tory governments.

Let us turn to a Pope for a bit of spiritual and secular guidance for how all this might be approached. Encircled by the tightening grip of Mussolini's state in the Italy of the 1920s and 1930s, just before the great social and industrial emigrations of the last half century began, Pius XI produced an Encyclical:**

> . . . Just as it is most unjust to wrest from individuals tasks they can perform by their own enterprise and industry, and transfer them to a group, so also it is wrong, a great injury too and a disturbance of right order to take away from smaller and lower societies tasks they can do, and for which they can take responsibility, and transfer them to larger and higher bodies. This being so, the state should confine itself to those tasks, which it alone can effectively accomplish, directing, watching, stimulating, restraining, as circumstances suggest and necessity demands. Let those in power be convinced, therefore, that the more faithfully the principle of subsidiary function be followed . . . the greater will be both social authority and social efficacy, and the happier and more prosperous the condition of the Commonwealth.

*The Town and Country Planning (Control of Advertisements) Regulations, 1992.
**Quadragesimo Anno – on reconstructing the social order, 1931, 80–81.

So, his late Holiness opined, the state should stay within its banks, and let people get on with their own lives. In other words – to borrow from that earlier Roman, Cicero – exist in a way which holds men together in companionable living in common. Both Pope and orator were right; both might have been Tories of the more thoughtful kind. To understand how to make those words live it is necessary to be quite clear how we got to where we are.

It is in the immediate post-war years that many of our present discontents – as well as some of our undoubted though contentious contents, like the NHS – began. Unfortunately since then we have not got the relationship between citizen and state right. If the major early-twentieth-century phenomenon we had to come to terms with was giving the franchise to everyone and all women to boot, then the huge growth in planning and public services have dominated its later years. Going on to this ground, as we have since 1979, has meant carrying the fight on to territory our opponents thought they owned, secure behind the borders they had defined for their creations. The Labour Party was the creator of the big battalions, big planning and in particular the public services which they have historically seen as their trump card. (The Liberal Party has also had a patch of territory, that of local community activity, where they have pitched camp. This is the strange and jargon-riven world of 'empowerment', 'cohesion', 'local action', above all 'community', which they have made flesh in the more prosaic world of pavement politics. It has often been to their credit, for this approach has had a considerable effect in winning and holding local authority seats.) But above all, people have been progressively promised too much, and thus have been persuaded to expect too much of government.

Why did Tories get into this complex and government-dominated world? Because of swallowing whole a belief in the wonders of central planning. This flowed first from the ideas of socialism. It flowered here in the 1920s and 1930s, finding many of its roots in the extraordinary growth of the now universally discredited communist creed. But they also found their imperative in the needs of war, simply keeping the country afloat in the perilous times between 1939 and 1945. Thus, then, to plan was all; the trouble is that the habit stuck. 'I plan, therefore I am' seemed to run the motto on the walls not only of Civil Servant or Labour Minister but many a Tory as well from the 1950s to the early 1970s. Founded thus in the theories of socialism and the practicalities of fighting a war, we produced a planned and producer-driven machine, benign in intention, generally malign in result.

The state, local authorities, and the burgeoning numbers of those in public services were asked to fulfil the rôle not only of regulator but purchaser, owner and provider of services as well. The doctrine of the day was that this then thoroughly modern approach was fair (because it allocated resources with that virtue in the forefront of the bureaucratic mind); accountable (because Ministers and Parliament became more and more in charge of the nation's life); and above all else efficient (because benign old central planning would end unnecessary duplication of provision). But these were grand illusions. It is worthwhile recording why. This was because the downgrading of competition, which is the automatic generator of quality and value, and the absence of choice, which is the well-balanced motor of accountability, debauched the dynamism which drives on organisations. The public producer emerged paramount over the consumer. In the end this meant that accountability upwards, to the producer, rather than to the user or consumer, became more and more a reality, 'they' being accountable more and more to 'them'. And, thirdly, central planning, with money following the plans, turned out to be much less efficient than the pluralities of the market-place. Insensitivity and remoteness followed as surely as dusk succeeds day. The whole machine grew and grew, becoming driven by provider organisations, with lives of their own. They were thought only able to do better with more money. Public expenditure was seen as a grand index of compassion. The measure of its size was thus in its turn apparently the only measure of the state's interest in this or that problem.

There were thirty Tory years of cohabitation with this; not a case of Whig measures and Tory men, but rather Labour measures and Tory men. A consensus was established, and Tories got on with the job of making Labour's big idea work for them. This was done with the best of intentions, and I am sure that if I had been a young politician in the 1950s I would have thought this was exactly right.

Since 1979 we have tried to turn those tables. Tory men and women with ideas broke the consensus, as Powellism which had fed Josephism whirled on into Thatcherism, building on the late-1970s feeling that had begun to stalk the land – that big government was not working any more, and would 'they' please stop bossing us around in a way now inappropriate to a modern and mature democracy. All of this passion engulfed and overwhelmed a very surprised left. They had rested their case so long on the invulnerability of the belief that, as everyone recognised in modern times that public services were necessary, then of course there was no necessity to consider criticism of the way in which they were delivered. Eventually it came to seem absurd that anyone other than the state should pipe water, or fly passengers around the globe, or mine coal. Very shortly afterwards, the true absurdity of these propositions was revealed.

Three startling lessons helped break up the tired consensus. First, the experiences of privatisation, even in their earliest manifestations, led to a slowly growing belief that the best way of improving the quality of public services was to transfer at least some into private hands. The bringing of sensible private sector management disciplines into what remained swiftly followed. Secondly, the spectacular economic growth of the middle 1980s not only boosted the living standards of the nation, it altered people's expectations. New services and goods were provided by the private sector. They deployed powerful new technologies of information and introduced new ways of managing to meet customer needs. As a result the gap between public and private sector performance often yawned much too wide. And, thirdly, the gap between what provider organisations like the National Health Service could offer, and the money available with which to offer it, yawned wider still.

Have the Tories thus helped change the national culture in this matter? The answer of legend – and sea changes in a nation's life are the stuff of myth and legend always – is 'yes'. In reality, it is as yet only about half yes, with our people only half deciding they have had enough of being provided for and pushed around. What is more, this process will not easily be brought to a satisfactory conclusion. Thus far, it is not so much a case of 'I know my rights' as in wartime England, rather 'I am a customer now and I expect a reasonable service.' In other words we have a kind of political Ralph Naderism creeping into public attitudes towards public provision and what remains in public ownership. Wishing to take responsibility, for much of what the state does still seems a very distant frontier by comparison.

We have not yet developed an adequate or understandable language to match the remarkable changes that have already been brought about. Neither 'privatisation is good for you' nor 'contracting out is fun', let alone 'a privately spent pound takes you further', exactly have cosy rings to them, unlike some of the corporatist but cosy and compassionate-sounding jargon of the 1940s, 1950s and 1960s. And exactly because of that, messages about 'it doesn't matter what you spend on a service, but what that money buys' have too harsh a ring to them still for too many people.

By comparison to these rhetorical challenges, for a Tory the answer to the question 'what should the state do?' is apparently easy to answer. The answer is 'as little as is necessary, done as well as is possible'. Exactly what this is in practice is much harder to define. The central functions of a state do seem at first glance pretty straightforward. All Tories would easily accept that the hard core of the state under the crown is to be found in the disciplined services at home and abroad (army, navy, air force, security services, police) and everything and everybody necessary to carrying out our foreign policy. Of course, these have altered in shape and style over the years. For example, army camps are guarded now by civilian security companies, and what police station does not have civilians answering its telephones these days? No police force refuses either to welcome the help of active citizens through the rapidly growing neighbourhood watches in their areas. (These are, as it happens, entirely new Tory-era, for the first was only formed in 1982.) Thus not only the private sector, but private sector disciplines have been brought in to make even hard-core and universally recognised state activities such as policing or the armed forces work better. Yet all that strange-sounding new-speak of 'contracting out' and, even more mysterious still, 'market testing', which properly bring into the public sphere some of the benign private sector disciplines, are even less well understood than privatisation.

Having defined the hard core, thereafter the challenge to define what a Tory government should and should not countenance is more difficult to meet. The state is already there, whether in principle we like it or not, providing beds for patients, teaching children, supporting the poor and the elderly. Those patients, children and elderly and their relations all rather like that. These things are seen in a modern state as good. They are there as facts of political life. The state's involvement in these sorts of issues is ancient. It is hard to think of scientific or even artistic endeavour not under some form of national patronage over the centuries. They certainly have been since the seventeenth century, when the 'civil list' paid out for all sorts of little pensions, annuities and grants to painters, sculptors, scientists, and even a poet or two. It is rather the scale of growth since 1945 which has been so remarkable.

While an exact definition of the boundaries of the state will always be difficult to draw, the true task for the true Tory in the twenty-first century will be first of all to determine to control the state's inexorable and apparently inevitable instinct to grow. Secondly, to continue to change the attitudes of the state's servants in the interests of the state's consumers. Thirdly, to let the state grow only in efficiency, and sensitivity, not in size nor number. For inefficiency, insensitivity and waste are generally characteristic of all organisations not subject to the disciplines of the market, and which are not under the lash of delivering a healthy bottom line under the scrutiny of shareholder and institution. It is the Tory task continually to review whether the state should be providing a service at the taxpayer's expense. If the answer comes back 'yes', we should indeed start to provide, say, universal nursery education, or continue to provide, say, central funding for the running expenses of the National Council for Voluntary Organisations; then the state's job is to see whether that can be afforded or continue to be afforded.

Government also should consider whether the state needs to do it; or whether the state should just ensure that it happens, with someone else providing the service or fulfilling the function. If government takes a decision to fund services for the public good with taxpayers' money it does not therefore automatically follow that the state has to provide them, rather that the government of the day needs just to ensure that it happens as efficiently and effectively as possible.

Remembering all of these pressing imperatives, those who control the blind workings of the state through government must do everything possible to break down the divide between the public and the private sectors. This is just as the manufacturing/service split is being broken down by many businesses now. How? By making the division between purchaser and provider central to early-twenty-first-century thinking throughout government. Indeed our aim must be that the distinction between public and private provision should permanently dwindle in significance. Why? Because this will not only be to the public good, and help greater efficiency, it will do much to end the harmful and elderly British class distinction that finds its roots in the thinking that there is a difference between those who use public services (lower class) and those who use private services (middle/upper class). It will also help to end thereafter the tendency of all state-funded services to be captured by the producer. Government should ensure that there is a clear separation between the public authorities whose rôle is to purchase the services, and those in both public and private worlds (and all those hybrids betwixt the two, like housing associations where voluntary effort melds with public and private funding) who will compete for the responsibility of their actual provision. The separation between purchaser and provider in that part of our national life which will be state run in the twenty-first century is absolutely central.

It must be equally clear that those whose duty it is to spend money on behalf of the citizen to buy public services must be quite free of any pressure to continue to provide employment for whatever provider-bureaucracies have historically existed. The bugbear of post-war public provision has been the confusion between the two. This has led to the capture of purchasing all too often by the self-interested provider. There is even an unlikely bit of jargon for this vice, called 'producer capture'. Such a fate can only be escaped if the state as purchaser can compare bids to provide a service which are truly competitive in cost and quality, from alternative and competitive suppliers in the provision of public services. In the twenty-first century it must be an iron Tory rule that it never matters who provides taxpayer-funded services, just how they are provided and at what cost.

This approach has one civic and two practical virtues. The two practical virtues are these: firstly, the process abolishes conflicts of interest and forces both purchaser and provider to define the nature of the service and the standard which should be provided. Secondly, it gives the public sector the means of access to private sector resources, private sector expertise and private sector managerial toughness. The single civic virtue is, by comparison, of great economic and social significance, for it puts the citizen, or those who spend on behalf of the citizen, in the driving seat. In other words, the education authority or social services department or health trust should become the advocate of the consumer rather than the defender of the producer. The post-war explosion in social provision for the needy was indeed an extraordinary sea change in our national life. But it was also a case of one step forward in provision followed by two huge steps back by turning over too much to the provider. There needs now to be a much bigger leap backwards in the interest of the consumer. Thus, to the public good, government and public bodies freed of a managerial rôle should in the future fight for the citizen. They should be their advocates pure and simple, for they are their servants. This process would also help to give back to public service some of the high esteem and standing which many in it undoubtedly should enjoy. Too often they have been thought to be followers of a self-interested doctrine and defenders of inadequate provision. At their best they are neither, and deserve our support and thanks.

What the state must do is be as business-like as possible; what it must not do is own and run businesses. Many of these have happily been disposed of. We should be rid of all that remain by the end of 1999, so government in the new century can begin with a clean slate. Those we had owned were sometimes accumulated by chance, as was the case in one of Disraeli's less glorious moments when he acquired the nascent telegraph network for the state in late-Victorian England. Other organisations were swept up on the post-war passion for 'nationalisation in the public good', everything from the Bank of England to the Covent Garden Market Authority and back again via Nuclear Electric. We still own them. We should be rid of them as soon as possible.

Such bodies should not be owned and run by the state any more than local authorities should own farms. Indeed it is a national disgrace that the assets of local authorities still top some £200 billion. 'Privatisation' has been one of the most successful policies ever pursued in Britain, widely imitated across the globe from Kazakhstan to France; wildly applauded from Chile to Indonesia. Tories need to be proud to have privatised; yet they also need to finish the task. The process since 1979 has brought stupendous improvements to the way that we live now and they must not be forgotten. Take British Telecom (BT). The old post-Disraelian creation, absent-mindedly acquired by the state like our Indian Empire, became progressively more and more producer dominated as the century rolled on. I cannot remember food rationing; but I certainly can in my adult lifetime recall telephone rationing with the dreadful queues to get connected that were there in some parts of the country even in the 1970s. Then, when you did eventually get a line, it was sometimes only to enjoy the extraordinary conflicts and chances of a shared, so-called 'party' line. I can also remember all too well the unworking phone boxes, often vandalised and long awaiting repair.

BT's past is not a pretty picture to conjure up in one's mind's eye – with one exception only to the rule that privatisation gives better results. That is the stark contrast between modern telephone boxes and those old red ones which, like warm beer, still do seem decent monuments to good British taste and production. Tories should be concerned about aesthetic matters in our crowded little island. There always used to be red phone boxes in most places, just like the red pillar boxes or grey-stone parish churches which stand inviolate still. Perhaps the next phase of British Telecom renewal may involve a certain amount of aesthetic re-fettling of their unpleasant-looking, if almost entirely vandal-proof, shiny boxes. The best one can say about them is that they provide easier access for a wheelchair user than their inter-war architect-designed forerunners.

Getting any new design right is, as it happens, one of the biggest architectural challenges of the twenty-first century. Why? Because telephone boxes stand everywhere in their tens of thousands, in city street and shopping centre, in country lay-by and by village greens. They do not have to look the same everywhere, or indeed even be painted the same – when Trollope was busy introducing letter boxes, some of them were green as it happens. The red telephone box was the sole triumph of the old state-owned telephone system. So, in every way apart from the aesthetic, the privatisation of British Telecom (like that of Cable and Wireless) has been a rip-roaring success. It gives a universal service, yet we have found that a combination of regulation (OFTEL) and competition (other companies) has led to the rapid and universal availability of the telephone service; happily calls are a third cheaper in real terms than a decade ago, and international charges have dropped like a stone.

Yet, back in 1979, as well as providing telephones, we were also an oil producer, a car maker, a steel manufacturer, the owner of an airline, and the runner of much road freight. The latter, however, was not a complete monopoly for Churchill's government too was keen on a little deregulation. This allowed the Right Honourable Enoch Powell to address the Road Haulage Association at Grosvenor House in London on 8 March 1965 with words which are both a period piece, and show how far we have travelled since: 'But for the Transport Act in 1953 there would today be no Road Haulage Association, because there would be no private enterprise road haulage. The idea that a private person or firm might actually be allowed to carry another person's goods for hire, would by now have seemed as outlandish as the idea that anybody except the state should be allowed to dig coal or install a telephone.' Exactly thirty years later, happily they now are able to do all of these things.

Even after the triumphs of privatisation, we have local authorities in our country owning hundreds of billions of pounds' worth of assets, and the state still has tens of billions of pounds' worth of businesses. Taxpayers' money is there, locked up in the Civil Aviation Authority, in Scottish Nuclear, in the horrors of London Transport and the entirely unnecessary Scottish Transport Group. And then there are, in mid-1995, more than thirty bodies classified as public corporations, running Letchworth Garden City and the Patent Office, owning the Docklands Light Railway. They should go as quickly as possible into private sector hands, in order to continue to improve the supply side of the economy. This imperative has nothing to do with any philosophical aversion to public sector activity as such, just a clear Tory sense that it is totally inappropriate for the state to own and run businesses.

However, though the money raised from privatisation is useful, the sale of public assets should not be pushed further and faster to complete the job just to deal with our still huge deficit. That has not in fact been the practice in the Tory years, for some of the peaks of privatisation proceeds occurred when there was little or no budget deficit to finance at all. This was happily – but alas briefly – the case in the later 1980s. The privatisation process is very good for the political process as it expels political considerations from areas where they should never have entered. Politicians make bad managers: for one thing they tend to look at life within the four- or at most five-year timespan which is imposed by the electoral cycle. This is not always going to coincide magically with the interests of efficient management except by chance. And, of course, sometimes good managerial decisions are bad news politically, so real managers labouring under the burden of some political chief of staff may be inhibited from taking decisions which would be embarrassing to their political masters. This means that managers are bound to play safe, with initiative restricted and vital organisational changes sometimes inhibited. It is of great political importance to keep these arguments in the mind of a new generation of voters as they lose their political innocence. If not, they may fall prey to the wiles of some latter-day successors to the elderly Harold Macmillan – whose wicked jokes were about flogging off the country's Canalettos in order to fund the annual expenditures of the state – and actually think that this might be true. The reverse is the case. In 1979 every family in the land was contributing £300 per year in today's money towards the financing needs of nationalised industries. Now, those that have been privatised contribute more than £2½ billion a year to the exchequer – a whole year's increase, for example, in expenditure on the NHS in England.

The pursuit of the smaller state and the spreading of ownership must not be thought to have ground to a halt in 1999 or whenever the ritual of the last privatisation goes through the Houses of Parliament, to equally ritual cries of protest. Contracting-out still has many laps to run; and once run, they need to be re-run every now and then in order to ensure that those services tested and done 'in-house' really do deserve to remain in that state. Contracting-out of local government services is well established and has been a great success. Like privatisation it was fiercely fought, though now is readily accepted as part of the Tory consensus. Quite often the in-house team gets the work – but they win by meeting the specifications for types of service which have been laid down. This means that they have to be just as tight on their management and other costs, in order to deliver value, as anybody in the private sector.

A decade or so ago, as a very junior Junior Health Minister, it fell to me to promote the first footsteps of this approach within the National Health Service. The arguments I had in various media about the virtues of privately versus publicly washed sheets had then, as they have now in my memory, a truly Kafkaesque quality. This is because to the patient it matters only that the sheets are well and properly washed. To the taxpayer it only matters that they are washed to the highest possible standards but the lowest possible cost. If the threat to the providers of the service of sheet washing meant they got better and more cheaply washed, then the common good was served. Because of these sorts of disciplines, for the first time in the 1980s and 1990s local authorities and hospitals alike have had to specify exactly what they want to see happen. They have to do this every time a contract is renewed to wash sheets, clean floors or provide hot meals. This is always remarkably laborious the first time it has to be done, but it is remarkably shocking in that it was never done before. This approach also means that the state or local authority can concentrate more on their core businesses.

Many major national and international companies used to think that they also had to do in-house everything connected with their business. This was an all-embracing business approach rather like nationalisation in style if not nature. Now the corporate tables have been turned. 'Out-sourcing' is all, which is the private sector's very own equivalent to privatisation. Wherever you look, whether it is to Cadbury-Schweppes, or to the Rover Group or Unipart or Nissan, they in their turn now often look out-of-company for their information technology, their legal services, their property management or their training and much else. Concentration on the core business or businesses is all in the modern corporate world; it should also be exactly the same in the world of the thoroughly modern state.

Following privatisation, and competitive tendering, down the track has come their logical successor, the introduction of private finance itself into public provision and on a grander scale. Private money has long flowed into housing associations, for example. Here government reforms of housing finance have attracted close to two billion pounds into the non-profit-making housing bodies for what is called 'social housing' – that is, flats and houses for those who cannot afford to buy their own or who cannot find anything to rent in the still much too tightly regulated world of the private sector landlord. By early in the next century, flows of private money into the provision of roads, toll bridges, schools and hospitals should be just as natural a part of our national economic and social fabric as privatisation and competitive tendering. The clearest example of what this can mean involves public payments for the use of facilities which are wholly funded privately. The private sector get all their costs back over a period, and make their profit, by charging the user. Cars paying to travel on privately contracted and operated roads are the textbook cases of how private finance can most easily work. The examples of possibilities can be multiplied. They should be legion in practice. By very early in the new century it must be the public expenditure norm that new day centres for the elderly, wings added on to hospitals, or sports halls run by grant-maintained schools should be funded privately, rather than be the brave and lonely exceptions. There is no reason at all why private sector provision should be confined to those projects where the full costs can be met by charging the user – as in the case of cars on those toll roads – provided the private sector takes its share of the risks as well as the share of rewards. The introduction of private capital into the funding of government or local authority must involve greater efficiencies – in order to deal with the fact that government can always fund projects more cheaply than the private sector (by about two per cent normally) – and risk taking. The introduction of private finance into the new century must not be allowed to become an exercise in creative accounting by government. Financiers of such projects cannot expect normal commercial returns and gilt-edged security to boot, either. The next frontier will be in giving our citizens vouchers for publicly funded services. The great virtue of these is twofold: they are transparent (you can see what the money is being spent on) and they cut out the middleman (which is why they are feared by Whitehall and town hall).

What all of this taken together – privatisation, competitive tendering, the market testing of activities carried on within government and the application of private sector disciplines to them, as well as the dreams of private finance being turned into the reality of bricks and mortar or vouchers into better services – means is the creation for the twenty-first century of a new 'mixed economy'. It will be in a truly Tory image. It is certainly the case that the United Kingdom used to be described as a 'mixed economy'. That phrase was often deployed to justify the tendency of Labour and indeed Tory politicians alike to extend their activities, influence and ownership to parts of the nation's productive life where they neither had the expertise nor should have had the responsibility. What the new, twenty-first century 'mixed economy' will mean is not the post-war, corporatist, dream of government essentially running the economic show as it did from the 1940s to the late 1970s. In the next century, the phrase 'mixed economy' should accurately describe a Britain where the distinction between public and private sector provision is simply no longer relevant. What matters in this new world is the ability of those who manage the provision of services, paid for by taxpayers' funds, to have the freedom to do so, or to attract private finance to these ends. This would truly be the meeting of public goals by private means.

There is one rather eccentric 'pseudo-privatisation' which needs to happen both to shrink the state, but also to bolster it. That is the Bank of England, which the state has only owned since 1946. It has such a strange relationship with the Treasury in particular, the pair of them making the ultimate financial odd couple. This change in status should take place as quickly as possible. No money needs to change hands because of expensive advertising on our TV screens. The Bank has a multiplicity of functions from operating monetary policy to selling government debt; it has collected this moss almost by accident over the years. It does not need to carry them all out. It should now be made independent in order to give a strong guarantee of present low inflation continuing as a permanent part of public policy, and thus usefully encouraging greater long-term investment at home.

A lot of changes have happened in the mid-1990s to help strengthen the grip of the Bank on interest rate policy, and thus take an even stronger grip on the scruff of inflation's neck. The Chancellor's innovative decisions to take advice on interest rate policy formally, decide on a rate change, but then give the Bank operational freedom over the exact timing of the hike or cut are revolutionary in recent British terms. The subsequent publication of the minutes of the meetings of these discussions, which show the ebb and flow of the arguments between Minister and Governor, is equally revolutionary. This is working well, so far. It seems a sensible half-way house, typically British and commonsensible in its approach. So, why go that step further and bother with more change?

The response to the question is quite complex, but can begin to be answered with a look around the world. Those countries that do have an independent central bank – take Switzerland, Germany, the USA, Belgium, the Netherlands, Canada or Germany – over the long run have had lower inflation and more stable currencies than the UK. To have such an institution in such countries is by no means a magic potion against inflation, but it has certainly helped to provide good preventative medicine. So the pragmatic lessons of other countries should appeal to most

Tories on those grounds alone; this is something which actually seems to work.

There are two further components to the simple answer. The first is that with an independent Bank the ability to manipulate short-term interest rates for political ends would be taken out of the political arena. In effect, in many ways this is exactly what recent changes to the steps in the Chancellor–Governor gavotte have brought about. But the opportunity is still there. This leaves in the back of the mind of the investing business community the doubt that they (i.e. the government) might start up the inflation racket all over again, for political ends. Secondly, lasting confidence to industry will be given that it really is worth investing in the long term because inflation will be kept low. If industry does not think we are serious about this, or that some other and more politically frivolous party might come in, take over and blow inflation up again, then investment will continue to be denied, or ploughed in abroad as a hedge. There is a lot of cash in corporate surpluses in mid-1990s Britain, representing about five per cent of our gross domestic product. So there could in the future be considerable medium- and long-term economic as well as monetary benefits, as this investment potential is progressively unlocked. An independent Bank has a prime political virtue for us as Tories, and that is, it will help to discipline socialism/Labourism in future. Should the electorate decide to have a Labour government, an independent central bank would make it impossible for Labour to go on an interest rate/inflation binge of any scale in future years, thus undoing a generation of painful, sometimes faltering but ultimately successful Tory endeavour on this front.

These seem three compelling reasons for having an independent Bank of England. They do not need to be dressed up in the clothes of some great constitutional change, either, for they are simply a pragmatic response to our passionate desire to keep inflation in its box and reduce the state. How might all this be done in practice? I do not think the government should give up sovereignty over the Bank. If we have to admit that, theoretically, there can be irresponsible Chancellors of the Exchequer going off in one direction, then by exactly the same token we must admit the possibility of there being an irresponsible Governor of the

Bank of England. This may seem unlikely in the case of the Jesuitically-austere Mr Eddie George – but who is to be sure? But all that needs to be done is treat the Bank of England rather like an executive agency, charged with going off and doing a job within a tough government remit, just like any other agency. Its task is certainly one on a grander scale than that of most agencies, and is conducted in a grander building, complete with pink waistcoated flunkies and some old-fashioned flummery. So the Bank of England should certainly not have complete freedom. It should be run by people with security of tenure appointed for a period by the government of the day. This should be five years, best starting off in the middle of a Parliament. So then it would not be easy for an incoming government of another colour to change its Governor and Deputy on whim.

There is a strong case for having confirmatory hearings on the appointment of the Governor and his or her Deputy in front of the House of Commons' Treasury and Civil Service Select Committee, as the Bank would be assuming a more independent rôle. At the same time the Governor and his men and women must not be allowed to assume god-like and overblown auras like monetary Roman Emperors. That is why the appointments must be made by the government of the day for a fixed period, in consultation with the clearing banks who use the Bank of England as lender of last resort. The Bank must be but a servant of democracy, and draw its legitimacy from the democratically elected politicians who form the administration of the day. Once 'privatised' and with the appointments made, the office holders need to work to a tough remit laid down by government. It should set the inflationary range that it expects delivered (I would favour 0.5%–2.0% as a permanent realistic target) and how it is to be measured, as well as the length of time for which the range must be maintained. The business of inflationary control would therefore be essentially technocratic; no politician should be involved. So if non-executive directors were to replace the present Court of the Bank, they should be in a supervisory and clearly non-executive rôle. The Bank, as it addresses these difficult and demanding tasks, must at all costs not be let off the democratic leash. Thus, hearings by House of Commons Committees would be part of their life under this prescription. The Bank already has, as a result of another innovation, an annual inflation report which it composes in an entirely independent fashion. This should be laid formally before the House of Commons by the Chancellor of the Exchequer with an accompanying statement, and be duly and solemnly debated. To get Members of Parliament seriously discussing inflation year after year in a great and competitive set-piece debate will help to lock an anti-inflationary culture into all our political parties.

The new Bank then needs to be shrunk in size. Being one of the last bastions of the seemingly untouchable in British public life there will be a great one-off opportunity for a bit of down-sizing amongst the marble halls. For a start, if the Bank is given the measure of independence recommended, it must be freed of any duty to look at government funding needs when at the same time it is taking what must be Simon-pure decisions about the level of interest rates or the tactics/strategy it must pursue to achieve those levels. Someone new thus needs to sell debt on behalf of the government. The temptation will be to put that task inside the Treasury, doubtless moving round pegs from one set of marble halls to another. There may well be better alternatives to this, but those are technical issues not central to the paramount need of bringing about a permanently low inflation, long-term investment economy. The Bank of England, when independent, will play much more than a walk-on part in this process. The state will as a result be smaller; the freedoms of its citizens will also be much better buttressed. It is one of the more important things a Tory government should do by the end of this decade.

All of these changes are going to be simple compared to the much bigger one that is now coming down the track. That is, that it should be an overriding imperative for the new century to persuade our people that it is a good thing to play their part as well as to own their property. Back to Pius XI; this means bringing about real social subsidiarity, and depends not just on good government ideas but whether or not our people wish to take the chance of taking back more responsibility from the state. We have not been bold enough thus far in giving them the chance. Tories have to take the thirty-year view of changes since 1979, and the things that are still to come. The first fifteen years have been taken up with what now seems to be the relatively easy part of the agenda. It may not have seemed so at the time, but to curb union power, to transfer ownership of housing on a mass scale, create a share-owning democracy and get rid of so many state-run industries was relatively easy. Giving people things, whether the chance to own their own council house or shares and thus shrink the state, was successful because people like to own things. This is certainly to the civic good as ownership underpins family and individual life, bestows freedom, erects a barrier against interference with them in central government or local authority. Very much more difficult and a task for the next fifteen years is to try to transfer more responsibility along with ownership. This is to give our people the chance to create a civic society for themselves, consistent with the fine old Tory principles of ownership *and* responsibility – also with the best of human nature. Giving people the chance to have more power over their own lives is a huge idea, which is still far from the end of the political runway. The more that the responsibility for running communities is in the hands of those communities rather than bureaucracies, then the better things will be for them. That Tories might take the lead in this and make it all happen might seem a fantastical suggestion. Yet did not the idea that the state might stop supplying telephone lines or making steel or mining coal seem just as extraordinary in 1978? To enable this to happen will have practical and civic virtues, for money will be better spent and local involvement promoted.

Whether people want to have this responsibility in the same way as they so obviously wanted to take ownership remains one of the bigger political questions of our age. It is rather more difficult to persuade people that their life might be better – rather than just full or busier – if they took up those suggestions. Any examination of how far the process has gone, and how far it might reach, could start with pondering one question put in the examinations of the summer of 1993 to undergraduates reading Politics, Philosophy and Economics at Oxford University. Their Modern British Government paper began, 'A hospital trust and a grant-maintained school are prime examples of subsidiarity in action. Discuss.' After discussion, the answer from the brighter sort of candidate should emphatically have been 'yes, that is exactly what these bodies are'.

The health and education reforms provide some of the best examples of devolving direct responsibility. But the problem is, at least at the outset, that many of the people who have availed themselves of these reforms are the self-same people who were already involved to some extent. How many more potential active citizens are there in the land? Quite a lot is the answer. No one now seriously proposes going back to a system in which governors are not in the ascendancy in running their local school. There have suddenly appeared active citizens aplenty to man the governing bodies of all state schools, whether grant-maintained or not. The vacancy rate for governors is extremely low, and that is a tribute to the selfless and largely unsung work done by so many men and women. Is it going to be much more difficult to bring more people and new areas of endeavour into the civic net? To make sure it is not, we need to explain how this approach will release people from a welfare culture, and how a dose of active citizenship may make life better for citizen and the community alike.

Our message should be that we wish in the new century to give you a square deal in life and to enhance your opportunities. We need to persuade people that to limit the rôle of the state does not mean being less caring and limiting responsibility towards others in society. Instead, this process allows for the exercise of far greater responsibility. To look to the individual does not mean the creation of some hedonistic society, in which each leads an atomistic existence doing whatever they want and ignoring everyone else. What we should seek for the new century is to parallel the reinvention of government by the reinvention of responsibility. This needs a little selling. We have got to help people to recognise that the state not only cannot but should not do everything in the social arena. This is just as we successfully persuaded people that the state should not play such a big part in the economic life of our country in the 1970s and 1980s. In the post-1979 years we have clearly and permanently won the battle that the government should steer, but not row, the economic life of the country; no longer do we have public sector oarsmen vigorously engaged in coal extraction or steel manufacture or piping water supplies to our people. Those public sector operatives have gone; what we now have instead is a much more appropriate style of economic management, with the Treasury and DTI checking that the economy sticks to its low inflationary course, and does not go too fast or too slow (or so runs the theory). Steering the economy is now all. But to be successful in the social arena in the same way means the state giving up power and involvement, exactly as it has done in economic matters.

The difficulties of this are twofold. Firstly, in finding people who want to take responsibility as much as they wish to take ownership. And secondly, in the equally daunting task of persuading local communities that because diversity and choice comes into the provision of a public service from taxpayers' funds, this is a good thing. For far too many, the thought is that diversity of provision must mean two- or three-tierism or worse, just because there is a variety rather than monochrome provision. But post-modern politics – for that is the change that the economic transformation of the last fifteen years has brought about – should be equally uneasy with universal state welfare provision. So the state needs consciously to turn to new ways of running things, shrinking itself on the way. Already Tories can claim some clear successes, although a number have barely been noticed. For some, compulsory competitive tendering seems to be about persecuting innocent local authorities for political ends; to others, it is dry-sounding and technical stuff. In fact competitive tendering is about as community-minded a policy as could be found, taking the part of the consumer as against that of the provider. Removing power from the provider, even if it means that it resides briefly in the centre before being redistributed, is invariably to the community good. For the communities and the individuals who make them up sit at the rim of the wheel of our national life. They are at the very end of those spokes of public spending coming out from the central hub of government, where they meet the grass roots. The hub must be as small as possible, the money and responsibility redistributed as much as possible down those spokes, so that the communities on the rim of the wheel can better turn it to the public good.

Some of this has already begun to be done quite successfully with the health and education reforms. In the case of the National Health Service, the redistribution of power to the patient is real, though thus far only through an intermediary. In doing this now we are moving towards an NHS that is not a nationalised service, rather one that is free at the point-of-delivery, whoever carries out the caring. It is the state who always pays. The new model National Health Service works a bit more on market principles. The patients who are the customers of that market have thus far been given a ticket of only indirect entry into the marketplace. Their interests are represented and their tickets punched by the purchasing Health Authorities (which are universal now) and fund-holding general practitioner practices (deciding to go down this route is a matter of choice for the independent contractors, the doctors, who decide to take the opportunity of operational freedom and finance or not). These bodies must be more and more responsive to patients' wishes. The patient is not yet personally 'entrusted' or 'empowered' save in being able to shop around a bit for their general practitioner of choice. General practitioners want to have more patients on their lists because of the capitation system, which means money following the patient; at the same time, they can refuse to have patients and there is no reason why this should not happen, choice and responsibility should be there for patient as much as for doctor. Not all doctors have taken the opportunity given to them. This is a pity, for the additional responsibilities matching the additional opportunities which fund holding entail have great intellectual weight; the moral case for them is overwhelming too. Putting the National Health Service under more local influence in this way is a start. Doctors and health administrators (nurses or surgeons could not function without their management skills) have started to take advantage of the route of freedom afforded by the health reforms. Those GP fund-holding practices are like little self-governing kingdoms. The problem seems to be that we have not had the courage of our convictions; general practice fund holding is the nearest we can easily get to transferring power very close to the patients in their interests, yet not all practices are signed up to this excellent way of doing things. They should be transferred lock, stock and barrel as a matter of priority.

Are there any further steps that can let the patient enter the National Health Service market more freely and get the services that they think they need? The answer is yes, by giving purchasing power directly to the patient through some voucher or entitlement system. This is appealing at first sight, but as yet probably tricky to operate in practice. This is because having something called a 'health care voucher' would indeed bring home to the taxpayer the real cost of our national health care service. Patients would turn up for appointments; less money would be wasted. It could be topped up by private insurance, which would bring more discipline still to bear. Yet these virtuous purposes would come up against the fact that people do not fall ill for an average period of time every year; illnesses and major traumas come and go. For some a life of permanent pain and difficulty is there, for others just one catastrophic accident or illness to be catered for in an otherwise doctor- and nurse-free lifespan.

Then there is the key issue of how to design a bureaucracy to administer this new system without steepling administrative cost. It is probably the case that however theoretically appealing such schemes are, more effort should first be spent trying to make those health authorities and trusts and GP practices as sensitive to local individual needs as possible. This certainly does not mean that they should, to use Labour's phrase, be 'brought under democratic control'. The thought of local councils or, even worse, special new local health councils, elected perhaps by less than a quarter of the electorate and bringing the issues of health care right to the forefront of local party political argument is not appealing. It might fill columns of local news print and provide employment for a new political salariat but is certainly unlikely to promote genuine and greater individual and community involvement.

So the first lesson to be drawn from the National Health Service is that it is sometimes less than easy to transfer power from the hub to the rim of the wheel. The process seems much easier with schools, where it is much simpler to bring citizen and choice face to face. Choice has a strong moral component, is a considerable civic virtue in itself. There should be a monument raised to it in a proud position in Parliament Square. This is because the effect of choice is always to raise the quality of provision. So choice serves a very public end. In education, as a result of parental choice conferred on them, mothers and fathers can send their boys or girls to better-performing schools. Already we can see, when this choice is married to a powerful school inspectorial system plus the possibility of failing schools being taken over by Education Associations, that bad and underperforming schools can go to the wall in a system dominated by choice. Equally the good and successful schools are allowed to develop, flourish, and possibly expand. All of this tough-sounding stuff is to the public good, for the public's children have only one school career and thus one chance to get a good start in life. As we know from bitter experience in this country, the phenomenon of encouraging and expanding the good matched by a drive to replace or remove the bad can never happen if the provision is uniform. So choice is a critical cog-wheel of both personal freedom and development, through helping to drive up the standards. Choice should also be the natural bedfellow of caring. The links between a compassionate and caring community and one where public provision is driven by the engine of choice are close, and the two should be symbiotic. This is precisely because it is compassionate to wish children to perform to the best of their abilities, reaching the highest possible standards that they can achieve. Churchmen and statesmen alike should be able to agree with this. Introducing choice like this is a critical part of the new politics.

Step by step, and rather successfully since the mid-1980s, Tories set about giving more choice to parents. We also began the process of giving more power over how schools are run back to schools and away from local authorities. Then, even more daringly, we have given the chance to local communities to take over schools and free themselves completely from bureaucratic control in a new form of civic endeavour. The first phase of the systematic empowerment of parents was by the introduction of what is known as Local Management of Schools. This devolves many powers of Local Education Authorities to schools; budgetary control follows that power. As a result a majority of schools in our country have direct control over about nine pounds out of every ten pounds which are spent on education locally. This transfer of power and responsibility to the schools – a halfway staging post to giving complete independence to them as grant-maintained if parents wish – was bitterly opposed by the vested interests of the educational world at first. It was excoriated as an outrageous attack by a wicked government. Yet, less than ten years since it was introduced, it is not possible to find anyone who wants to reverse the trend. Governors and Head Teachers, once they have got the hang of controlling their budgets, helped by the obligatory computer, seem to flourish under their new-found freedom. They spend money where they judge it best spent with the knowledge that only the truly local can have. They can decide whether to carpet classrooms or to spend more on the core curriculum. That is right.

The very success of this once 'wicked Tory policy', so attacked by the neanderthal divisions of the education establishment, means that now this very freedom is used as an argument against the logical next step for schools, proceeding to grant-maintained status. The intellectual bankruptcy of people who argue thus is staggering. For this second stage means that parents can vote whether they wish their school to be state funded, but independent. If a school is performing well, enjoys community support, and already has command of nine out of every ten pounds that go to its pupils, then it is rather like a nearly mature fledgling perched on the edge of the nest. It can and should now so easily fly alone. When this decision is taken, it is normally a remarkable expression of local community involvement, putting flesh on the arid bones of all theoretical but often meaningless jargon about 'empowerment'. These grant-maintained schools become self-governing: teachers, parents, business people and others, all active pillars of the community join in to run them.

One of the reasons for introducing grant-maintained status was to help to fulfil our nascent but underdeveloped Tory commitment to empower individuals in more areas of social life. What has been the experience thus far? Well, self-governing grant-maintained schools have certainly engaged the commitment and the expertise of parents and other members of their local communities. Many accountants and lawyers have come forward with their expertise, for example. These people have ensured that money is spent wisely on those things which the school independently judges it most needs. They have been able to target money and to do so quickly, not waiting for an official in County or Town Hall to act on their request. Greater responsibility has meant greater commitment. It has resulted in greater local pride. Little things in political life sometimes stick in the memory, and one of those was visiting an infant school in southern England where the just-about-to-retire woman Head Teacher took me into the cloak-rooms and showed off the fresh tiling behind the basins. She told me, 'They were always a mess before I had these put in, and the local authority simply wouldn't do the job for ten years – we are now getting on with running our own school.' The result of this local unleashing of responsibility has been better and more efficient schools. That is as it should be. It is a consequence of giving power back to the locals. There is a grave danger that, despite the enormous shift in attitude achieved through local management, there will be a big effort by bureaucracies, promoting the reinvention of a culture of dependency. A culture, that is, in which schools are made to feel that the dark secrets of the management of change are known only to a select few. Rather it is the understanding of the problem and the will to change which are critically important. The technical know-how is much exaggerated. External expertise can be important for a business as much as for schools, but they do not, for example, need local authority 'pre-inspection reviews' nor 'post-inspection counselling'. Such bureaucratic interference is costly, patronising and debilitating.

The extent to which grant-maintained schools target money in the best interests of pupils and teachers is borne out by the results of recent surveys of grant-maintained schools. These record that, since acquiring grant-maintained status, nine out of ten secondary schools have increased their pupil numbers; eight out of ten were employing more teaching staff, they were increasing their provision for pupils of special needs and spending more on books and equipment. Little wonder perhaps, given the greater freedom that schools enjoy, that ninety-five per cent of these schools had no problems in recruiting and retaining governors, with many happily reporting an increase in the number of parent-governors seeking election. That is exactly how it should be, when responsibility is transferred.

Matching this is the information that is now provided in order to enable local people to make their choices in education soundly. It is essential to provide full, accurate, and up-to-date information about how public services like schools are run, what they cost, and how well they perform. No information; no real choice. Those performance tables of school and college examination results have had an electrifying effect on school performance, and made so many more people interested in what is going on in them. The evidence for that? It is in the acres of newsprint which each year are now used to publish supplements in our national and local newspapers of just how schools and colleges have done.

Just as over the introduction of the now universally accepted Local Management of Schools, the producer lobbies in the shape of teacher unions, and some educational experts, were in full cry against them. Even when they rapidly recognised that once the information cat is out of the bag, the media for one will never let these figures be suppressed, the campaign continued on fresh ground, to make adjustments of results on 'social and economic grounds'. These 'adjustments' will of course be made by 'experts', whose aim will be to wipe out all difference and try to explain away the reality that it is not money alone which ensures a good education. If money were the answer, many of our inner city schools which have formidable sums of money spent on them, by comparison to other areas, should by now be spectacularly better than they are. Yet only a few out-perform not just their local, but the national, average. This is because those schools themselves have chosen to set demanding benchmarks and then drive towards them. They do not make 'socio-economic adjustments' for themselves and their pupils, rather they face the educational realities of life.

Schools like these recognise that pupils have to make their way in life on the basis of the grades they have actually achieved, not those that the experts want to attribute to them. If it is good enough for children to have grades, then it is good enough for schools to be graded on their basis. There is a wealth of evidence to show that a school's performance is not automatically and directly dependent on such things as money or the social background of its pupils. In post-war Britain, there has been far too much secrecy about our primary and secondary schools; it is the publication of information which has broken down the walls erected around the educational secret garden. The performance of grant-maintained schools has been exceptional. If the principle seems right, and the practice effective, why have these benefits not been universally applied? They should be, in the life of the next Parliament, starting first with the country's four thousand secondary schools, and then rapidly moving on to our twenty thousand primary schools.

This should be paralleled by the introduction of educational vouchers, easier to bring about than in the NHS. They would have the great practical benefit of being transparent. Parents would see exactly what they are spending their money on. Their economic as well as educational virtues would be that what the state pays would not get raided by town halls and siphoned off to pay for the army of non-teachers funded by the education budget. (In some areas there are now more than two officials for every three teachers.) Their great civic virtue would be that parents will be able to choose to buy what they want up to the value of the voucher, not be told by the state what to do.

The same sort of active citizens who have helped to run our schools are also trying to do their bit up and down the land to prevent crime. Here we can also do more to improve twenty-first-century life, by transferring some responsibility to the community. Probably nothing threatens the security of any government more – after the threat of job insecurity – than the fears of electors about crime. In the politics of crime, it is usually a mistake to underestimate the anger of voters. Capping the inexorable post-war rise in offending, and the matching growth in the petty incivilities which make life unbearable, is a vital task. Detection, condign punishment and the principle of putting the victim first make a virtuous trio.

Our people have a broad sense of what leads their neighbours to crime. Most crime is indeed neighbour preying on neighbour; so it is first prevented in the neighbourhood, and by the community. There are no excuses for crime; there is no victimless crime. City fraud, for example, may rob the nameless but rob them it does. Our people want us to be tough on crime, but they also want an acknowledgement that the rich man may more easily resist stealing than the destitute man. It is very important that we continue to mobilise the community against crime. 'Citizens to arms' is one way of helping people recreate a more civic (and civil) society. The mobilisation that we have seen dates only from the early 1990s with Neighbourhood Watch schemes. Now there are more than a hundred thousand Neighbourhood Watches with scores of thousands of members, sometimes lively, sometimes becoming moribund, but overall doing more than their bit in the battle against crime. Where Neighbourhood Watches are effective, they have an impact in deterring burglary and theft in particular.

Keeping them going demands a lot of effort for the police organisers (often civilian these days) and the active citizens who volunteer to become their local co-ordinators. But slowly, almost imperceptibly, a little power goes their way as a result. This is first of all because of the way in which those notices go up saying, 'This is a Neighbourhood Watch area'; then by the reports that are given to the police of potential or actual local crimes, helping both deterrence and detection. There have been some very welcome recent additions by the Home Secretary, in the shape of the new parish constables. This excellent idea means more 'specials'. They are no longer deployed anywhere in a force area, but only in their home streets or village lanes which they know, and where they are known. This reinforces the involvement of the community in policing themselves. So far, so good, and having travelled so far over such a short period of time, Neighbourhood Watch is no longer excoriated as a sort of nosey-parker business by the left-wing councils who so disliked them setting up in their area. As late as the late 1980s, some like Cleveland still conducted guerrilla warfare, by banning the erection even of harmless 'Neighbourhood Watch' signs on lamp-posts. Those little organisations are now thought to be both politically correct and benevolent by all sides of the political community. Nationally, this is yet another example of the swift (and realistic) rightward movement by those in the Labour and Liberal Parties who once thought this wholly admirable idea was representative of repressive policing or shot through with Tory dogma.

The movement to mobilise citizens permanently to prevent crime needs to go deeper and wider in the new century to deal with the reality of offending. This is, that most crimes are committed by young men, with the tendency to give in to temptation reaching a peak in their mid-teens. It is in the run-up to this stage that maximum community effort needs to be concentrated. Here is a new task, which can only be done within the community, and can never be satisfactorily carried out by statutory services nor the police force alone, however numerous. That task is, to try to prevent criminality amongst the young in the first place. In other words, identifying those likely to get into trouble and trying to help them not to do so. This approach has long been talked about in the upper reaches of government. In the past it has kept bubbling up to the surface of government action, but has never broken the surface. Successive Home Secretaries in quite recent Tory years have worked on quite well-developed plans to begin this task, only to find those plans side-lined by successive Tory Prime Ministers.

What 'preventing criminality' means is addressing the causes of crime, at its roots. This in its turn means starting a process of long-term change. It is clear that our traditional responses cannot by themselves provide the whole solution to the problems of crime and criminality. It is young individuals who commit crime; thus it is their attitudes and behaviour which will need to change if it is to stop. Some action to encourage young people to keep out of crime should be as integral a part of the total response to the problems as is the detection and punishment of offenders, crime prevention, and the support of victims. Criminal prevention should be an integral part of dealing with crime.

'In the old days', people are often fond of saying, people listened, did as they were told, and got a thick ear if they did not. If there ever was a golden age where youngsters were helped not to give in to the urges of criminality and thus drift into a career of crime, it was probably the much more lightly governed 1920s and 1930s. Victorian England was a pretty lawless place, particularly in towns; and in the UK, as all over the Western world since the 1950s, reported crime has gone up year on year. In between – doubtless helped by the shock of the killing fields of the First World War – was an epoch of relative civility, where authority figures stalked the land. A sharp word from a park keeper or a bus conductor seemed often then enough to stop some minor incivility, and from minor incivilities and yobberies crime springs. Then a couple of PCs managed a football crowd with great ease. Those authority figures, thanks to the introduction of everything from technical changes (automatic ticket machines) and manpower cutting (in the proper interests of greater efficiency and economy), are not around in the numbers that they once were; and, if they were, their natural authority would be much more likely these days to be viciously challenged at worst, or simply ignored at best.

It may be hard to recreate that half-mythical inter-war age with all its custodians of the public peace and civic virtue. It is, however, possible now to take a longer-term view of preventing criminality, tackling both the phenomenon itself and the hopeless feeling which abounds that 'nothing works'. What is needed is to build up a greater sense of responsibility for their own actions amongst the young before they leave the primrose path and start to grow crooked rather than straight. In other words, to seek in a thoroughly modern way to reinvent those boundaries constraining behaviour which used to be there. Certainly the available evidence is that the volatile chemistry of crime is complex, with no simple litmus test to say exactly when it is going to break out. But if criminal behaviour is to be nipped in the bud it needs to be tackled not just by the state and bigger government before it starts, but by those who first observed the problem – parents, teachers, police, churches and many others – in conjunction with those who can help to solve it. And these happen to be the self-same parents, teachers, police, churches and others. In the end, a small proportion of young men commit a disproportionate amount of crime. They should be the target for criminal prevention work. Like weeds, they spring up each year, as new generations grow into the offending years.

The impulses which seem to move some young men first into crime are strongest between the ages of eleven and fourteen; they turn all too often into full-blown repeat offending for a small number of them by fifteen or sixteen. If, by continuing effort, they can be kept out of trouble, then there will be fewer victims and less troubled communities. To do this needs strong local leadership, and a local framework quite specific and of long duration. So, *criminal prevention associations* could be of great value and do enormous good, bringing state servant and active citizen together at this task. On one side of the table head teachers, youth leaders, probation officers, chief constables, local authority chief executives and social services workers would be gathered; on the other, would be churches, voluntary organisations, chambers of commerce, Neighbourhood Watch co-ordinators, victim-support schemes and the rest. Their aim? To identify the nature of the local problem, for in different parts of the country offending patterns seems to vary. Having identified the problem, then to work out co-ordinated but local plans of just how to deal with diverting youngsters from crime.

If this indeed recreates the best of the past, using formal and organised methods, while not trying to take away youngsters' freedoms won over the post-war years, that is no bad thing. It does mean identifying children and young men in particular who are at risk. The answer to dated and pathetic *Guardian*-esque cries of 'this means stereotyping' or 'that is authoritarianism' can be pretty brisk. If to identify children clearly at risk of going off the community rails is stereotyping in some way, then so be it. For that is exactly the same sort of stereotyping that takes place if a child is identified as at high risk of asthma, or of being abused by a parent or suffering dyslexia. Crime is just another manifestation of human disease and, like any malady, if it can be nipped before the bud breaks then that is practical caring and compassion at work. If it is thought authoritarian to organise diversionary activities for potential offenders or having fierce little words with children who are about to frighten society's horses, those who think thus need just to go to one of our gaols. They can there look at the results of inaction. There are too many people in them, too young, so sad, too much ignored, simply hopeless. Often having been victimised by their parents' lack of firmness, or lacking love, they might just have been helped out of their dilemma if someone had done something.

So, for the Conservative Party to face the new century with hope of capping the post-war crime wave which has so disfigured British and all other Western societies, it is not too early to start on this task now. This means putting alongside better detection, fiercer punishment and the primacy of the protection of victims some real criminal prevention amongst the young. 'Criminal prevention associations' are needed in order to provide a focus for the shared civic responsibility of preventing criminality. As a result, over a period of years, there should be less crime, and perhaps less will have to be spent on law and order services. But none of this will happen unless government realises that it is a snare and delusion to imagine they can do it all; instead they should recognise that part of the answer may be paradoxically in shrinking or refocusing state activity. The other part is not to forget the traditional Conservative moral attitude to the punishment of justly convicted criminals, that this should be done because it is right and even if it can not be 'proved' to reduce crime levels. Our citizens feel right and well protected if they can see that criminals have been properly treated by the courts.

At the other end of the spectrum from the young offender are the elderly, as well as the disabled of all ages and those with mental infirmities who need better care. This need could well be met by similar bodies, called *care associations*, to help to put communities, volunteers, and the private sector back into the driving seat where historically they always were in social provision. Here there is a model that works for all to see in our Housing Associations. These are sometimes criticised for becoming too large and over-bureaucratic. But they have been vital in helping to shrink the state's rôle in social housing. They have spent taxpayers' funds pretty efficiently. Progressively they have also helped to take housing out of the political arena.

'Let us take the politics out of X or Y' is the immemorial cry of many a politician on a television or radio panel show who has either run out of anything to say, or who wants a quick burst of applause, or both. It is not always possible to do that. But if the provision of housing has been depoliticised to some extent by the introduction of Housing Associations, then care associations could have the same effect. How? In part of a city, the whole of a town, a slice of countryside or a stretch of coast, there is no reason why the state cannot shrink the local authorities which it funds in order to better deliver the care which society rightly feels must be provided. This is there in varying amounts for everyone from those in need of a little bit of help (a home help two or three days a week to clean a bit and cheer up the old man on his own, who welcomes the hot meals – and the kindly enquiry after his health just as much – when they come from the WRVS lady who delivers the foil-covered containers Monday to Friday) to the truly helpless (the severely disabled or elderly and doubly incontinent who are cared for at home by loving but exhausted relatives who need all the help they can be given).

To assist people like this is fine and desirable; very few want to be wrenched away into a home or hospital unless it is inevitable. Yet putting all our eggs in the statutory basket, even if we enjoin social services departments to co-operate more with the voluntary and private sector, does not yet seem to have produced the goods. When we have county councils who in 1995 complain that they cannot manage to provide proper care in the community even with the massive increases of funds that they have been given, then that is a sure indication that we need to look elsewhere.

Many Conservatives thought that it was an error to give councils this task in the first place. They believed that it would store up problems precisely by building up the state, when the reverse was desirable. Why might 'care associations', modelled on housing associations, do this job better? 'What about statutory duties,' the vested interests will cry; 'these have to be fulfilled.' Of course they do. But housing associations which have taken over some of the statutory provision to provide shelter when a local authority's houses and flats have been transferred to housing associations lock, stock and barrel following a tenant's ballot, do their job well. And there are those already involved in social care, like the National Society for the Prevention of Cruelty to Children, who have long undertaken precise statutory tasks within the law, and to universal acclaim. So care associations should be encouraged in order to take over part (just the disabled; just those moved into the community from long-stay mental institutions; just children's services) or all of the provision of the social help that is needed in different areas, according to local demands. To do this would be to return to the grass roots much of what is directed from the offices of distant County or Town Halls. To do this also would shrink the state further in its local manifestations, giving renewed life to community endeavour.

This approach to the provision of education, fighting crime or helping the needy means that politicians and bureaucrats locally and nationally really must remember to steer more and to row less. The problem is not of finding people to undertake these tasks. It is often the case that every time some fledgling organisation is thought of, wiseacres say 'you'll never find people to do the job'; yet thirty years ago housing associations as we know them were barely thought of, and ten years ago there were hardly any Neighbourhood Watch schemes in the country. Give the British people the chance, make the task appealing, and many will respond. This does mean however that we must explain what these movements mean in an appealing way and with clear language. This is not concerned with ideological-sounding 'privatisation' (though co-operation with and the provision of services by the private sector is to be welcomed, wherever it is more efficient and less expensive than any other sort of care). It is rather a process which is concerned with what is described by two other bits of unlovely jargon, 'enabling' and 'empowering'. In reverse order, this means giving to local people the chance, and the money, to do their bit. The process would require new legislation and new organisational frameworks. However, it does not require more bureaucrats or more money – the history of this sort of endeavour is one of seeing a pound stretching further. The simple message is that the taking back of the running of things is not going to be just cheaper and more effective, it is going to make your quality of life better. The community should be better housed, there should be higher educational standards, less crime, and more sensitive forms of care for those in need.

Thus should the state be shrunk by a Conservative government. The Tory message as we open up this second front for a new century is that local and mixed, rather than bureaucratic and politicised, provision is best. It is also that direct, deep and continuing responsibility is something communities should welcome. We must spell out how people's lives are going to be made better by this process. Happily there are all those examples of those high-performing grant-maintained schools, those effective Neighbourhood Watch schemes with their parish constables and those housing associations as points of light to show the way. This approach, we must explain, releases people from the worst effects of dependency culture, and frees them from the iron grip of bureaucratic state welfarism, even if in order to do this the state collects in and redistributes taxpayers' money back to those carrying out the tasks at the rim of the wheel. The Tory message for the new century is that on the social as much as on the economic front not only will we give you a square deal, we will enhance your opportunities and quality of life. The moral message which parallels that is that we wish, if you wish, to transfer much of the responsibility the state took over from you this century back to you in the next.

By comparison, for Labour, apt these days to be embarrassed by the crumbling of its post-war statist dreams, the promoting of 'community' means something very different. For them diversity is something to be abhorred. This is because the presence of diverse forms of provision is always thought by Labour to mean that there must be some which are better and some which are worse, just because they are different. Secondly, Labour feels that in the end wise and all-seeing state-employed people must run it all, or it will not work. Labour is the national Party of officialdom. Labour is not the natural party of community. Indeed, most of Labour's criticisms of so-called 'quangos', ludicrous though they are, could equally be applied to local bureaucracies. What Labour wants to do in its plans for community is, rather, to recreate the past, but without recreating hard-core municipal socialism. They want to have an approach which can have a new name, but has no Derek Hatton nor any Ted Knights. They certainly do not want to have any real devolution of power, nor any diversity of provision. Labour wants the recreation of municipalism behind a veil of community rhetoric. To ask the Labour Party in the end to kick the habit of trying to run things for people is exactly like asking them to give up the narcotic addiction of spending other people's money.

To reinvent or recreate the opportunity for responsibility means shrinking the state, and reducing its local manifestations as well. Government and individual Ministers, as well as hard-working local Councillors and officials, will always have a rôle to play, but it should in the new century be a different one. Local elective democracy needs to be kept in fine fettle, but joined by much more active local involvement of communities and the private sector in running those things that they are better suited to do. The two are not mutually exclusive; they rather run on two parallel tracks.

This reinvention of responsibility should be part of the essence of thoroughly modern twenty-first-century Conservatism. It will follow from the deepening of Conservatism in social policy in the next two decades, just as we deepened it so successfully in economic policy in the 1980s and 1990s, thus underpinning the lives of individuals and of families.

5

The British Family

We should shrink the state to leave more head room for the family. Then we should bolster that institution. We should support the community in order to provide support in its turn for the family. We need to get the balance better in the twenty-first century between the family, the community and the state. At the moment it is out of kilter. If it is a mark of social and economic imbalance to have an ever-growing social security budget, then it is also a mark of the progressive collapse of a country's cohesion to have its families in decline.

Since the Second World War we have let government grow too big – blindly expanding, seemingly almost omnipresent. Partly as a result we have undermined family and community alike. One of the greatest threats we face in the new century is not some particularly vicious economic manifestation of Disraeli's two nations. Rather, it is likely to appear from the deep division between those who have enjoyed and benefited from a stable and caring upbringing in their families, and those who have not. The undermining of the family, and the attack on the strong family and responsible individualism has meant the balance of state power has gone rather against the family as an institution. It has also gone against the tradition of duty and ties to the community

which is part of its rationale. As much as government can influence such matters, we should concentrate on economic and social
policies that support the two-parent family. At the same time we
should make sure that we always attack weak claims for public
support and not weak claimants.*

Families have always been there. So have communities, but we
have seen the ties of community eroded as they have developed
over centuries and across generations. The very basis of civil society is that of the family of parents and their children, extending
outwards to the wider community. Between them they have provided timeless bonds of civility on which responsibilities, duties
and obligations rest; they have also helped supply the practical
arrangements by which these could all be fulfilled. The point of
the family apart from love and mutual support has been to protect and raise children from infancy and through vulnerability
until they reach self-sufficiency and contribute themselves. Then
they can take their turn just as their parents did, as responsible
adults – and parents of the next generation. Families need
fathers, not just as breadwinners but to give positive male examples to that most potentially troublesome and criminal of classes,
the young and teenaged boy. So should values cascade from one
generation to the next, and so communities should develop and
strengthen.

Some of the often unwitting attacks on family life have been
due to changes in attitude; on other occasions it has been because
of distorted attitudes to the family as an institution. The family
cannot flourish unless it has a decent amount of economic freedom. One of the absurdities of post-war life that will need to be
demolished little by little in the new century is the belief that
what government does with the money it takes from people's
earnings is altruistic, and automatically 'in the public interest'.
This same line of thought says that what individual men and
women do with money is, *ipso facto*, greedy. It should be an iron
rule of government that the state should not interfere in how parents bring up their children, and should also avoid taking away

*For a brilliant exposé of this in the United States, see David Frum, *Dead Right*,
New York, 1994.

parents' money in a way which impedes their essential right to spend their earnings. The family is a moral good. Money helps to support the family. Some of that money comes from public expenditure, whose ever growing size has led to debate being conducted in terms largely of how do we 'restrain public expenditure' (now well above three hundred billion pounds a year). The first question to ask is, rather, not how do we stop the juggernaut of public expenditure rolling out of control, but rather what is the moral basis for public expenditure in the social arenas of our nation's life in the first place.

We need to restore much greater economic liberty for the family in the new century. We need thus to concentrate more on the family, and be less than neutral as between married and unmarried families in our taxation and social policies. A more than plausible case can be made that by default and through best endeavours, much of contemporary social and taxation policy works against the stable family. If the family is put first, and is thought to be worthwhile nurturing, then this should leave any Conservative politician imbued with the desire to give back to the family more chance to spend their own money. We have to draw a line across which the juggernaut is not allowed to proceed – for reasons both moral and financial. If we do not do this and subsequently hold that line, then public expenditure may well destroy what it sought to help in the first place. That will lead to government out of control, and families being robbed of their self-reliance to the point where they are destroyed. Various valiant attempts have been made to begin this task these last fifteen years, but are mere skirmishes compared to the lengthy war of attrition which needs to be undertaken.

Conservative social policy has evolved traditionally on the basis of Conservative governments respecting the right of the individual to look after themselves and their families. The often unspoken theme that ran through this is that over and above taxation for the essential duties of government – defence, law and order and the rest – governments should leave people to spend as much of their own earnings as possible on themselves and their families rather than spend it for them. That is why, in the 1920s and 1930s, Tory social thinking, reflecting changing times and increasing 'needs', led to government concluding that it should ask individuals to insure when they were earning. This was thought prudent in an age when costs of living were increasing in parallel to standard of living and aspirations. So, anyone in work should insure himself against a loss of earning leading to unemployment, should certainly insure against sickness, and should put down some money against old age. Churchill thought like that when he was Baldwin's Chancellor; and so did Chamberlain afterwards. They certainly were not concerned with any nascent social security system which viewed redistributive taxation as a public good. Rather they saw such schemes as not only meeting need but increasing self-reliance and incentive for the family and the individual. So, statesmen of their time and ilk respected the fact that a civilised state needs defence and domestic policies for internal and external security. They also quite rightly understood there should be provision for the poor or the less well-off. Interwar Ministers would have thought the modern mid-1990s welfare state inconceivable in its size and reach.

There are three separate forms of public spending. The first is where the state takes responsibility for common concerns. On the one hand there is defence and foreign relations and on the other upholding the law at home, policing, catching and punishing those people who break the law. Second, there is that redistribution of wealth where government uses the funds the better-off have to help those who do not have them. The third area is one where government decides to provide services to families and individuals, which might otherwise be providing for independently. These are everything from insurance against unemployment and contributions to pensions to providing services like education and health. The government has a responsibility to protect the sick, the old, the unemployed, the handicapped and others in need. Tory social tradition, at least until recently, was that people should be encouraged to meet and pay the cost of many of these needs through contributions, rather than by simply depending on other people's money being redistributed to them. One of the biggest changes we have seen has been the tendency of the state increasingly to ignore the contributory element and to treat everyone, whether they have made contributions or not, as potential supplicants at the state's door. Thus the balance has been tipped sharply against the contributor.

So, the early principles on which a welfare state system were developed owed much, as Beveridge himself recognised, to notions of self-help by the individual for himself and his family. That is why the welfare state had a tax and National Insurance system to reflect this. Taxation involved an element of redistribution, while National Insurance was a matter of paying to insure so that you and your family did not suffer. The problems have come later, in the blurring of the distinction between these two types of public spending. There will always be those who depend on the help of others, and that help must be given by redistributed taxation. But in terms of government policy this is a very different matter from encouraging individuals to take more responsibility where and when they can to look after their own families. We too easily lose sight of the fact that the wider framework of taxation, benefits, and social policy should always avoid discouraging incentive. We should also always avoid measures which undermine the responsibilities which individuals have and bear towards each other.

Then, in the 1930s and early 1940s, the natural companion of the promotion of self-reliance was small government. That was not thought to be just a practical aim, but something which was seen as morally right in itself. That is exactly how we should see things anew in the twenty-first century. That attitude should mould our whole approach to reform of the welfare state, before it swamps public finances and private families alike. It should be a Tory article of faith in the new century that the tax system and the social security system should be designed to wholly virtuous twin ends – to support the family, and to encourage self-reliance.

Earlier in the present century, Protestant England with its traditional work ethic and Catholic Rome with its support for cosy Christian democracy seemed to be at one; secular thinking and religious thinking were congruent. The influence of Popes like Leo XIII* across Europe was strong. He exhorted governments and the rulers of state that the state had no right to tax a man

*See his Encyclical *Rerum Novarum*.

and spend all his money for him, rather than allowing him the fruit of his earnings to spend on himself and his family. From this flowed the equally strong view that the state should never abrogate to itself the responsibilities over children which belong to the family and to the parents of those children.

Secular and deeply Protestant English social thinking went along much the same lines. Sir William Beveridge, if he were resurrected today, would be horrified at what has subsequently been done in his name; a level-headed and entirely coherent concept has been kidnapped by politicians and administrators, in an essentially blind fashion. I should think it unlikely that Sir William Beveridge ever had a Papal audience, or read any Papal Encyclicals. But his thinking was the same as that emanating from the Holy City. He argued time and time again for only a minimal contribution and insurance scheme on which individuals could build for themselves, and their families if they had them. Government, in his view, had no right to take money and spend it above a minimum level. It certainly had no right to eradicate the incentives to work and earn, let alone to look after the family.

It was pragmatic stuff, built on the ideas which had proved quite successful for their times earlier in the century. Underlying all those insurance schemes to cover against loss of earnings through illness and unemployment, as well as pension schemes for retirement, were some great assumptions. For example, that most people would be in work most of the time. And of course Sir William's time is a foreign country to late-twentieth-century Britain. His thinking was moulded by a society which did not have serial marriage, endemic divorce, nor many of the never-married single mothers with one- or two-children households, that so characterise the world half a century on in the United Kingdom.

The point of this approach was that it kept the state small; kept the state's fingers off an excessive amount of individuals' own money; and kept the state out of the front parlour as well, so it had a minimal rôle in family life. Contribution was at the basis of this way of looking at things; funding everything from general taxation was thought to be positively bad. The idea of contribution was that it gave the contributor a stake in his or her scheme as of right. If there is a contributory basis for any scheme, it must also mean that costs are kept under control. That is seemingly why Beveridge proposed that the contribution should be a flat rate, and the benefit that accompanied it equally flat. Thus employees or potential pensioners would be left with their own money to take out additional schemes to suit particular circumstances, present family or future pension needs. Equally, while playing its part through the benefits, the state would self-consciously guard against taking money and spending it on behalf of the citizen, reflecting a strong moral imperative. It seems a tragedy that the original compulsory comprehensive scheme suggested by Beveridge was not in the end operated by private societies and companies, exactly as he wanted. They could have used the opportunity to sell additional annuities, policies or schemes. If that had happened, we would have had a genuine mixed economy built into our social security system from day one, rather than seeking to create it now as we must.

Beveridge's ideas were right, in tune with recognition of a citizen's personal responsibility – and equally supportive of the small state. Two things have gone wrong since. Firstly, the notion of a framework for social security that both supported the family and did not discourage incentive has gradually become eroded. And the idea of contribution as the basis for benefit has ebbed away. That is why, by 1994, the benefit bill in this country was running at eighty-five billion pounds a year – substantially more than the amount raised that year from income tax and corporation tax put together. So not even the redistribution of income and corporation taxation can meet the bill which the contribution of National Insurance has long since failed to do. It now yields not much more than forty billion pounds a year – indirect taxes like excise duties on tobacco and drink or VAT bridge the gap.

Secondly, government is now a huge business compared even to that of wartime England; Government Departments have grown in number and size. Policy has become more ambitious as new thinking on social issues has become more ambitious. Welfare spending spirals. The post-war consensus was that big government and large Departments had to be high spending to meet newly perceived needs. Yet big government reduces through its social spending the risks that used to be there, automatically attached to those who chose not to be self-controlled or cautious. As a result, people can indulge in new and sometimes destructive behaviour without facing the consequences. The habit has sometimes grown little by little, in the way that Joe Kirwan observed, 'Ministers are using money that has been taken compulsorily from the taxpayers, ostensibly to cover the costs of government, to give to coteries to enable them to impose their tastes on other people. Monies raised in taxation ought to be used exclusively for the necessities of government including provision for the otherwise uncared-for poor ... also to be avoided is state support for causes which Ministers choose, or have chosen for them by committees composed of willing spenders of other people's money, or have imposed upon them by vociferous groups. The task of governors is to govern wisely. It is not within their competence to scatter largesse.'* Such 'largesse' that can be accumulated is best spent rather on supporting the family.

The family certainly is not a perfect institution. Families can be unhappy, disruptive at worst, sometimes stifling. But the nuclear family is a near-universal social unit. It meets a basic human need. It is not some passing phenomenon, but rather a fundamental part of social relationships. Secular (and occasionally religious) self-styled visionaries in their time have recommended alternatives, everything from free love to communes, from multiple to serial marriage. None of them lasted as has the family. Most of us still spend most of our childhood in a household headed by a married couple. Despite all the problems that there are with family life, most of us marry and most of us have children. The family is far from dead, despite the buffetings it has received from everything from earthquakes in social attitudes to changes in the social security system. Yet there has certainly been a decline in the numbers of our people living in a traditional family. Over the last twenty-five years, the shift has been from about eighty-two per cent of the population to seventy-five per cent of the population living like this.

*J. Kirwan, *Subsidiarity, Government and Taxation*, CPC, London, 1995.

There has been a substantial growth in 'consensual unions' as they are known. Those participants in these thoroughly modern versions of the trial marriage are usually young, have never been married before, and do not yet have children. What normally seems to happen is that they live together for a short while and then either go on to marry or break up and go off to some other relationship. Cohabitation in this way has not replaced marriage for most people; it has generally become, rather, a prelude to it. Overall, as public opinion surveys show, the British population still believes that people who want children ought to get married even if they do not do so themselves. It is the same with attitudes towards religion. The vast majority of British people, when questioned, want their children to be brought up knowing about Christianity, even if they do not go to church themselves. The retention of those old attitudes is comforting, and does leave something to be built upon.

This continuity in the family as a central part of British, let alone European, life has been paralleled by some dramatic changes however. We now have the highest ever divorce and illegitimacy rates the country has known. And with these are associated social horrors and human tragedies. The first is the heart-breaking plight of children who so often suffer emotionally, psychologically, physically, and materially as a result of growing up without the protection of both parents committed for life to each other, and so to their children. Children need loving mothers, and they need the authority as well as the love of their father. If one or other is not there, or if the adult players come and go in multiple relationships, then children *always* suffer. This may seem a deeply politically incorrect suggestion to some, but it is true.

Governments cannot and should not seek to become involved in the turmoil of personal relations in any way at all. But governments also have to face up to implications of family breakdown for public policy. These are particularly clear in the high levels of homelessness and poverty which so often result from family instability. A family split up demands two roofs where one was enough before; a joint income which goes a long way where a family is sharing it, does not stretch so far when it has to accommodate the needs of those now living apart, who used to be together. And then there is that cycle of delinquency which is so often related to insecure family background. First of all, children fail to achieve as they might at school because of unhappiness. They often then slip into truancy, and if they avoid subsequent crime, which may be hard, then they may not find it difficult to slip into unemployment after leaving school.

Governments of all political colours cannot be blamed for the post-war changes in attitudes which have brought this about. For too many years smart social scientists and glib members of the chattering classes have encouraged generations to look upon changes in family structure as not only the inevitable, but probably beneficial, result of progress. Traditional attitudes to love and marriage needed updating because they are outmoded, went the argument. This was a good thing because the flowering of individual liberty would be helped. Hypocritical bonds which locked couples into loveless unions at considerable cost to their own happiness and that of their children (and how wrong that has turned out to be!) would be brought to an end. Such approaches flew in the face of the reality of marriage, as recently neatly summed up by a forty-something French female tax inspector talking to Theodore Zeldin. 'The family is an institution,' Colette told him, which requires 'constant effort to sustain it. It is important not to want everything to be perfect. Couples divorce because they expect too much from each other, refuse to make concessions, can't wait patiently for better times.'* This is high-octane reality, even if some of those who do really recognise it, and then strive hard to stay together, feel that they have to go to the divorce court in the end.

Governments were very much involved in the public policy responses to these pressures. Understandably perhaps, they reflected them to an extent, and did their best to legitimise them. Taxes and benefit arrangements came to be framed in order to help those who were, in practice, simply the casualties of the new thinking. What this meant was that those who stayed together in

---

*Theodore Zeldin, *An Intimate History of Humanity*, Sinclair-Stevenson, London, 1994, p. 58.

traditional families came increasingly to be seen within a new framework that was more and more designed for those families who split up. The families who stayed together began increasingly to cross-subsidise those who did not, or who never ever had formed a lasting two-parent relationship under one roof. This means that families increasingly lost out economically – though for the best of motives of course.

Public policy now must be aimed at doing all it can to cap, then reduce, the growth of single parenthood amongst young mothers and the parallel growth of divorce in the United Kingdom. It will do this best by being positive, encouraging family life, and being realistic about single motherhood and divorce. It must not attack or marginalise those who sometimes, although not always, are in such a position through no fault of their own. The United Kingdom cannot and must not be proud of the fact that it has more single mothers than any other European country, and is the divorce centre of Europe.

Since the 1960s there has been an extraordinary increase in the rate of single parenthood amongst young mothers. Now a quarter of all mothers under twenty-four in the United Kingdom are single, and have never been married. They are concentrated in areas of economic difficulty in our capital and cities like Manchester or Liverpool, much more than in rural counties. This is compared with only about ten per cent on average over the rest of the European Union. Life is not easy for the single mother, emotionally or economically in most cases, though some flourish. It is a grievous political mistake to attack the 'single mother' both for the craven political reason that there are a lot of them and they have votes; and for the more compassionate reason that if you marginalise any group then that militates against the social cohesion of the country. Public policy should always start on the basis that all people are good, that no sector of society should ever be decried – except the criminal, of course. None the less, everything that goes on through public policy, community development, education, the work of the churches and voluntary organisations should be aimed urgently at helping cap and then reducing this trend early in the new century. All the evidence – without apportioning blame on the mother or some absent father, and certainly without reopening the wounds of old political debates about whether single parents are 'guilty' or not – is that despite the efforts of many single mothers who do bring up their children well, *on average* they are likely to perform less well at school, and more likely to drift into delinquency and crime. Thinkers on the left joined thinkers on the right in the early 1990s to agree that this is in particular because of the absence of fathers, and thus of a consistent male rôle model and authority figure.

It is the same in the case of divorce. About a hundred and eighty thousand divorces happen every year in this country. A third of marriages are now likely to end up in the courts. There is a classic study of what has happened to children born half a century ago in 1946 after their parents divorced, then a very rare business.* This followed the life stories of about five thousand of those now forty-nine-year-old men and women whose parents parted. It found that fears about the malign effects on children were no fabrications but, rather, tragically fulfilled. Those immediate post-war children of divorced families were twice as likely to have had a criminal history by the age of twenty-one, had a greater likelihood of emotional disturbance, and achieved much less at school. They were even more prone to serious disease, remarkably enough. These problems seemed to hit the boys of such marriages particularly hard, for they had significantly lower income throughout their lives. They were three times as likely to be unemployed. And, when those of both sexes married, they were likely to divorce themselves quickly if they did.

The divorce rate in the 1940s and 1950s was running at about ten thousand a year. Now it is closing fast on two hundred thousand a year. That means that the personal horrors that the 1946 generation faced with the emotional distress, the stunted economic chances, the greater likelihood of drifting into criminality and the rest are likely, alas, to be reproduced in spades for those born of divorced parents over the last couple of decades. If history

*M. Maclean and N. E. J. Wadsworth, 'The Interests of Children After Parental Divorce', *International Journal of Law and the Family*, vol. 2, 1988.

repeats itself, as sadly it is likely to do, then between two and three hundred thousand children are going to be born in 1995 whose parents either will never marry or will end up in the divorce courts – however much of a lilt there was in their step when they went down the aisle. The problems of this year's divorced children are going to be one of the great challenges of public policy lasting, possibly, much of the twenty-first century. It is in the hands of future governments at least to stop the trend getting worse. Governments cannot make people love each other or stay together with their children. What they can do is recognise that every time they have reformed divorce law to date, this automatically has led to a fresh surge in the numbers of divorces. It is clear that there is a causal link between every liberalisation of the law, and the following dramatic rise in the numbers of divorces.

Those are the simple facts. They should make it astonishing that government ever again in the twenty-first century might seriously contemplate easing divorce law further, whilst simultaneously expressing anxiety about single parents, their children's problems, and the health of society at large. All our past experience shows that changes in divorce law have created the very problems that government now struggles with and will have to for much of the next century. (An old-fashioned and shell-backed Tory might be pretty pleased at all this, for it surely demonstrates that truly 'all change is for the worst'.) Reforming divorce law certainly saves neither marriages nor money. It pleases absolutely no one in the end, outside some in the narrow legal establishment who are always coming up with new ways of making bad situations worse.

Is this a cruel criticism of the austere members of the Law Commission who have led the charge on this issue over the years? No, but they are part of the problem. The Principal of St Anne's College, Oxford,* was around at the time in 1969 when their influence was most malign. She knows what she is talking about now, for she held a post then with that self-same Law Commission which helped to formulate the Divorce Reform Act,

*Ruth Deech, *Divorce Dissent, Dangers in Divorce Reform*, CPS, London, 1994.

1969. While the learned Law Commissioners were coming up with their ideas, divorces were running round about seventy thousand a year. When their thinking passed into statute in the Divorce Reform Act of 1969, overnight another forty thousand divorces with all the attendant problems suddenly came out of the closet. When the Act came into effect in 1971 more than a hundred and eleven thousand couples then split themselves asunder. This just magnified the same experiences that followed earlier from the 1937 Matrimonial Causes Act; that year there were six thousand divorces; in 1938 suddenly there were more than ten thousand.

The architects of these changes in 1969 said that they wanted to promote 'The stability of marriage, reconciliation, maximum fairness, protection of children, and the economically weaker spouse . . . The tragedy is it just did not work out like that. Not only did the numbers of divorced people shoot up, but the numbers of children born out of wedlock exploded as well; yet the measure was brought in expressly to regularise what were then called 'illicit unions' and hopefully legitimise those so cruelly called 'illegitimate'. It was indeed suggested that the level of divorces might fall back as a result of this reforming legislation. The precise reverse happened, and we did not learn from experience. Then there was the introduction of the Special Procedure in 1977, which meant that some parties no longer had to appear in court under certain circumstances. Once again, the effects on the numbers of divorces were electric. The one hundred and forty-one thousand divorces of 1976 shot up to one hundred and seventy thousand the very next year. Now, the mid-1990s arguments for divorce law reform which are still to be heard from the Law Commission are a reprise of what they were saying back in the mid-1960s. They want to make the law 'understandable, efficient and respected'. Now, as then, they predict that should this or some future government implement their recommendations then of course there will be no rise stemming from these new laws. Then, as now, they would be wrong. It was realising this fact that caused a few within government in 1993 and 1994 apparently to make such a fuss privately then, that the proposals being brought forward to follow their recommendations were happily stillborn. They lurk still menacingly on Whitehall's capacious shelves. These plans should be given a decent burial.

If a country really believes in the welfare of children, then any law that might risk an increase in the divorce rate should always be avoided. Equally, it should do nothing to promote serial marriage in society, for we cannot afford it. Most men simply do not have the resources to support the wife and the children of the first marriage if they remarry, so they become a charge on the state. It has been an unspoken political convention between the parties that having a go at making divorce less easy is totally unacceptable 'in modern society'. That may be so, but there should be now an equal consensus between the parties that we will never make it easier either. It is a politically correct conspiracy of silence that while a public debate rages on single parents and the problems of their children, the fact is submerged that over half of these children are the result of divorce and separation. Since the middle of the last decade well over three and a half million adults have been divorced, some of them more than once. About 1.7 million children have grown up during their parents' divorce over the same period, some children have been affected twice by the same experience within that decade, for sadly, second marriages are even more likely to end in divorce than first marriages; a third marriage even more so, we are told. The financial costs to the state are enormous, several billion pounds a year.

It is the emotional costs that are more important than the material ones, both because of the pain they cause, and because they lead to those personal problems which linger on through the generations thereafter. It must surely be accepted as an iron rule of social legislation from now on that if a government introduces changes to the divorce laws of the day, then the divorce rate will automatically rise. As bad, and equally automatically, more and more children will suffer, and more and more costs fall on the state. Further reforms will increase the long-term benefits bills for one-parent families. The unstated effect of too much policy since the 1960s through government of both political colours has been to hallow the destruction of families by making divorce easier; we should at least stop doing the latter, and instead concentrate more on underpinning family life. Otherwise the social as well as economic costs by 2020 and beyond may be unbearable.

Criticisms of Toryism by commentators since 1979 have often concentrated, wrongly I believe, on the fact that Conservatives were supposed to have let individualism rip, and selfish individualism at that. In fact changes both in the law, as well as in public spending and social policy have, since the middle of the 1960s, encouraged another sort of individualism to strike at the long-held basis of obligations within the community and thus at the heart of the civic society. Just as there must be all the understanding in the world for those people who can simply no longer live together, and who make the irrevocable break despite all the problems for them and their children which they know will follow, so we must be the same in our attitude to 'single parenthood'. This is not, and should never be a term of abuse. Widows and widowers often struggle wonderfully well to deal with loss and the subsequent problems of rearing children alone. Deserted men and women do exactly the same with their children. Single parents can be of all ages, but what seems uniquely British is the huge explosion in young single female, one-parent families since the mid-1960s. The problems for their children can be very much the same as they are for the parents of divorced children.

The government's chief medical officer has not yet ruled on the effects of single parenthood on children, but in his annual assessment of the nation's welfare published in September 1994, Dr Kenneth Calman highlighted the social, educational and health problems suffered by children from broken homes. To pick just two of these, Dr Calman said last year that girls under sixteen in step-families are three times more likely to leave home because of disagreements or ill feeling and four times more likely to marry before the age of twenty than those who continue to live with both parents. And, even worse, girls who become part of a step-family by the age of sixteen run twice the risk of becoming teenage mothers and giving birth to their baby outside marriage. It therefore looks as though divorce itself is a potent engine in the formation of many of those young single parents. Nearly three-quarters of single-parent households in the United Kingdom in the mid-1990s depend on state benefits. These are almost always given to mothers who themselves have paid little if anything by way of contribution towards those benefits. In effect, the tax-payer has become the husband of all of these young mothers, who have married the state.

The last census in 1991 showed that there were rather more than one and a quarter million one-parent families in the UK, with about two and a quarter million dependent children in them. The cost of support for lone parents last year amounted to well over seven billion pounds, which is an increase, taking into account inflation, of more than 175 per cent since 1979. Over the same period, and in step with those huge rises in expenditure, has been a quickening in the strike rate of teenage conception. Between the 1981 and the 1991 censuses these increased from fifty-seven births per thousand teenage girls to sixty-five births per thousand teenage girls. This is despite the blizzard of sex education, the explosion of sexual knowledge, and the cheap and easy availability of contraception on demand.

It is wrong to suggest that all those young unmarried women have children just to get a council flat or house, and thus all the benefits which follow for those faced with rearing a child on their own. But the very existence of such benefits does make being a single-parent family much more feasible than it was. In the old days – the not too old days, just back in the 1950s, and 1940s, let alone earlier – economic realities forced unmarried girls to think long and hard about lone parenthood. If they had a child, then adoption often followed. The inevitable conclusion is that, just as with trying to halt the seemingly inexorable rise in divorce, there should from now on be no further new particular advantages given to single parents. Everyone who can, must be encouraged to make a contribution to the children they have brought into the world. This is, of course, a lot easier to write than to do.

The rows following the introduction of the work of the Child Support Agency, a good idea which almost floundered on the rocks of poor introduction and implementation, show what it is going to be like. The men who marched in mid-1990s demonstrations against the Child Support Agency have sometimes done so not because they did not wish to support their children but because they thought they had struck a deal with the courts and that had then been overturned by these new arrangements. And 'the man facing up to his responsibilities' has quite often meant in practice that his second and perhaps subsequent families have found themselves suddenly suffering in the interest of bringing a bit of relief to the already deprived children of the first family. Some even argue that if the Child Support Agency really were to succeed, it would have the net effect of making some of those second families much less viable. In the end as a result they would be forced to look to the state for money for the basics.

The approach underlying the Child Support Agency is in principle quite right; it is wrong that men or women should know that if they abandon their children, then there is always going to be someone to pick up the tab. By the same token, however, knowing that you can hitch up with the state matters; we must realise that the availability of easy insurance (all those state benefits and all that local authority housing available) does have subtle influences on attitudes and behaviour. It will take a generation of determined effort to bring about the necessary benefit and fiscal changes slowly to right the social and economic balance between those who benefit and those who foot the bill. The see-saw has tipped strongly against the conventional two-parent family. There is an increase in the net burden imposed on them by the state. The scale of support for lone parenthood has increased greatly, and that increase has been funded quite substantially by the taxes on, as well as National Insurance contributions of, married couples. At the same time the fiscal benefits that used to be there to encourage marriage have been diminished. In less than a century we have seen the momentum that drives taxation policy switch from supporting the family as the priority to supporting the single. Both may need society's help. But the social see-saw has been allowed to hit the ground to the general disadvantage of families. In making the case for fiscal and benefit changes, let alone alterations to any legal framework, it is important to keep right in the middle of the political radar screen the exact reasons why we are concerned about the realities of the family. So a precondition of any full discussion of funding matters must always be based on a clear Tory philosophical approach to the family, why the family is so good socially for the country – and indeed why it is an important motor of the economy.

The big difference between right and left of centre views on this matter, even at a time of apparent political convergence, is the Conservative belief in the family underpinning the community. The Conservative respect for the family is founded both in the institution as a reservoir for traditional popular wisdom, and in Judaeo-Christian morality. And Conservative social geography locates it as the place most likely to be where helpful attitudes are learnt and good manners are inculcated. Conservatives also believe in authority. Though the family appeals as the place where authority is exercised, undoubtedly this can sometimes be erratic, careless or wayward. Hopefully, however, it is usually genuinely loving, firm and productive. Socialism at root really does not much like the family as an idea, however much the veneerism of modern Labourism may pretend it does, because families are about authority. At their worst, socialists tend to feel that the exercise of authority is oppressive. These miss the point. The family that makes a point of eating together – rather than browsing through the day – and talks together, learns to be understanding, tolerant, and respectful – not just of each other in the family, but also of authority generally. All of this means less public expenditure on social workers, policemen, judges, prisons and the whole expensive paraphernalia of what has become modern state-run social, rather than family, control.

So not only are good families happy families, they help calm or enrich communities. They may also cut costs on the state. What is more, it is too easy to forget that there is a very strong economic case for the family as well. Economic history since the early Venetian and Dutch empires show that economic vigour goes hand in glove with social stability. It is economic failure, not economic success, which leads to social breakdown. That is why we find traditional family ties at their weakest in the inner cities and bigger outer-city housing estates, the unfortunate and often innocent recipients of deadly blasts from the twin barrels of industrial blight and high unemployment. The correlation between areas of high unemployment and those with high numbers of single parents is striking. The only alternative to an ever growing dependency culture in those places is economic growth and renewal there. If there is no renewal, then there will be more and more benefits paid out and more and more members of a shadowy 'underclass' appearing, those contemporary menaces to the perceived security of the middle classes. These, like the beggars of the Middle Ages or the threats of syndicalism and then communism to late-Victorian England, are more imaginary than real. So to twenty-first-century Tory Chancellors of the Exchequer, sound economic policy will always for sound practical reasons have a bias to the family. This means that the politics of the family must not be left to idealists, religious zealots or, worst of all, liberal social scientists.

If it is accepted that how children are brought up contributes to the social stability and economic growth of the country, then it becomes crystal clear that the philosophy of twenty-first-century Conservatism towards the family should drive taxation and benefits policy. The rot set in with Rousseau. In his beautifully written but endlessly damaging *Emile*, he laid down that all children are naturally good and only made anti-social by the corrupting influences of society itself. By the 1960s, this had not only been swallowed hook, line and sinker but turned into reality. Politicians, including some Tories, thought that there was too much discipline about, punishment was all rather difficult. Of course many in the emerging new educational establishment thought this must be right. Discipline and competition to them were obviously coercive devices, encouraging an entirely undesirable searching after personal attainment.

The surroundings of children naturally influence them. To that extent, Rousseau may have been right. But children are inherently potential savages at the beginning. They need to be taught restraint, how to be sociable, how to abide by laws. By not supporting families adequately, then, the state undermines one of the family's most important rôles. So the strong approval which parents and families may give to children because they work quite hard, are pretty helpful, generally tell the truth and have got relaxed good manners, is vital in showing the young and then fully grown-up adults the social and economic attitudes needed to make both community and economy hum. The twenty-first century will not be a pluralist society where absolutely any form of behaviour is broadly acceptable that some 1960s thinkers pre-dicted. Indeed, in a world where personal services of various sorts will be more and more motors of economic betterment, then manners will be vital in the armoury of social skills that will help underpin economic opportunity.

Conservative thinkers and doers over the next twenty-five years must put the family at the centre of economic things. They must never forget, either, that the family is vital in the education of children. That fact should inform our changing attitudes to the provision of child care and nursery education. The guiding prin-ciples for the government must be that the state should be neutral between mothers who choose to go out to work, and those who wish to stay at home and look after their children full time. There is nothing absolutely right or absolutely wrong about either way of life, and a lot of mothers and some fathers do a bit of both at different stages of their working life.

It is clear that some types of anonymous and institutionalised child care are not much good for other than the housing and feed-ing of young children. What can be good for children is high-qual-ity child care or nursery education. The two are not exactly the same. Both however have low numbers of children looked after by lots of carers or nursery nurses or teachers in friendly and homely surroundings. It is a very ambitious agenda indeed for public expenditure to contemplate universal provision like this on demand. Equity indeed demands that mothers who stay at home should get the same opportunities as mothers who want to go out to work. To do that would make it even more expensive. It is worthwhile remembering, however, that the ideal child care or nursery education environment – those small numbers of children getting close attention from warm and stable adults in friendly surroundings – is exactly what the ideal family plus its network of friends and neighbours is like! To recreate this at the state's cost is economically impossible and socially damaging. It would be even worse with additional state provision being made for fathers to have statutory paternity leave, as many in the European Union would want. The idea of paternity leave, like 'child care' and 'nursery education', is one of those measures which some on the left in particular now demand as a 'right', and also as an apparent show of support for the family. The reality is exactly the reverse, for if taken to extremes it could harm the family. If we have this sort of state provision, then the non-wage labour cost of businesses would shoot up. Taxation would increase. There would certainly be higher unemployment from the higher costs. Some employers might be turned off from employing young married men, because they would be more expensive. In the end the family would just be taxed again in a new way, in order to give even more of its money to the government to spend on the family's behalf. Married families would undoubtedly suffer the worst, as they would also be contributing to the costs of paternity leave for those at the margins of work, who would be unable to make proper contribution themselves. Being the 'Party of the Family' as speaker after speaker proclaims in Conservative Party Conference after Conservative Party Conference does not mean taking more and more money away from the family to recycle it around the social benefit system again. The best way of helping families is smaller government and lesser taxation.

Such families are of critical importance to the economy, for they are likely to provide many of the best-educated children eventually entering the workforce. Public, political, and business life in this country is stuffed with examples of those men and women who perform at the highest level, having freed themselves from the difficulties of circumstances and background by a combination of education and ambition. Ambition is, like competition, a very good thing. So it is a very good thing that Tory governments since 1979 have given children and their families greater opportunities than they generally had in the previous twenty years, for example by the introduction of some appropriate education policies and the publication of information about the results of all the taxpayers' money that is spent on teaching our children.

These policies must continue to reach the children in those parts of the educational system where they have been let down with poor schooling. This has often been reinforced by that most hopeless of all educational knee-jerk reactions, 'they come from a poor background or difficult family, so you cannot expect them to do well'. Two American thinkers have produced a picture of exactly how they think this sort of approach is likely, in their view, to finish off many American communities (this would happen by the increasing segregation of social groups, rich marrying rich, poor consorting with poor).* Happily, what happens on the other side of the Atlantic does not always automatically happen here. In the United Kingdom, we tend to be linked more closely to social changes and norms on the mainland of continental Europe. But it is instructive none the less to pause for a moment over their vision of a future US urban hell. They see the country rigidly divided by intellectual ability and educational attainment. Thus there will be two sorts of urban ghettos. One will be for those, sometimes of an ethnic minority background, on whom the education system has given up. Poor white or black alike, they will be a dull lot, marrying their kind, and producing an ultimate lockout world – no education, no jobs, no communities. The fuel for their communities will be welfare handouts; drugs and crime will be their daily lot. The other group will be made up of the bright and well educated, marrying each other, ensuring that their children do the same. They will be encouraged to be ambitious and brought up to love education in good schools. They will return to safe areas at night with their high-earning mothers and fathers.

There are some hints of this picture having emerged in small areas of London, Birmingham, Manchester, Liverpool and Glasgow in particular. Hints must not be allowed to turn into reality. The only way to stop it is by good education. That is why closely monitored and rigorous standards and the driving on of children are so important in these areas in particular. Some schools in East London or Liverpool which adopt this approach are spectacularly out-performing the glum expectations of pessimistic professionals as a result. Schools in inner cities get substantially more cash than schools in leafy, prosperous suburbs to educate each child. Some of these have more problems so more money, up to a point, may well be needed. But all the money in the world will not solve the problems. Tests, examinations, and the publication of results are important to expose not only the

*Charles Murray and Richard Herrnstein, *The Bell Curve*, New York, 1994.

under-performing but also the high-performing schools in inner city areas. These should be seized on as rôle models by the rest. But no amounts of money nor effective new educational policies are any good without high expectations of children. We need inspirational head and other teachers, determined to expect just as much from a child living in difficult families and appalling circumstances high in some tower block as they might from those in a comfortable middle-class ghetto. It was a very wise school inspector who said of the teachers in one such school that rather than telling children who did their homework 'well done', simply because they did it at all, they should say, 'That's pretty good but let me show you how to make it *even better the next time.*'

In the end, people in such areas can only pull themselves up by their own boot straps. The most effective public effort that can be made is to strive to give children being born and brought up there the same state educational opportunities as in more comfortable areas. There, the middle classes have long, and with subtlety, brought about selection in schools through the cost of housing. Thus they have found a cast-iron way of passing on educational and so social advantages to their children. In some parts of London, and in some British university towns, it is extraordinary to hear of parents boasting as though it reflected civic virtue that they 'send their child to a state school', when those neighbourhood schools they colonise have effectively institutionalised selection by house price in the area.

The cycle is reinforced by what we and their teachers expect of our children. Examinations always favour the well taught, and teachers like to teach in such places; teacher assessments generally favour the outgoing and the well brought up, who can express themselves clearly. Such are not the initial characteristics of some pupils in many city schools. Extra cash goes to them, to help those children. Too often it does not produce results. Pioneering legislation exists in order to take over some or all of these schools which are failing there despite the much higher sums of money spent on them. A body called an 'Education Association' could take over and control one or all of the schools in such an area, bring in teachers with high expectations, sometimes on short-term contracts (and paying them more) to break the cycle of disadvantage for once and for all. It is desperately sad for the children in such schools that with the means to do this on the statute book nothing has yet been done.

Such radical approaches would certainly never be taken by a Labour government. They are not as a Party attracted by a civilised meritocracy which would accept that talent is important to an individual's chance in life, but also which wishes to celebrate the self-improvement of that talent. The whole attitude of the left since the Second World War has been essentially deterministic. Labour believe that large sections of the urban communities are pre-ordained to failure – and to vote for them. If they are to get out of the circumstance which has hampered them they can do so only by having yet more money spent on them or by the system being rigged through positive discrimination and 'adjusting' results to reflect 'socio-economic factors'. It is impossible to think of an approach to a major contemporary problem which offers less help to those who need it most. Educational despair and political correctness are part and parcel of the social but also the economic problems of the inner and outer city, undermining family life.

This should not be the Tory way. We have the way to help these areas break out of this cycle of despair by revitalising their schools. We need to give families the chance to grasp at a better education for their children than they ever had. It is politically and personally patronising to suggest that they would not. If they could do so in 1861, surely they can in 1995. Commissioner Goode's views on parents in Victorian Newcastle then should reach down through the years to that same city's problem estates in a new century. Giving evidence to the Royal Commission on education in that year he said, 'It is a subject of wonder how people so destitute as labouring parents commonly are, can be such just judges as they also commonly are of the effective qualifications of a teacher. Good school buildings and the apparatus of education are found for years to be practically useless and deserted, when, if a master chanced to be appointed who understands his work, a few weeks suffice to make the fact known, and his school is soon filled . . .' More than a hundred years of state education of all our children in Britain has helped breed a people, in some parts of our country, quite indifferent to education. That indifference will be turned into interest only if the opportunity is there which families can recognise on behalf of their children.

It is instructive, as it always has been since we have had immigrants entering this country, to look at how some of our minority communities value education because it is a family icon for them. The Jews who came in waves first of all to London, and then spread across the country in the nineteenth century, have education as central to their family life. Go to some of the areas they once colonised, or visit some Muslim families in both east and north-west London, and you will sense that same veneration for education. It is seen as a powerful mechanism for economic and social advance, and is entirely based within the aspirations of the family. Some other minority groups struggle to identify with being British, and play a full part in the economic life of our country. That is why it is critically important to make sure that the children of such families are taught English first and foremost, and are taught in English throughout the school day. If they do not have a firm grasp of reading and writing in English, and cannot speak standard English with some mastery – whatever their accent – then they will suffer. Children of such minority communities, like their parents, need to know the language of the country, and they also need to know the customs and history of Britain if they are to integrate themselves in the place where they now live. That is why it is essential for the children of minority communities to know about the history and constitutional arrangements of Britain, just as it is important for reasons of family piety for them to know about their own roots back in the country from which they came, or from where their parents travelled to settle in this country.

Conventional wisdom always says that more money must be put into such places and such communities with such appalling difficulties. Thus are contemporary consciences easily satisfied. Thus also is much contemporary money wasted. Future support through the taxation and benefit system in the twenty-first century should rather concentrate on support for the family and getting better value for money. All the evidence points to this being the best way to spend money to greatest effect and to have most benefit on the moral 'health of the nation'. We hear a lot about the health of the nation in its physical sense; its moral well-being is, or should be, of equal public concern. It is a very short-sighted government that will take decisions about social policies funded through taxation on the basis of penalising the major contributors in favour of the non-contributors. Since 1945, the demands and obligations imposed by big government with endless ambition have left a lot of those on the fragile margins of living via their own resources more dependent on the state than they would otherwise have needed to be. It is a sad reflection that post-war governments have taken a lot of their money but not given them a lot of choice. Now is the time that those post-dated dreams of mid-century social reformers, such as the god-like Beveridge, should be realised – for top-up schemes which would allow contributors to state systems to lay down more against possible loss of earnings, to build up a bigger pension, obtain better health care, or get better education for children.

Families need to be taken out of the fiscal firing line. They have been the biggest victims of big post-war government, especially those with one modest earner and two or three growing children whose contribution and taxation bill make real independence from the state very difficult. People like this are often double-losers; they lose out on having enough to look after themselves, as they are contributing so much to others, but they also have no other choice than to take what local authority or state gives them by way of education and health care. These facts are enough to justify lower taxation which is something for the moral good and welfare of families, and thus the nation. But low taxation is not sufficient in itself. While we should, as a compassionate country, have a bias towards the poor in trying to help them, as a sensible country we should also have a bias to the family. This is in order to help the very unit which most contributes to binding our local communities and nation together.

It was the case that from the days of Pitt the Younger until the late 1970s when the last Labour government started phasing out the arrangements that existed, our tax system always took account of the costs of children, through a child tax allowance aimed to help families. Since then, the balance of advantage has moved against the conventional family with children. Look at a married couple earning £18,000–£20,000 a year, and living in some midlands suburb in 1995. With a heavy mortgage burden, and substantial National Insurance and taxation contributions, their net income, after the taxation and benefit merry-go-round has stopped, is likely to be no greater than that for an unmarried and out-of-work couple living together with some children in the same area, supported entirely by the state. This system seems odd. It does not help the married family, and thus the stability of the country. It may well nudge some married couples in this situation into greater dependency on the state. Set the diminishing fiscal awards for being married against the increased burden of taxation and National Insurance, and the earning family has a smaller proportion of its income to spend on its own welfare and children. This is socially unjust.

Low taxation is a good thing. An uncomplicated and straightforward taxation system is also a very good thing. Conservative administrations since 1979 have done brilliantly in bringing about a more straightforward taxation regime for companies and businesses generally; industry and commerce are complicated enough without having to deal with the fiendishly complicated system containing the morass of reliefs and allowances that we used to have. A simple business taxation regime is critical to the effective workings of business, and employment. In exactly the same way, any measures which bring about happy and productive families with cheerful and ambitious children are critical to the supply of hard-working and stable adults. If families have a bit more of their own money left, this is likely to help produce just those results, and thus better sustain the economic as well as social fabric of our land. Tories in the twenty-first century need to perform exactly the same trick for families that they have done so well for businesses since 1979.

Besides restoring the taxation advantages of marriage, in order to right the balance that has been so upset since the 1960s, this means looking hard at child benefit. It is impossible to consider ever-increasing real child benefit *ad infinitum* throughout the new century. The money to do this will never be there. Yet children are a burden, and the old child tax allowance recognised this. Children are most a burden before the age of five, when they are physically very demanding and their families are under the greatest of financial pressure, with mortgage payments at a peak, and often suffering the loss of a mother's earnings for a while. Realism has always marked the Tory approach to taxation policy; and we should be as realistic in no longer automatically uprating child benefit for older children, letting those payments progressively wither on the vine. This was the approach used to reduce mortgage interest tax relief, itself in its turn once thought to be a political task impossible. The additional money left can then be concentrated on helping children at the time of greatest need.

Much more demanding than children on private and public purse alike, will be the increasing cost of old age. The new life-span in the next century is likely to be four score years and ten. Some of these will be very elderly and frail. One of the triumphs of twentieth-century civilisation, brought about by improvements in nutrition, cleanliness and health care that have resulted in people living much longer than we ever expected, is going to turn into one of the most intractable of twenty-first-century political problems. Looking after the elderly is a proper duty of all of us. The days have long gone since a statesman like Lord Lansdowne could feel that expenditure on the South African war was a better investment than on old age pensions, because war improved the moral fibre of the country, whereas pensions weakened it.

At the last census in 1991, there were 8.8 million people aged over sixty-five (about fifteen per cent of the total population). More and more of these go on into their eighties and nineties, needing increasing help in order to live independently. And that help will cost more and more money – certainly far in excess of the contributions most of these nonagenarians will have made to National Insurance or private pension scheme.

The post-war pensions settlement certainly will prove inadequate to meet the personal needs and spiralling expectations of those people who will want more for their sometimes unexpected last years. The pensions schemes that were introduced after 1945 were based on the ones which had been pioneered and piloted before and then following the First World War. The concept was of contributions funding the scheme through insurance, plus taxation. The idea behind it was that any scheme should be minimal, leaving the employees with income to meet their own particular circumstances and wants. It should not discourage incentive. Since then, we have seen the contribution principles withering, and general taxation supporting much of the undoubted need. But what we need to do in the future is to ensure that the state's rôle in pensions is to help those who are in the poorest families, rather than operate a scheme which in some respects just copies what the private sector does, or should do. 'Full funding' for them will never be a possibility; others will have to 'pay-as-they-go'. This is a good way of financing the public sector pensions where needed, provided that the transactions are absolutely open.

Beveridge was right in his concept of 'social insurance' – meaning that National Insurance contributions one year will finance National Insurance expenditure in that year; the same goes for the contribution of taxation to pensions, provided the transactions are open rather than opaque. For others, less in need, the obvious solution is to move more and more towards personal pensions. This has the added benefit in turn of making the employment of older people much more flexible. Most pension schemes purport to offer a pension linked to the salary earned in the last year of work. This is only a good bet for the winners. Under our calcified pension system these are the men and women who sit tight for forty years working for the same firm. It is also a pretty good bet for those who are better paid. Who are the losers? They are the ever growing proportion of those who will have to move more and more freely between jobs, helping to pay for the winners as they go. This is because moving from one company scheme to another is more or less like redeeming a life insurance. The more often they move, the poorer value they get compared to what they have put in. There is a slow-burning political fuse here, for as the new job market dictates all those job changes, the penny will drop in many minds that as far as their pension contributions are concerned 'they have been robbed'. Like negative equity, the resentment will smoulder. It may catch fire when some of those who had expectations of a decent inheritance from their parents' property find not only that it has to be used rather to buy an annuity to pay their rising nursing home fees, but that it may not even be enough as they reach their eighties or nineties. So some direct contributions out of their children's income may have to be made.

The twenty-first century should see the Tories promoting personally owned individual retirement accounts, with tax relief for them in recognition that these are independent personal financial savings, specifically aimed at retirement. Just as in the balance between families and individuals, that most promiscuously used phrase in the modern political lexicon, 'natural justice', demands that those who can provide for themselves are as fairly treated as those who cannot. To reach this end will mean that the old but good ideas about topping-up schemes to meet your own needs, that were there in the thinking of mid-century social reformers like Beveridge, could well reach reality, but by a different route. This way, people will be encouraged to provide more for themselves, and families of people of pensionable age will have a greater independence.

Reality may even demand the raising of the age of entitlement to the retirement pension a little further, and putting some of the money saved into higher rates for the over-eighties. A paramount principle, however, must be that if expectations of future payments for which contributions have already been made through National Insurance are diminished, then that should be recognised, and compensation duly paid. Tories need to be clear that in the twenty-first century the greatest concentration of effort will have to be at each end of the life cycle, for the under-fives and the over-eighties. They should also be clear that the financially and morally most beneficial route will be to channel help through the family. The family should be the focus of taxation and social security policy alike, even though much of the burden will be met through the contributions that come from business, industry and the rest of the economy.

6

The British Economy

The overriding duty of any government, to strive to preserve sound money, is of the same order as its duty to provide security at home and defence from foreign attack. The monetary system of the United Kingdom owes its very being to the government, which says that it can exist in the first place. If there were no United Kingdom government, there would be no pound sterling.

So a Tory government must guard the integrity of money not only as a central but an almost sacred task. This is because there is just as big a transfer of trust from the governed to the governing as there is when the country's subjects give to Ministers the task of defending our shores. Governments have never had an unblemished record in the matter of preserving the value of our money, any more than did medieval kings. Take the situation when the scholar Nicholas Oresme, an economic commentator in fourteenth-century England, wrote, six hundred years ago.

> Every change in money involves forgery and deceit and cannot be the right of the prince. The amount of the prince's profit is necessarily that of the community's loss; and if he should tell the tyrant's usual lie, that he applies that profit to the public advantage, he must not be believed, for he

might as well take my coat and say he needed it for the public service.

This is just as true now, though it is a truth which is harder to penetrate in modern times. It has become progressively more and more difficult over the years to see what has been going on with our money. The development of financial instruments and the complexities of banking have made it much easier to conceal the true facts than when princes clipped their coinage, or circulated smart new batches made up of silver mixed with a bit of tin. Sometimes moneyers and forgers did the same on a smaller scale. The latter, if caught, were burnt; the former generally reigned on unscathed.

Modern monetary complexities may leave the average elector cold but they no longer bemuse him or her. They now understand much better the basic principles, just as the medieval shopper could spot a clipped coin at a hundred paces. Why? The experiences of the 1970s and 1980s have ensured this. The inflationary shock of the 1970s had a devastating effect on the lives of a generation of British people, giving some apparent and uncovenanted capital gains as housing values were pumping up like hot-air balloons, but conferring on others a more difficult old age. This was because inflation tore through their hard- and long-earned nest eggs, and the fixed incomes flowing from them, like the white terror.

Having gone somewhat cold-turkey on the after-effects, that 1970s generation has seen inflation ground down to acceptable levels. They never wish to see it go up again, as much as they can have any say in the matter. Inflationary expectations influence behaviour. Thus people now no longer regard roofs and gardens like a store of value to be bought at all costs as a hedge against inflation. That voracious buying at cheap rates was initiated by lax monetary policy and promiscuous lending by the banks. Too much money chased too few houses and flats. This had a volcanic effect on house prices and thus eventually ensured the destruction of the very prize itself.

The rise in property prices, like any other form of inflation, is inherently bad. Like most bad things, it has the habit of creating a good feeling for a while. Yet if there is an increase of a few per cent in the necessities of life or consumer goods, gloom and doom overcome the public and media. Excuses pour forth from the government of the day. Why did increases in house prices in the 1980s seem a good thing? To the two-thirds of our people who owned their own homes it was the generally mistaken cosy feeling that their material wealth had been improved. A snare and delusion this, given that somewhere to live is a necessity. Thus surges in property prices tend to benefit those relatively few who own more than one property, for in any move from one property to another the actual price is not the issue; the difference between the one sold and the one bought most certainly is.

It is now seven years since the residential property market reached a peak in the mad summer of 1988, after years of price increases leading to that peculiarly British cocktail of housing hysteria (must buy now while stocks last; mustn't miss out) and euphoria ('look how many "K" I'm now worth') helping to inflate an already buoyant economic situation. Like the worst speculative eighteenth-century bubble, it promptly burst. Human misfortune followed inexorably, as the results of over-borrowing at high interest rates reached their deadly conclusion. Alas, with it too came the failure of many smaller businesses, whose cash flow had been hard hit by suppliers and customers alike not paying their worth. They were often also locked into the housing market, with all those family homes pledged as collaterals sometimes having to go back to bank or building society. And, like the Black Death, the spectre of negative equity soon stalked the land; all too many plague crosses were scratched on all too many front doors, and forlorn *For Sale* boards stood outside them.

Despite the efforts of estate agents periodically to pump the market since by predicting huge booms in prices just around the corner and the return of the 'good' – but actually bad – old days, we seem to have returned to normal. 'Seem' is the right conditional word to use, but there does indeed appear to be a will by governed and government not to want this to happen again. This may be good for a generation, just as people seem now more realistic about not asking for more pay than they know can be afforded. That is a straight trade-off between pay and the preservation of a job. Are all of these changes the last act staged in a thoroughly modern and self-righteous morality tale; people who have been greedy, pushing up house prices or demanding huge wage increases, and reaping the reward of inflation or unemployment, coming at the last minute to realise the error of their ways, and thus defeating the demon?

The answer is certainly not. For these manifestations are largely symptoms, not causes, of what is always in the end a government-induced or -encouraged malaise. This central Tory tenet we have forgotten once or twice. We must never do so again. 'The defence of sound money' has an old-fashioned or theoretical ring to it; in fact it is an historic responsibility which we have thrown over-board twice in my political lifetime, in the early 1970s and again in the mid-1980s. I must take my share of the responsibility for the latter event as an enthusiastic member of government which became so beguiled by 'growth' that we lost control of inflation. I can plead in mitigation the memory of the late Mr John Smith, as Shadow Chancellor, coming to the despatch box to reply to Mr Nigel Lawson's budget speech – which cut interest rates at the height of a boom – to demand that they be cut even further. Then, some of us were so bemused by foreigners with interesting formulae and the sheer fashionability of it all that we entered the Exchange Rate Mechanism. Again, some mitigation can be plead-ed, everything from technical inexpertise to intense pressure from businesses, whether small in constituencies locally, or large in the CBI nationally, demanding that we did indeed 'go into the ERM'.

No government can dodge responsibility for its own inflation-ary sins; to assert anything else than the reality of government's overwhelming responsibility for controlling and creating inflation through its spending and borrowing is to kick sand into the eyes of the electors. That is why it is always inappropriate for govern-ment Ministers to moralise on economic issues, for government spending seems to cause inflation always at least at twice the rate of any so-called 'private sector' inflation. Tories have, in my life-time, flirted with the idea that a little inflation is good. It is not. It is economically, politically and morally bad. That realisation should stay with us throughout the twenty-first century. Our people now generally realise this. What they often refuse to recognise is the other side of the coin – that their demands for government to 'do something' to meet some lobbyist's demands, and thus spend more money, can help to rack up inflationary pressures – if there are not off-setting savings. Because of the difficulties presented by the political unpopularity of turning down flat some of these demands, it is all too easy for any government Minister to connive, a bit, in this process. Thus is sand kicked in the eyes of the people from a different angle. There is a temptation for government to pretend that something is affordable, if not now, well then, soon. Thus are created warm political mirages entirely made up of good intentions that can have dreadful monetary consequences. So, little by little, money is spent that cannot and should not be afforded unless off-setting savings are made, or extra taxation raised.

How very tempting and easy it is to satisfy these ambitions at a greater rate than can be paid for by increased productivity, taxation or savings. How very simple it is then to borrow and increase the money supply rather than looking the idol of priority straight in the eye and making it clear that if this nice thing is to come along faster, then there will have to be rather less of that thing. In other words, and in the appropriate higher-flown language, it is the overriding moral duty of Conservative governments to assess the demands that people and lobbyists make on them within the total of the money which can be properly provided from taxation and borrowing – which adds to inflationary pressures by expanding the money supply.

This does mean that we must control public expenditure both to reduce inflationary risks and to leave more and more money in the people's own pockets. After the control of inflation, our overriding economic aim must be to cut taxation and keep it down. To do this is economically good, and also preserves or bestows the 'democratic space' in which people can do what they want freely, take their own risks, exercise their own charity; it is an integral part of not being interfered with by 'them'. Tax reductions therefore are not just cheap and vote-gathering populist moves, feeding greed. They also have considerable moral force. They go with the Tory grain, and our attitudes to the individual and ownership.

The difficulties of keeping public expenditure under control are, however, very difficult to face up to. Going on a public expenditure binge is so much easier. Viscount Montgomery, when he was with Eisenhower working up to 'Operation Overlord' and the invasion of Normandy, used to look for officers who were willing to 'binge'. These were, in his rather quaint use of that word, thin not tubby staff officers. They were physically and mentally fit, had a glint in their eye. They wanted to go out, kill Germans and win the war.

Public expenditure bingeing is the reverse of that, and is soft-optionism writ largely. The post-war phenomenon called 'Butskellism' was a consensus which was partly about growing welfarism, and therefore growing public expenditure. It started quite small, like those first and uncertain drinks at a teenaged party which may lead to full-blown addiction in middle years. Government and public alike may have decided that they both understand and wish permanently to control inflation. They have not yet been successful, alas, in creating the vital other half of the virtuous consensus that public expenditure must be restrained, too. There is a latent and deadly temptation in all governments to go on public expenditure binges, rather than conduct a much more demanding and warlike campaign against its excesses. Some say that the government had the public spending binge of all time in the four years between 1988/1990 and 1992/1993. In the last of these years it shot up by more than five per cent. It certainly has used up any 'public spending slack' for years to come. Dreadful consequences would follow any re-run of these events. Trying to provide a framework for the British economy remains for government a delicate balancing act just as it always has been, in times of feast as well as in times of famine. We have now got controlling inflation at the very centre of our national economic war aims. It will be our historic duty in the new century to keep those memories fresh, for all the world like a Napoleonic-era nursery nurse reminding her charges what Boney would do if they did not consume cabbage or go to sleep on demand.

An independent Bank of England would greatly help (but not guarantee) both to keep the bogey of high inflation at bay, and also to entrench in future generations the same anti-inflationary instincts. National economic management is not a totally single club matter, even if controlling the money supply is by far the biggest club in the bag. On this depends inflation, interest rates, the value of the currency and much unemployment. Compared to inflation, our aims on public expenditure are much less clearly laid out and therefore much less clearly listened to. Barrages of annual accusations of 'cuts' have helped to ensure that. So the pressing need to continue to bear down on public expenditure is much less accepted by the voting public. It is easy to see why. People prefer to have what they think are free goods from government, rather than finding the money themselves or restraining their demands on the state machine. Governments have a human face. They have a duty, as well, to individuals, hurt by the world recession or structural changes in the job market alike, to go through their own personal transformations. The extra costs of all those extra benefits have had to be borne by extra expenditure. The burdens of either the economic cycle (say the cost of the last recession) or new and interesting demands (say extra help for the disabled) always mean that the pressure is naturally upwards. That makes certain that the illusion which stalks the land is there are not really any limits. Even worse, there is the feeling that if you cannot have what you want this year, a spot of campaigning will ensure that you get it the year after.

We must ensure that the British people are just as persuaded about stopping public expenditure rising, as they seem to be of the importance of stopping inflation going up. We can look back to a golden age in the otherwise much excoriated 1960s for an example of how low levels of modern government expenditure could be. Back in 1964 we bequeathed to the then almost minority Labour government a level of public expenditure standing at about thirty-seven per cent of what the country produced. Thirty years later, it stands at about forty-four per cent. We have set ourselves the target of getting back to the levels that the Labour Party in their turn bequeathed to us in 1970, then forty-one per cent. That is our aim by the financial year 1998. We will have to make heroic efforts just to hit this target. If we do, it will still be too high then. We need a clear national sense that there must be a cap on what the state should take from and spend on behalf of the taxpayer and corporation taxpayer.

We need the discipline of an unbreakable national ceiling on public expenditure. This should be that government should take and spend no more than forty per cent of what the country produces. It has a symmetry with the top rate of personal taxation. What is right for the individual should be right for the state. Such a realistic and entirely attainable target is both an economic and a moral good. It is economically right for it will prevent the state overblowing itself and giving in to the perpetual temptation of crowding out the private sector. Such a target is morally right because it stops the state overflowing its banks, into the areas of freedom where individuals and companies should have to make and to spend. A cap on possible public expenditure is also a barrier to unaffordable lobbyists' wish-lists turning themselves into expenditure realities. Economic, public and moral realism will all be well served by such rigid restraint.

This means politician explaining to elector that there can be a guarantee of their keeping a fair slice of income, and also having reasonable help from the state if they need it. It also means explaining that if more than four out of every ten pounds that the nation produces is state-spent, then that balance is disturbed. It should be even less if possible. If public expenditure grows too high, well so will debts, inflation and general misery. It also demands that most difficult of political tasks, saying no. It means repeating that often the state cannot afford to spend this or that on your behalf and if you want it, well then you must pay for it. It is a good thing to have a target in order to help to get and then keep the balance of economic management right, and to get the message across to the consumer of the political product, who may want government to 'do more', that this always means spending more.

So if Tory governments are to be allowed to sermonise on economic matters at all at the turn of the century, it can only be to reiterate the simple fact that there are no free policies: every successful pressure to get government to do something has its costs. This is politically unpalatable stuff. But it is vital to get a national understanding of this stark reality, if we are to get an equal understanding of the realities of twenty-first-century life. It has the great merit, for Tories, of treating the electors as well

informed and realistic. It also has the benefit of putting Labour
on the spot. Do they have similar targets, and if not, why not? If
they do have higher targets for public expenditure consistent with
their policies, what are they, and how much will they cost to
fund? For the Tories, this clear capping of public expenditure is
both economically and politically virtuous. It should drive home
that the question 'who pays?' must always be asked. Of course
the correct answer is always and inevitably 'the taxpayer does'.
No Tory government should give in to the temptations of
rewarding vigorous political lobbying with splendid social
largesse.

The challenges, however, to the British people and the British
economy in the twenty-first century are not only the latent enemies of inflation and public expenditure within. There are also
new and dangerous economic dragons abroad. These are not just
found in the competition that is there in the Far East and other
emerging economic dynamos, but in the simple fact that today all
governments are none the less at the mercy of events in the larger
economic world over which they can have little control. These
days, billions and billions of pounds flow across international
borders every trading day, and there are seven of those each
week, for most of every twenty-four hours of each day. In some
ways governments are lucky not to be reduced to bit-part players,
just enjoying walk-on parts now and then on the world economic
stage. The world markets have to a large extent become the judge
and jury not only of worldwide enterprise but also of national
economies. This is because of the eruption of world capital markets at the same time that communism collapsed, coinciding with
the extraordinary expansion in the immediacy and cheapness of
communications across the globe.

In parallel with this has come the globalisation of more and
more companies. Firms have expanded and contracted, production activity has been reallocated between regions, countries and
continents. Manufacturing that almost died in some sectors in
some countries in one decade has been revived by foreign investment and ownership in the next. Take British-made motor cars,
for one example of this. When I walked the streets of Oxford in
the run-up to the 1979 election contest, the burning local issue

was how to manage the decline of the local motor industry. The feeling abroad was if the Tories got in, the area would probably become an 'industrial desert'. Debates raged about how much government subsidy should go into each Morris Marina, riddled with bad design and worse quality control, built by that decrepit monument to the sweet deceptions of government-led 'industrial policies' called 'BL'. I had to support the local product, just as much as Labour felt it had to support the trade unions who ran the assembly lines at BL's Cowley plant. Together with weak management, trade unions formed a debilitating little alliance to run William Morris's once world-beating and entirely British dream almost into the ground. But who would have predicted then that the Cowley plant, a by-word for corporate awfulness and industrial anarchy in 1979, would be called 'Rover' in 1995, owned by a German company, and be completely riddled with Japanese working practices, turning out world-beating cars? I certainly was not able to predict that then. It has all happened; globalisation has worked and beneficially.

These sorts of activity have led to the spread of corporate operations, with their money, across continents and national borders. It parallels exactly the way in which the money markets have been globalised. Investment has become more and more international and footloose. There has been much more collaboration following that footloose but highly directed money. Product development, sourcing and manufacture are all now much more international. The service industries have begun to go along the same path; auditors and architects in Pakistan or India can do routine accounting work or architectural drawing at a fraction of North American or European costs; fast following the fax, which makes this possible, are the information superhighway and interactive media. Such operations become more and more possible. We have an emerging global workforce now; work can be done almost anywhere by almost anyone. Any government attempting to manage economic matters must recognise this, and it must be part of the Tory economic stamp of character for the twenty-first century.

These are not the international or imperial challenges which a

Peel or Disraeli had to deal with. In their day there was of course a sort of globalisation (our accidental empire, and the trade which came with it) and technological change (steam; telegraph cables under the oceans); but it was chalk to what is the late-twentieth-century's new economic cheese. There was then no globalisation of and by big companies, and certainly there were not any totally free global money markets, trading at the blink of an eye. For us these changes bring both pleasure and problems. Pleasure when we welcome a BMW or a Japanese motor company moving into British manufacturing; problems when we recall all too recently the devastating effects that gimlet-eyed serial currency-killers at work in front of their screens can bring, as we found on Black Wednesday. It used to be only a little like this when rumours of war caught the Edwardians at the beginning of our century. Lloyd George spent much time calming the City. Asquith wrote of financiers faced with fighting, 'They are the greatest ninnies I have ever had to tackle. I found them all in a state of funk like old women, chattering over their tea cups in a Cathedral town.'

These days the City faced with rumour is rather more stalwart and it is one of our greatest national strengths; rumour is much the stuff of the financial as of the political worlds. But try though the Germans might to bring us down at the close of Edwardian England, there was no similar chance of the money markets doing the same at the time; they had neither the capacity nor the speed of operation necessary to do so. Whether rumour or reality, the Tory stance toward all of these rapid changes in the future must always be shaped by the national interest, that of a nation state in a European framework at the mercy of, but also helping to shape, international events, seeking to maximise our economy for the advantage of our people.

The same view of events must inform the leadership that we give not only to Europe but to the rest of the world on unemployment. This has replaced the plague as one of the most widely feared contemporary phenomena. If it is thought to be stalking the land and thus about to hurt the presently employed, then no government will reap easily the rewards of economic growth. Few feel good even with money in their pocket today, if they also feel threatened, by losing their job tomorrow. They have seen it happen to their neighbours, or at work in a big company where they have felt the chill wind of 'down-sizing' as its rush carried away their contemporaries. They want a government to say they are going to stop this sort of thing happening to them. They do not these days so much expect government to do this by directly employing them in bloated bureaucracies, nor by bottling the Trent or Severn, but rather by better maintaining the framework in which work can flourish. Just as the experience of the 1960s and 1970s may have educated many of our people on the causes of inflation, so those deadly decades have also taught our working people that governments cannot create jobs; that only work and enterprise can. None the less, learning to live with the lurking threat of unemployment and the uncertainty that a number of job changes in any career may bring, does at the same time create considerable political uncertainty.

In the days of high inflation, and thus inflationary wage settlements, people 'felt good' in a usually self-deluding way. To a great degree, fool's gold was being poured into their banking accounts; now, with more realistic wage settlements and low inflation people cannot get that feeling – just at the time they realise that there is no longer a guarantee of a job for life. This newish economic insecurity is matched for intensity only by the parallel social insecurity caused by the increasing levels of crime. Government is wholly responsible for neither. But a Tory Party which is able to persuade more of the electorate that it has got most of the answers to many of those insecurities will dominate the politics of the first part of the new century.

So, as with public expenditure, another key Tory task for the new century must be to explain why we wish to see as decent a set of working conditions that are compatible with having as light a load on employers as possible. In other words, why having 'low non-wage labour costs', as they are known in the economic trade, is a Tory imperative. Such a balance helps to create jobs; but it is also deeply realistic by recognising that high non-wage labour costs can be job destroyers. Of course we can look to economic growth to play its part in reducing unemployment. But we have also to explain what structural unemployment is, and how it can only be dealt with by bridging the yawning gap that opens up between the pressure on us to adapt in the UK and our willingness to do so. This is a fundamental challenge as the pressures caused by new technologies, the globalisation of companies, changes in money markets, and intensifying international competition gets fiercer by the year. Thus far, we have helped to show the way, to the great credit of Tory thinking since the late 1970s – though as yet neither opposition parties domestically nor our European partners abroad have been remotely fully persuaded.

All of this has to be set against a background of rapid changes in where the new jobs have been coming from at home. There are too many people, still, in the public sector. Most of the new job growth in the next fifteen years will continue to come, as in the last decade, partly from high-technology industries, even more from business, finance, insurance, and certainly a whole range of personal and community services. And self-employment will continue to make a striking contribution to job creation; part-time employment will take an ever-growing share of total employment. Both these changes are good things. But alas, they also contribute at the same time to that feeling of voter insecurity – working for me rather than for them, and perhaps half-time, is a less secure business for the voter who was brought up to expect one of those fast-vanishing jobs for life. With some change, the challenges and the reward are enticing, but the risks equally offputting. This is not surprising, as so much post-war life has been centred on getting rid of personal risk. The rewards of risk taking need to be centre stage.

We have not yet done enough to explain what does *not* lose jobs. The three bugbears are usually thought to be cruel competition, unfair and low-cost imports, or wicked new technologies. None of these things really matter too much to too many jobs in the United Kingdom. Treating them as illnesses when they are not will make the unemployment disease worse, not better. Competition is rarely cruel, rather it helps to create jobs. There is much more of it now because of globalisation, forcing industries and services to become more and more efficient. Competition will become sharper still in the new century. To attempt to reduce its intensity would mean erecting barriers like financial controls or halting mergers or imposing ludicrously tight job-security provisions. Exactly the same sort of barriers would have to be used to deal with 'cheap imports from lower-cost countries'; but trade barriers in the end destroy trade, and if trade is destroyed so are jobs.

Equally, technological change has never produced jobless growth save in the minds of Captain Swing and his early nineteenth-century adherents, who sought to preserve old practices by smashing new machines. It is a fantasy to thing that advances in technology will help to destroy rather than help create jobs. They could only do that in a world of perpetually restricted demand or wholly saturated wants; these are a fantastic set of circumstances to imagine at the beginning of the twenty-first century. So, when the going gets uncomfortable, we must recognise clearly that the causes of unemployment are not this trio. The answers to it must not be sought by slowing or stopping technological advance, or through organised work-sharing, and certainly not in protectionism.

Only some latter-day Luddite would wish to slow the rate of technological advance in this country behind a wall that kept out globalised companies. These increasingly provide the power behind growth and are always – whatever their products – research- and development-led. This is the same from drugs to motor cars and back again. As costs of communication and transport have dropped, so research and development costs have shot up; the increasing burden of these has become the very sign of a highly sophisticated economy. Only a socialist would wish organised work-sharing, for this views the economy as a cake of fixed size, the slices of which can only grow larger at the expense of other people. That is exactly how Tudor economists believed things to be. Work-sharing means not just reduced income through rationing work, but is a wholly artificial business, increasing the number of jobs with no more economic activity.

Worst of the deadly trio of tired non-answers to the unemployment problem is, however, protectionism pure and simple. This would attempt to take part or all of the domestic economy out of the world economic mainstream. And that would encourage domestic monopolies and inevitably increase costs to consumers.

International competition from the killer economies of the Far East, and from the North American Free Trade Organization, presently made up of the United States, Canada and Mexico, but likely to become more and more fierce (as well as uninhibited by pan-American monetary union), must be met head on.

What will help to create more jobs, and to tackle structural unemployment? First and foremost is a determination to adapt freely to change, and thus to be more competitive. This means making sure that management skills and education keep pace with the possibilities presented by better-managed and more technologically advanced economies. It is all very simple to say that the British companies must improve the productivity of their operations and the workforce must be better educated and trained before and throughout their working lives; it is of course much harder to bring this about.

Secondly, we need to be realistic about where new jobs are likely to come from in a Britain which is getting rid of those policies that hamper job creation. These jobs are not going to come – and must not come – from the public sector. If jobs in the twenty-first century were ever again to be created on any scale in the public sector, that could only be done by taxing people and businesses more; in other words by deliberately rocketing through the forty per cent ceiling on what the state takes and spends from the productive part of the economy. All policies must be directed at helping, not hindering, private sector job creation.

We must never allow ourselves to be diverted away from that central task, by thinking that there might be some new and easier nostrum which will get us out of whatever hole we see ourselves in – in the past we have tried social contracts, and a host of other fixes. The latest of these seems to be the idea of an imposed, European-wide single currency. 'Beware of economic nostrums which find their roots in supposed political imperatives' is a good rule. The impetus behind this particular idea is largely political, with a bit of bureaucracy to spice the pudding. Those who want to bring Europe together, and particularly who wish to bind Germany into Europe, think that a single currency is the best way of locking that continental economic giant into a perpetual democratic embrace. In addition the idea of running anything from the centre is the blameless ambition of central bureaucrats, in this case those in Europe from Brussels who wish to turn the European Union into a sort of Greater Belgium. The killer economies of the Far East, already dead set on not binding themselves into a harmonisation arm-lock imposed by high non-wage labour costs, are even more certain that they do not need any sort of single currency.

Looking the other way across the globe, we see the United States and Canada, two countries who formed their own free trade zone more than six years ago. As a result, they have the closest and largest trading relationships of any two major countries in the world. They have now been joined by Mexico in an enlarged North American Free Trade Area (NAFTA). Yet the Federal Reserve in the United States has certainly not thought it necessary to merge the dollars north and south of the fifty-second parallel, let alone lock those two giants into some shotgun monetary marriage with the uncertain Mexican peso. NAFTA is efficient and effective. The barriers to a similarly more efficient and effective economic working by the European Union countries are certainly not monetary. Economic problems in the growing European Union are often rooted in cultural differences. These are understandable, excusable, and always likely to be there; they are found in varied legal systems or codes, and in structural and fiscal differences. If individuals and companies in Europe want to have a parallel or common currency embracing all or some of their countries, there is nothing wrong with that at all – philosophically, constitutionally or practically. But let demand and the market drive the process. That would be a realistic way of proceeding.

Even with such a voluntary and incremental system, perhaps starting with the payment of credit card bills denominated in both the local national currency and the parallel currency, practical issues would crowd in. For example, there might well be problems of acceptability in spending a unit of common currency alongside the lei in the streets of Bucharest, let alone next to the pound sterling in London or the schilling in Vienna. No currency has ever flourished unless it is wanted, and has been backed by a sovereign state. Thus only if sovereignty was severely diminished amongst the nation states of the enlarging European Community could such a currency grow to ascendancy.

The effort put into the search for new economic magic potions is better spent on preventing job-destroying measures creeping in, and by looking to the creation of new jobs. Some of these will be brand spanking new, hardly imagined now, just as the independent financial adviser was a new thought in the mid-1980s. Others will be found in activities formerly performed inside manufacturing companies but now increasingly done outside – much design work, for example.

The very distinction between 'services' and 'manufacturing' will blur as the twenty-first century rolls on. Outside the service sector pure and simple, British companies which make and trade in goods will have increasingly higher-level requirements. They will be unable to cling to low-wage labour products in the face of inexorable competition from even-lower-wage but ever more efficient economies which start from a cleaner industrial slate. To flourish in this world and to create and sustain more new jobs will depend on the quality of our people in the new century. We can only have a high-productivity, high-wage Britain if we have internationally competitive, highly qualified people, imbued with a personal competitive spirit, entering new jobs; these jobs cannot be created without exactly these sorts of men and women. To do this will require an act of national will, and much understanding between educator and employer of the changing nature of employment, demanding lifelong learning and re-skilling.

The generation just entering work in the United Kingdom in the mid-1990s can expect to change their jobs four or five times, as they move from the nervous and well-dressed first-day new boy or girl, to the contented recipient of whatever the mid-twenty-first-century equivalent of a gold watch will be. It is inconceivable that many in the future could expect to enter into a potential job for life as I did aged twenty-four in 1969. Shortly afterwards I was told by the bursar of my Oxford College exactly what the pension rights and entitlements would be when I retired, aged sixty-seven as it happens, some forty-three years later. Critical to the way we do things will be educating people how to learn in this new environment, to acquire and then reacquire skills through their working lives. It would be better to drop the word 'training' from the early-twenty-first-century economic and education lexicon, and just use the simple and accurate 'education'. This education must not just be in particular subjects or skills, but also in the business of how to acquire knowledge. Lifelong learning and education need to become the central characteristic of a high-skill, high-wage British economy. This is easier to write than to achieve, that is why the *National Education and Training [sic] Targets* are not some cosy insider concept between government, CBI and trade unions alone, but rather should be part of a national crusade. Other economies are already racing far beyond our modest benchmarks set by these targets.

For too many, 'education' is still thought of as a matter purely to be gone through in school and college. It is also still considered to be a burden on some companies, as an unwelcome cost. Education should be neither of these things. We need to account for what is being done to improve things. The government has started to do this, with the publication of the results produced by every secondary school and Further Education college in the land. The other side of the page is as yet blank. Shareholders and the general public do not generally know what companies do to educational ends; and the public sector is an equally closed book to the taxpayer. We have done a lot in the United Kingdom of late to reform our accounting standards in the interests of financial reality, as well as probity. Yet there is an information blackout in most companies' annual reports and public statements, except in the most general sense, as far as education is concerned. Investors in financial market are used to looking at the assets of a company that they fancy; they might now usefully demand that these also account for the stock of skills in that company's assets; the same goes for the public services.

Our own excellent Accounting Standards Board has proposed in the past that companies should declare discretionary expenditure which is largely for the benefit of future periods. Research and development is one part of this discretionary expenditure, as is major maintenance and advertising. Education should also be included as a key enhancement of future company profit-potential. There may be difficulties in defining and quantifying the costs of education programmes, particularly for multi-national companies operating through numerous subsidiaries distributed around the world. But the stock of the workforce and the state of its education will be seen as an essential part of any thoroughly modern twenty-first-century company's statements. Brain power has finally overcome the muscle power that provided nine out of every ten jobs in late-Victorian England: it now needs accounting for.

That very transformation which characterised the twentieth century has, in its turn, led to the creation of an ever-growing 'middle class'. It is vital that the Tory Party, which has drawn so much of its core strength from middle-class, middle England continues to take the lead in a transformation of their attitudes towards work and education. This is a vital political task for two reasons. First, because these groups are growing so fast. In immediate post-war England it was a matter of pride for a village if one of its young people could 'go to college' or 'go to university'; fifty years on, the majority have those opportunities. Secondly, because entry to this broadening band of British life, which once brought with it the guarantee of something like a job for life, no longer carries this near-certainty with it. For the first time this ever more politically powerful class faces the serious risk of unemployment or the challenge of having to change their jobs. White-collar workers, losing their jobs, losing self-esteem, losing their potential, losing investments, and sometimes as a result losing faith in the government as well, are something new in post-war political experience. Most voters not already in this income group want to be there, too, enjoying its perceived fruits and status despite the obvious and new insecurities. This is both a human tragedy and a political threat. Therefore we must persuade people that they will need to adapt, and explain why. But we must also help arm them with the educational weapons to do so. The traditionally placid and comfortable vision of 'middle-class life' is being transformed into a still very rewarding, but much harsher, reality by these changes. Conservatism needs to respond if it is to retain ancient electoral loyalties.

A climate of hope and entrepreneurship amongst the unemployed or those forced into it is the key to economic and political success. Some other people have work, but want now to earn their living in a different way. They want to start up their own businesses, grow, take on more men and women, and thus snatch out of unemployment some with the skills and drive to do those jobs. So, any Tory 'industrial and employment policy', based on sound money, must be devoted to two ends only. First, such little public money as is available should never favour the big firms at the expense of those that are no more than a glint in the eye or are yet a bright idea of a man or woman. And, secondly, public policy, particularly over regulatory matters, must be on constant red alert to remove red tape, regulations and practices that impede entrepreneurial spirit. The sad fact is that as soon as one undesirable practice has been suppressed, others seems to pop up.

Just look at how difficult it is still today to start up that most innocent – and most wanted – of facilities, local businesses providing for pre-school children. A combination of repressive attitudes by local planners, and the dislike of private endeavour by all too many in the statutory social services, has meant that we have fewer such facilities than we should. There are fewer small businesses employing fewer people as a result; it is more complicated for some mothers and fathers to get to work as a result. The problems facing nursery provision are just one example of where the 'cat's cradle' of controls that the then Sir Keith Joseph used to rail against in the opposition years of the 1970s seem to come back to life again all too easily. Only last year, the owner of a pavement coffee house and restaurant in Nottingham detailed on BBC Radio 4 how many hurdles he had to leap before he was allowed to open and provide a service and jobs. It began with a City Council official apparently asking, in response to enquiries about how this business might get going, 'why on earth do you want to do such a thing, no one in Nottingham will want to sit outside to eat and drink'. It is the reverse of that attitude that we need to promote, as the President of the Board of Trade so clearly recognises.

If we wish to see a competitive as well as a contented society – and we cannot have one without the other – then we need to look at the education which will underpin all future economic activity. Three areas are critical, overlapping the one with the other. Firstly, there is the quality of compulsory education: just how fit for the purpose of producing a competitive economy is it?

Secondly, how young men and women can best leap from school – and increasingly college or university – to work. And, thirdly, how working skills can be refined and renewed throughout the working lives of men and women as they move from their twenties to their sixties, and on to retirement. These are critical, for our natural resources are few, save oil and gas. The battle for economic survival in the first quarter of the twenty-first century will be one almost entirely based on the knowledge, skills and competitiveness of our country's human resources. They are a part of the supply side of our economy which we have not yet got right. The uncomfortable fact is that our economy is still not competitive enough. The even more unpalatable truth, particularly for the educational world's considerable and powerful vested interests, is that our educational system is not competitive enough, either. And in a world where, in the twenty-first century, knowledge will equal economic success, that cannot be allowed to continue.

We need only to look east for these lessons. In the year 2000, let alone 2020, the countries of the Far East will be a bigger market than either the European Union by then extended, or the NAFTA as recently extended to include Mexico. Go to Malaysia or Singapore – admirable places with admirable economies – and you will find GDP growing at eight per cent plus this year. Thailand's sixty million people are taking the same route. And of course greater China, including Hong Kong soon, is joining in. Foreign investment pours in, with countries like Taiwan shooting up the league tables of international competition. They know there, what we know here. That the world has about a billion 'haves', and about four billion 'want-to-haves'. Satellites beaming programmes with their advertisements shown throughout the world means that demand everywhere will be pumped up. The worldwide business opportunities of this media explosion are enormous. The four billion 'want-to-haves' are going to want lavatories that flush, telephones that work, and the rest of the apparatus of a consumer society.

Why all this economic geography? It is because we are now up against people using the latest technology because it is cheaper than current technologies. For the moment, they have succeeded in abolishing endemic Western economic pessimism and have sidelined Malthus. Where Singapore has led, Thailand and Indonesia are going fast. Vietnam, the Philippines and Burma and others are stirring behind them. Extraordinary social, commercial and industrial changes are occurring which leapfrog generations of development experienced along the classic patterns of Western advanced countries. Our historic route now seems a time-warped way of development by comparison. Thus Asians, on as yet much smaller incomes than ours, are using cellular telephones before they know what a fixed line is; the most significant technological development is this convergence of 'fixed' and 'cellular systems'. These are the growing knowledge and therefore economic highways of Asia. Indeed, telecom links are probably more important to their development than road links in some of these countries. They will be a crucial agent for growth in the new pattern of rapid development. This will happen soon in China. That giant aims to raise the numbers of its telephone links to three times the size of our home network – from thirty to one hundred and thirty million connections – by the year 2000. Fixed cellular systems will slash the cost of installing this basic infrastructure.

It is exactly the same with commerce and retailing; the leap is now not from street market to shop via supermarket to out-of-town centre. It is straight from street market to Seacon Square, Asia's biggest shopping mall, opened in the summer of 1994 in Bangkok. It is the same as far as manufacturing is concerned: microchips are harvested where once tapioca and other crops were grown and exported. This presents the economic context in which the reform of Europe must be seen. We should forget arguments about a two-speed Europe, and rather persuade the European Union not to regulate itself into one of the slow-lanes of a multi-speed global economy. Those people in the Far East have encouraged foreign investment, been fiscally responsible, saved much of their income and kept their inflation low. Above all else, they have worked very hard, they venerate learning, and have exceptionally competitive education systems, using increasingly innovative technologies. The next frontiers will be in high-quality learning for adults as much as for pupils in front of interactive screens in college or home alike. Parents anxious about their children's state of progress will get educational psychology assessments down the line.

The people of these killer economies are thus very productive, making high-quality goods at competitive low-pay rates, too. The big strategic question for the UK and Europe is how on earth can we avoid being overwhelmed by the economic power of the ASEAN (or NAFTA) countries? How did all this happen? By learning from us? Of course, British motor expertise founded the Japanese motor-car industry. By their leapfrogging unnecessary intermediate steps in development? That is right. It is what we are seeing in front of our very eyes with those fixed cellular phones and shopping malls. By having all the advantages of lower wage rates? Why yes, of course, their high-quality products are produced by people with pay rates less than ours. Hard work? Go and sense the buzz in the seven-day-week economies of a Hong Kong or a Singapore, as you drive from plane to hotel. Is there a missing ingredient in this heady eastern cocktail? No, it is all there, including that ancient respect for learning and a deep cultural sense.

The street scene in Kuala Lumpur in Malaysia is full of beguiling advertisements on billboards of young men and women in caps and gowns advertising the opportunities of this or that college. Parents would march in the streets in such places if teachers stopped testing, or stopped driving children as well as caring for them, or tried to avoid publishing their examination results. In Singapore, bursaries are available to encourage talented youngsters to read some humanities subjects. This is the exact reverse of the difficulties the UK has in persuading more of our top-flight youngsters to go into science and technology – particularly engineering; we have to provide bursaries to do the latter instead. Talking to sixth formers in 1994 at Raffles College in Singapore, an elite and high-performing institution, was enjoyable (because they were so lively and challenging in their questions) but also chilling (because of the ambition to do well which they showed, and the impatience they had with any teacher or government that would not help them on the way). Of course this sort of atmosphere may not always be to individual or common good, and mindless worshipping in front of the idol of competition has its dangers. But these are human emotions and motives on the right side; they stand in sharp relief to the impression left by the words of one distinguished Schools Inspector, who said of a school recently inspected in England that it was 'caring, sharing – and failing!'

Is this why last year's World Economic Forum *World Competitiveness Report 1994* put Singapore first in the world for having an educational system which meets the needs of a competitive economy? The answer to that question seems clear. On our part, we need to question why our educational system was ranked at thirty-seventh in that report. The UK stands just below Mexico and just above Argentina.* There are always problems with the comparability of international statistics and their interpretation. Injustices can easily be done by the way statistics are gathered or the methodology employed in their interpretation. Very well then, allow for these possibilities, and put the UK up by a round ten slots, to twenty-seventh place. That places the UK just ahead of Thailand. If we carry on assuming that statistical injustices have occurred, and move the UK to seventeenth place, we do get our nose just ahead of India on these criteria. Alas, that telling and frightening graph does not show us, say, in seventh position, ahead of Germany, and just behind Japan. It does not, even though we spend more of our gross domestic product on education than both of these countries. In the years ahead, we need to redouble the undoubted improvements of the last fifteen years, to use all that money better and produce a more competitive educational system.

First, look at what can be done further to improve compulsory school education. These days there is a fashionable debate over nursery education. To some, the place of parents is in the home, for that is where children spend their formative years, and will be best informed by their parents. There is nothing wrong at all with that approach to child rearing. Others want 'nursery education', not particularly because they want the teaching of their three- or four-year-old, but rather because they want child care on the

*The World Competitiveness Report, World Economic Forum, 1994, figure 8.28, p. 595.

cheap. Some policy makers may want exactly the same, because they wish to have more working women entering the labour market at a time of a slowly ageing workforce. They are worried that more than eighty per cent of those who are going to be working in the year 2000 are at work already. Still more want it because the French have it and why shouldn't we, as we are just as advanced a country? Then of course there may be votes in it. Thus it is every party's big idea, subject always to the rider 'when resources allow'; and thus entirely consistent with the new economic realism.

In examining whether or not nursery education is good for the country we have to separate care and maintenance 'child care' from formally educating children in their very early years before they go to school. In the United Kingdom, along with the Dutch, we have the earliest start for full-time compulsory schooling anywhere in the European Union. These days most children rising-five get school places in most parts of the country. The hard question which needs to be asked is, accepting that it may be nice for children, convenient for parents, and have some votes attached, does nursery education improve the life chances, and thus the economic performance, of the children of our country? On this question the jury is still out. There is no evidence anywhere in the world that the beneficial effects of pre-school education are sustained throughout the later educational performance of those that have it. What is clear, however, is that special attempts to assist poor and disadvantaged children aged three, four and five do, for many of them, pay off for a period in their later school career. They certainly integrate better into school, make fewer demands on social services – and the law and order services – and perform better. So there is an educational kick-start for them; but the effects of that chance of a better start in life seem to run out of steam by the age of eight or nine. By then they are like their classmates who did not go to nursery school. That is not to say that these benefits for those children are not worth having, by making a rotten infancy better. It is just that the strict educational and therefore economic benefits of experiencing nursery school are not as yet clear, as are by comparison the results of rigorously given, and parentally supported, mainstream education from five to leaving school or college.

In this respect, British education is certainly very good in parts; but overall it is still not right. It is not competitive enough – that 'C' word is still a very dirty one in educationally correct circles. Is more money the answer? There is no evidence for this. We spend a great deal on education in this country, fast approaching thirty billion pounds a year. About five per cent of our nation's gross domestic product goes to the education of our children, college and university students. And we know that this is more than is spent in Germany or Japan, the latter a country where computers are a rarity in comparison to the classroom-plenty of the average British primary school, and those classes sometimes fifty strong.

Our teachers are reasonably well paid. Yet all that money and all those teachers do not seem yet to be delivering enough even of the basic skills needed for the twenty-first century. Look at the harsh fact that four out of ten students in our Further Education colleges need help with their basic literacy and numeracy, once they get there from school. This is to our national shame. And there are those regular and sadly accurate newspaper stories about major employers refusing to take on school leavers. Why? Because they cannot write a decent job application or speak standard English in an interview. Or because they have poor time-keeping or no idea of the work ethic – whether puritan or not – which is so vital to our less than puritan nation's economic future.

Where does the problem begin? It begins in too many homes, with too many parents who do not take enough interest in their children's progress before and during compulsory schooling. Fifteen minutes a day spent reading with a young child, or teaching them the alphabet, can transform the prospects of a boy or girl. Instead, far too many children arrive at school for the first time aged four or five, possessing scant familiarity with the printed word. So it is no wonder that such children struggle at school, when they are allowed by their parents to spend more time in front of the television or video than they are now expected to be in the classroom. Such parents have failed in their civic duty. Teachers cannot be left to pick up these particular pieces, or be blamed. By the same token, however, their job is to piece together for our children all the strands that make up a proper schooling. Something is not quite right here. To deny this is to fly in the face of the dreadful reality that about six million people in our country today are thought to have some difficulty with reading, writing, spelling and basic mathematics. That means about one in ten of our fellow citizens are functionally illiterate – in other words their standard of literacy is not up to coping with every-day life, and thus more challenging work. The younger they are, then the more likely they are to be like this. There are some in this country who are absolutely illiterate. For far more the problem is to be found in an inability to use language and figures at a level necessary to function properly. For these men and women, writing a decent letter is difficult or impossible. A tabloid is completely defeating.

The number of these that the education system has let down – for low IQs cannot be used to explain away the educational underclass that has grown up in post-war Britain – is more than half the population of Greater London in size, more than five times the population of Birmingham.

This is the stuff of human and economic tragedy. The ability to read and write, to make oneself understood, is essential both for the well-being of the individual, and for the spiritual and economic health of the nation. Put simply, literacy means full integration into the community. Those who cannot communicate properly are, *ipso facto*, not going to find it easy to be part of the community and be economically productive. Though they may live in our world, they may not be able to make full sense of stories that appear in the newspapers and probably will not even look at them. They cannot compose letters to far-distant relatives or to potential employers nearer at hand, seeking work. They cannot write to local stores to complain, to local councils to request some form of action. And if the local authority or social security office writes to them, incomprehension is the response – not just because the communication may be written in officialese. Alienation is often the result of this educational deprivation.

Alienation is also just as economic as it is personal. If some of our people are functionally illiterate, then the job opportunities are severely limited. Not only desk jobs are out, but many vocational and skilled tasks as well. This is a dreadful barrier to human progress. It is a brick wall between a man and a woman and their social and economic advancement. Literacy is not just good for the individual, it is vital also for the wider community. The greater the capacity for communication, the greater the ability to discuss, and to resolve problems. The greater the capacity to understand what is going on around you, the less likelihood there is then of feeling outcast. The greater the ability to speak standard English, then the greater will be the opportunity to take part in national and local life, and not to be sidelined into some sub-class. Literacy and numeracy are essential to creating a more contented, cohesive and responsible United Kingdom – as well as a more productive one. In short, literacy and numeracy are the dynamics of social mobility and economic success in equal measure.

The economic cost of the endemic failure of our educational system to eradicate functional illiteracy is high. At a minimum it has been suggested that it stands at over five billion pounds. How is this suspiciously round-looking figure, which comes from an excellent body called the *Adult Literacy and Basic Skills Unit*, made up? About half of it is put down to rectifying mistakes. A lot of the rest is due to lost custom and cancelled orders through poor services. These are costs that Germany or Japan, spending less on education than we do, seem to refuse to bear. That same body reported, in January 1995, that people educated in the 1970s and 1980s have more problems with reading and arithmetic than those who attended school in the 1950s and 1960s, before 'modern teaching methods' took a grip on the educational throat of the nation.

What is to be done? A lot of the education reforms, starting with the 1988 Education Reform Act – and Mr Baker's Act was of at least equal importance in its time as Mr Butler's Act was in 1945 – have done a lot to begin the long haul to internationally competitive standards. Since then we have seen the introduction of a National Curriculum and of regular national testing. Depressingly they were bitterly opposed when introduced by producer-led educational interests. Happily they are slowly becoming part of the warp and weft of our educational landscape. It is an odd reflection that we did not get going earlier on all of this. But, with 20:20 hindsight, it is even odder that we did not deal with teacher training in 1979, just as soon as we got the chance. That is where we should have begun the task of stopping the rot in British education. This set in during the 1960s. By 1976, even Mr Callaghan, and then a rather unwilling Mrs Williams, were forced to concede this. In the event, we waited – and I was one of the guilty men for not encouraging earlier action – more than twelve years before we really began even to think seriously in government about the issue.

The reform of the way in which teachers are educated is the task we should have started with precisely because it was in many – though not all – of our Teacher Training Colleges that some dreadful and damaging practices began. These have affected a generation of children. What went on is reasonably summed up by the phrase 'progressive teaching'. Never was an adjective so misplaced. With 'progressive teaching' we rather took countless retrograde steps. Even after recent legislation carried through Parliament in the early 1990s, in trying to improve teacher education, the problems of theory dominating practice remain. How else can it be explained that in 1993 half of recently graduated young teachers felt, after four whole years in college or on a university course, that they were not adequately prepared to teach reading to children of primary age? This is less surprising after examining the fare they may have been fed at college. A glance at what three teacher education experts (Kimberly, Meak and Miller by name) wrote in 1991 to help students to get pupils to read explains a lot:

> Within a psychosemiotic framework the shared reading lesson is viewed as an ideological construct where events are played out . . . children need to learn to position themselves in three interlocking contexts.*

What is this psychobabble all about? A 'psychosemiotic framework'? 'An ideological construct'? 'Interlocking contexts'? Where

---

New Reading: Contributions to an Understanding of Literacy, A. and C. Black, London, 1991, p. 38.

does the alphabet fit in exactly? And what, pray, about reading and writing? The publishers of this tome should be ashamed of themselves, and arrange a public burning of available copies by way of expiation.

Too many people have recently left teacher education establishments conversant in the rituals of progressive orthodoxy, but half of them saying that they do not know how to teach infant children to read, because of jargon-ridden claptrap like this. Some teacher education is at present the source of too many of the problems in state education, and also the home of a culture which is endemically anti-elitist, anti-testing and at times apparently opposed to academic rigour or structure in teaching and therefore learning. This means that the country is not going to be able to be as competitive as it should be. Yet all too recently in too many teacher training colleges there was a twilight world, in which paranoid academics could be heard to compare the introduction of even the entirely innocent National Curriculum – most countries have had them for years – and regular testing, to fascism and Stalinism.

What now needs to be done is to take a long view of the effects so as to build on recent reforms ensuring that by the beginning of the new century a majority of our would-be teachers get their training substantially in school. Many, it is to be hoped, will not be fresh-faced and college scarf-wearing youngsters. Rather that they might be thirty- or forty-somethings, who have had two or three of those job changes, bought their home, and want to give as well as to take. For teaching is a noble profession at best, and is intensely demanding as a task. It is also a task that sometimes may be better done by those who have experienced a wider world than the school-college-back-to-school path pursued by too many Mr, Mrs, and Miss Chips. Of course the education of would-be professional teachers needs some theory as well as some practice. It also needs to be rooted in particular experiences as well as particular subjects. Teacher education is best placed in the best schools in the country, including independent schools; it needs to be moved away from people who are overtly hostile to practical teaching methods of any sort. This hostility is the root of the obsession which still exists in many primary schools with 'topic' work. Alas – blame entirely the trainers not the teachers whom they have trained – too many teachers in too many of our twenty thousand primary schools do not like subject work very much simply because they have not been taught adequately to teach it. They often prefer small group work to whole class teaching, despite the fact that these methods are well known to be wasteful of teacher time and undemanding on boys and girls. All this undermines educational performance.

Learning on the job is better by comparison. Many independent schools train young teachers just out of university or college in just this way. We need more co-operation so that the best of good state and independent schools can produce the best sorts of teachers for a new century. We have a long and honourable history in this country of 'teaching hospitals' where young doctors learn their profession; it would be good to see boards set up outside schools conveying the same sort of message that here the education of teachers is a speciality. For many, however, at the endemically politically correct end of the teacher-training spectrum, any form of co-operation with the independent schools is regarded as a betrayal of the great programme of social levelling that they see education as being primarily aimed at. Some will not send their students on to teacher practice in public schools. Anyone on a teacher course in such places who remarks on the impractical educational clothes worn by the child-centred emperors, running too many teacher departments, gets short shrift. It is vital for the next century that we have applied and rigorous teacher education. This must produce teachers who are equally applied, rigorous and in favour of levering up standards year by year. They need to be dedicated to caring, but also to competition. On those firm foundations of ever improving standards, more diverse schools can progressively emerge.

It is vital for future economic success that the recent reforms are fully used. The muscle that the newish government agency charged with the oversight of teacher training can apply if it has the will, to close down bad courses and institutions by withdrawing approval, is weighty. No approval, no funding – for funds follow the students joining approved courses. The same muscle can be used to encourage the placing of teacher training in the best schools in the country, whether state or independent. Just as with the skirmishes on testing or the National Curriculum some in the educational establishment will do all they can to subvert these changes, and keep control of the educational agenda. This is because professional trade unionism in the late twentieth century is not just about pay and conditions but control of the professional agenda as well. Power over what happens next is, for most professionals, almost as important as pay. This attitude is uncommon in the Far East and most European countries. But it is certainly not unique to the United Kingdom. Just listen to one recent mid-1980s US Secretary for Education, William J. Bennett.

> For three and a half years, my efforts to challenge American education met well-organised institutional resistance, most often from the educational establishment: teacher unions, educational lobbyists, and bureaucrats – all groups skilled at the exercise of narrow, self-interested political power. Early on, their opposition appeared as a form of denial – the schools were not so bad as they seemed. A little later the opposition took a different tack, admitting that things might be bad, but insisting that they could not be fixed in or by the schools – that first 'society' or 'the system' must be altered. More recently we heard what might be called opposition by extortion, the false claim that fixing our schools would require a fortune in new funding.
>
> But the fundamental problem with American education today is not lack of money; we do not underspend, we underproduce. A review of some 150 studies shows no correlation between spending and educational achievement. The American people have been remarkably generous in their contributions to our schools. In 1990 we spent $414 billion on education, roughly $140 billion more than on national defence. In the international competition on education spending, the United States wins the gold medal. In absolute terms we spend more on education than any other nation in the world. And expenditures keep climbing. In 1950, we spent (in 1989 dollars) $1,333 per student. In 1989 we spent $4,931. During that period we probably experienced the *worst* educational decline in our history.*

*William J. Bennett, *The Devaluing of America*, Touchstone, 1992, p. 55.

In the UK too, we spend much more per head, on books, equipment and teachers than two decades ago. The picture is nothing like as tarnished as that Secretary Bennett painted for the United States of America. But it is an odd reflection on the new shape of our national life that, having gone through famous set-piece battles like those with the National Union of Miners, so many 1990s manufacturing or high-tech or service companies will have good conditions for their workforce, and barely feel the wind of belated union power that once blew so strongly. Yet the seed-bed supplying new workers from our schools still does. There is an urgent need for the members of the numerous teachers' unions to reform themselves just as much in the interests of their own standing in the community as of their salaries. These are now worth half as much again, even taking into account the inflation of the intervening years, as they were in 1979: teachers' status has not risen in parallel. It is easy to see why. A useful start would be to drop the dread word 'union' from their nomenclature to be followed by the formation of modern professional bodies to represent their interests and raise the public's appreciation and understanding of what teaching at its best means. This might start with the formation of 'colleges' of primary teachers, of maths teachers, of science teachers, devoted to self-regulation and high standards.

These could become distinguished and diverse 'Royal Colleges of Education' of different sorts in the early twenty-first century. They would help to lever up professional standards, get professional opinions really listened to in the highest councils of the land at the earliest stages of policy formulation. They would also do more to weed out the poor teachers in our schools, who jog along without much jogging their pupils' elbows. In this respect, burnt on to my memory, is saying to the great ones of one of the head teachers' unions that I had been told there were too many poor teachers about, and hazarding, nervously, as a guess that 'about ten per cent' might be the number. This was greeted not with roars of abuse but roars of laughter, followed by the suggestion that the real figure was 'at least twenty per cent', but 'nothing really can be done'. It should be, as Her Majesty's Chief Inspector of Schools pointed out early in 1995.

There is another sad fact which will bring joy only to those who want to do better than us, which is that for a number of reasons – everything from sloppiness and sentimentality to ideology and back again – too many teachers and some parents are reluctant about having pupils submitted to regular, rigorous testing. Without such testing and thus the comparisons which are made possible, it is all too easy for pupils to be allowed to drift through their schooling so that not only are they not stretched but do not even reach the basic levels of education that they should. The evidence for that is found in all those millions upon millions of our fellow citizens who have been let down, and are wholly or partly functionally illiterate. The losers are the masses of underqualified and undermotivated young people who, despite the opening of a second front in education post-1988, are still currently being produced by some of our schools. This is one of the worst cases of misapplication of resources in contemporary Britain. The National Health Service is a veritable paragon in terms of what it produces in outputs compared to those of our national education service. More must be produced by our education system for the pounds which are spent on it. This is essential if public spending is to be kept under the forty per cent ceiling, above which lies much economic peril.

It may take decades to produce a truly 'education culture' compared to many of our competitors. Parents must be better persuaded that the testing of their children is not harsh but helpful. That choice and diversity in schools are not confusing, do not mean two-tierism but rather bestow great national advantages. City technology colleges, technology colleges, and other specialised academic, as well as comprehensive schools, competing with each other as well as co-operating with each other, will raise national educational and thus economic standards. A few employers have made a noted contribution to developing education. Listen to John Neill, one of Britain's leading industrialists, speaking last year:

> If we find that our local schools are bottom of the league, then I believe that will be a powerful catalyst for action.

Businessmen will see clearly and objectively that the products of their community schools which they employ, will incur them in enormous retraining costs or leave them at a competitive disadvantage. That in itself will be a catalyst to business to put quality-time and resources into their community schools, to help them produce a better product.*

We now have the published results of school performance at GCSE, A Level, and vital new vocational qualifications. They tell us exactly which schools are, to use the words of Mr Neill, at the 'bottom of the league'.

We also have a long way to go before the opportunities offered to our young people by manufacturing are fully appreciated by them. Listen to Mr Neill again, on the same occasion:

... My company commissioned some private research amongst a thousand young people where we have our major business operations and the results were worrying. Eighty per cent of young people thought manufacturing was vital to Britain's national prosperity but less than ten per cent of them would consider a career in manufacturing. Seventy-five per cent thought the Japanese were very good at it and only three per cent thought the British were any good at it. The reasons they rejected a career in manufacturing was because they thought it was dangerous, boring, uninteresting and badly paid.

We need to change a century-old adverse view of making things as a career into the rewarding reality that the best of manufacturing in modern Britain presents.

Part of the secret of doing this is getting our children well taught in mathematics, exposed to science early enough, and given the chance to pursue it throughout their career. All our boys and girls now get compulsory technology up to the age of fourteen, uniquely in Europe, though the first children to have journeyed thus through the National Curriculum will not have

---

*John M. Neill CBE, speaking at the CBI Eastern Region Luncheon, 14 September 1994.

finished their educational voyage until the dawn of the new century. Industry also needs to steer talented youngsters their way. This will be done not just by paying them well, but also by getting involved in the schools where they are educated. Just as the active citizen may be essential to revitalising neighbourhoods, so the active company – an intelligent and learning company – should be in close contact with the schools where it is located. Companies from motor manufacturing to retailing have got used, in recent years, to forming long-term partnerships with their suppliers. This benefits both, and the consumer. One of the most important 'suppliers' for any company are the schools and colleges who can produce the core skills that employers need. Enlightened businesses should look at schools in just that way. Sir Christopher Lewinton, the Chairman of a highly successful UK-based global company, said in 1992:

> Engineering is the vital means to an end. Until you can make something and then sell it, no wealth has been created. Financial services, on the other hand, are only an enabling mechanism. If they, rather than industry, attract the lion's share of the best brains then industry will falter and fail the rest of us. At present, some of our manufacturing base is trapped in a destructive and repetitive cycle of educational deprivation. That circle starts from the fact that not enough good brains are involved in the process of wealth creation through industry. Because too few of our brightest and best are involved, the culture of many of our manufacturing firms remains hesitant and averse to innovation and risk taking.*

This is true. But all too often big employers can reasonably complain that when a new entrant is taken, they bring with them a basic training cost or levy. They have not come equipped with all the skills that might be expected. The harsh and difficult business of telling under-performing schools to perform better is one task

*An address by Sir Christopher Lewinton, Chairman TI Group plc, called 'Industry's Decline Arising from the Secret Brain Drain', given at the seminar on Engineering, Employers and Education, held at the Department of Education and Science, London, 13 February 1992.

that cannot be bucked by government or employer alike. Advising schools and helping them is however an immensely rewarding business for companies. The virtuous triangle between government, school, and business, needs to be as explicit as possible.

If business needs to ask more of schools, governments may need to make much more use of their 'asking power', by constantly bringing together leaders in industry and technology to create a shared vision of the next steps in becoming more competitive. Every benchmarking study shows that British industry could double its performance. This is just a first step in a never-ending process, not a new and thereafter relaxing plateau once it is reached. The UK is fortunate now, thanks to inward investment, in having a critical mass of world-class Japanese and American firms from whom much can be learnt. Change on the shop floor is occurring, through training following the examples of world-class companies and their suppliers. Some now have on-site and open-access colleges, like the Motorola 'U', or the Unipart 'U'.

Critical to the success of this approach is the creation of programmes in our secondary schools to teach the skills of team working, problem solving and process analysis that match the technology curriculum. To parallel this, a huge effort is needed by industry and government alike to show the young how appealing are the results of and opportunities in firms that have made these changes. The myths about modern industrial life remain legion.

Further Education colleges are vital in the task of creating a better-educated workforce, and of making an easier transition from school to work. The five hundred or so FE colleges in the country have taken an extra quarter of a million students over the last three years – not just the young, but those of all ages. This is a revolution in education and opportunity. When taken together with the technology and science for all that is now available in all our schools, we could jump a competitive generation if we take the chance. These colleges are yet in the mere foothills of the mountain which we need to climb in pursuit of the twenty-first-century dream of what is becoming known as 'lifetime learning'. They are vital to provide the setting for some off-the-job learning as employment and industries change. The Training and Enterprise Councils (TECs) are as vital to improving competitiveness, too. The results of these endeavours need to be closely linked with all the other inputs into a successful company, like new capital investment. Lifelong learning is essential to the high-skill, high-wage economy to which we aspire. This means a shared vision of what is necessary, and a sharing too of the costs of lifelong learning between business, the public purse and also the individual's pocket. None of this is or will be cheap, and government, via the taxpayer's contribution, cannot be expected to do it all.

The essential elements are in place – the National Curriculum, the colleges, the universities – knitting together more with service and manufacturing industries. It is easier for governments to orchestrate progress in schools, Further Education colleges and TECs than with the universities. In their case, national needs come up against academic freedom. This is why, having so radically increased the numbers of people going to universities old and new (from about one in eight back in 1979 to one in three in 1995), it is now vital to pause for a big academic and economic breath. Academic freedom is a good thing. Universities are rightly independent. They cannot be twitched this way or that at government's whim. But neither can they be directed into this or that activity, save by the rubber levers of the funding council which distributes the academic loot to them annually. Even where man-power planning is king – as in the case of setting the numbers of dentists, doctors and vets to be turned out annually – the results are not always a perfect balance between supply and need.

Any 'picking of winners' by Whitehall in academic life is just as likely to be disastrous as it was when those who thought they knew best did this in industry in the 1960s or 1970s. But universities must respond better to the signals that knowledge-led industry sends out in a new century, offering skills as well as the re-skilling of people of middle as well as teenaged years. Tory governments, characterised by both continuity and momentum, can sometimes usefully rest on their laurels. They do need now to rest on their university laurels as far as promising more places is concerned, and draw a firm line under the numbers of universities that have been created. It is not in the national interest to have any more. The enormous new system that has been created needs to settle down, improve its standards, offer diversity and choice, as well as serve the needs of the economy as closely as possible.

The attitude of the government should be to encourage more and more explicit diversity amongst the hundred universities that are there, everywhere from Strathclyde to Sunderland, from Imperial to Plymouth and back again. There is much to be gained by greater diversity and choice in the university system, just as there is as far as schools are concerned. This does not mean different 'tiers' of universities; just differences. There should be 'teaching' universities doing just that. To teach well, at the highest levels, is a very demanding task by any standards. Other universities might teach and do some of the applied research which smaller firms and regional economies need. And then there will be a few essentially research-driven university power houses. These world centres of academic excellence are already open-access and elite outfits demanding elite outfitting. The country can only have a few of those. There are not more than a couple of dozen worldwide.

Universities are one of the four pillars of economic life in the country, along with industry, the City and government. In too many of these for too much of the time the effective working links between them are too tenuous. In France they are systematically arranged to the point of intellectual, and sometimes economic, incest. In Germany and the United States, industrialists senior and junior jump into government and back, then into academia and back into industry again. This sort of movement in the UK is still not much promoted by government. In the academic world it is too often regarded as the mark of someone who is not quite serious about his scholarship. The industrialist told they are to be seconded out of the company think that means that they are being diverted off the promotional fast track. Here is the stuff for serious debate between the architects of these pillars, the universities included.

It certainly should no longer be the stuff of manifesto pledges, to promise further that there will be an even greater participation rate for university students. Institutional improvements in standards rather than institutional expansion should be the university norm. We simply do not need extra battalions of BAs in the new century, as much as marching regiments of the rapidly re-skilled. This means a host of part- or full-time courses, sometimes provided by universities, more often by the Further Education colleges in conjunction with TECs, which are rightly moving centre stage in our national life. They should be the powerhouses of continuing lifetime education, if they are developed properly. No sensible government will cede to the Further Education colleges any greater freedoms than they enjoy now. The notion of academic freedom has been developed quite as far as is decent or desirable in the late-twentieth-century university world. The second- and third-rate must never be buttressed by the freedoms deserved only by the best. Rather we need to continue to put right a national deficit in basic, directly applied vocational and advanced skills. The Prince Consort accurately recognised this in our country all those years ago. Alas, that the years in between then and now have not been as full of effort as should have been the case in order to turn Prince Albert's message into the reality that it deserved. This is where the national focus should be concentrated, to get as well-educated and re-educated a workforce as anywhere in Western Europe. As the Party of capitalism we should realise that capitalism will be driven in the new century by knowledge and education alone, shaping the country in the future.

7

A British Future

Prosperous, safe and clean is how most people want their futures to be in the twenty-first century. Many would also like as much space as possible in which to live, and to be as mobile as may be. They want to be bossed around by government or local officials as little as possible. Most will wish to own their own homes. They hope to feel secure in them, free of passing burglars, vandals, and the petty incivilities that can make life disagreeable. More and more they will want to have horizons which go beyond their front drive or car park. Personal mobility will be quite as important as economic or social mobility. Geographical liberation will be all. Most of them, as well, will want a 'decent environment', that phrase which trips so easily off the tongue but can mean so many different things to different people. It can embrace the disagreeable visions of the eco-terrorist and the new pragmatism of the eco-Tory, or be symbolic of the conservation of the old and the realisation of a dream. In other words, everything from national park to theme park and back again.

The problem with meeting all these hopes is that most of the United Kingdom is full. One of the major political problems throughout the twenty-first century for Tory politicians will be to reconcile all these ambitions with the smallness of the stage on which they can be played out. When a few years ago there was some undesirable development threatened in and around the edge of Oxford's green belt, 'full' was the motif chosen to characterise a campaign against it. Repeated speeches began with the same clearly expressed wish that the signs on the M40 leading to Cowley, and its Latin Quarter down amongst the dreaming spires in the city centre, might read, 'You are approaching Oxford. Please do not attempt to stop and relocate here. Please drive on to . . .' The campaign got legs because the idea so neatly summed up the pressurised reality. The problem is that Oxford is not a unique case. Oxford certainly is full. It is tightly packed within its gloomy but efficient encircling ring roads, with barely an open patch of land to be seen from the air, save from the odd green of a college quadrangle here or there.

The rest of the country, to varying degrees, is just as full. The politics of the good life that people will wish to lead in the twenty-first century is going to be more and more determined by the fact that the United Kingdom is one of the most densely populated countries on earth. It is under intense pressure because our slowly ageing population is growing in prosperity and therefore in mobility. For a minority, they hope that a second home might follow the second car. That means that they want bigger and better roads to bring closer together those two potent symbols of what many aspire to. Indeed, it is one measure of the transformation in prosperity that has taken place since the 1950s that simple home ownership has been replaced by second-home ownership as a goal for some. For the majority of our people with their one flat or home and their one car, the aspirations will also be for a bit more space. For some that means a house with a garden rather than a flat. The 1980s were the decade when gardening joined shopping as a major leisure pursuit. The two have been brought together in that most quintessential of late-twentieth-century British developments, the 'garden centre'. For those with less green fingers, the demand for other places to go to gets stronger and stronger – shopping mall, leisure centre or golf driving range. The twenty-first century will see these intense centripetal forces, pushing out from towns into the surrounding countryside, becoming ever more land hungry. This is one of those step-changes in the way in which we live, which will be seen to be quite as remarkable as the initial eighteenth- and nine-teenth-century rush from country to town. The political implications are enormous.

It is easy to be nostalgic about the dimly perceived past. The country has always been relatively crowded. It never has been easy to find total peace in the countryside. It is a lively enough place. Nature is noisy. There is always the dawn chorus of bright-eyed birds as well as the tractor legitimately going about its seven-day-week business. It is, however, much harder now to find a dark sky at night. Over most of England, and some of the more developed parts of Wales, Scotland and Northern Ireland, the persistent reflected white or sad sodium-orange glows of lights strung along arterial roads or around the roundabouts, that are the wilder dreams of traffic engineers, are thrown up against the clouds. Such light bounces up from town or out-of-town shopping centre straight up into the night sky. It can create a vision on the horizon that was once there only when London was burning in Great Fire or Blitz.

By day and night people dash from home to work to leisure or shopping centre (sometimes the two conveniently combined), stopping off at the weekend at a theme park or popping into a dis-count club, complaining all the while of the longer and longer time it takes to do this. They feel the strain if they venture on to the M25, which was meant to take the strain away. They pass business parks (sometimes sensibly these days with attendant housing developments), which may be built like an Assyrian zig-gurat thanks to fashionable architectural façadism. They go to shop in retail sheds which hide their supermarkets behind the frontage of some neo-Theban temple. If they can resist temptation to take their four-track leisure vehicle on to the Downs but rather take to their feet on the chalk, they are likely to find it rutted by the ubiquitous trail bike whose snarl comes over the crest of the next-but-one hill. By-passes have nasty little taupe brown signs inviting one to pop into some business centre or another, shoe-horned into set-aside farm buildings which somehow still meld into the surrounding prairie-farmed fields. Or, heavily rebuilt, they might stand stark within the relatively well-manicured golf course which has moved in. Balls are now hunted where once hounds put up and pursued the hare.

Even where the farms are still worked, a farmer's life is made the more difficult by the masses of generally urban-dwelling people exercising their legal and historic rights to walk on established footpaths. Too often, however, despite all the fashionable eco-babble they will let their dog off the leash. They might leave a gate open for some Suffolk ram to go through in pursuit of mischief, or drop the plastic wrapping of a taut plastic supermarket sandwich box to be chewed by Holstein heifers. Sometimes the chance to walk has been, in the way in which the word 'right' has become the most mischievously used word in the English language, replaced by a self-assumed 'right' to roam. To the more extreme, this means going wherever and whenever you like on private property of the country dweller. These would-be 'roamers' are usually just the thoughtlessly politically correct and more gentle cousins to the hunt saboteurs or animal liberation frontists. Their reaction, should some farm worker's boots return the compliment down their own front paths or up their own back garden, can only be imagined.

It is in the nature of a town to devour the countryside. It always will be. Out of town is where people more and more will want to go, to live, to shop or to recreate themselves. They want space. This is the space which the country dweller of generations wishes to defend so he or she can farm in peace. The more recent in-comer wants to halt some road or housing estate proposed for his or her back yard, too. It would destroy the view, it will break the peace which is what they had sought in the first place. The pressures of the town are not just on the diminishing space in the countryside. New roads bring nasty urban habits. The Neighbourhood Watch and Farmwatch signs that now adorn many a lane and hamlet give a hint not just of the traditional and minor *Archers*-like crime of rural England but demonstrate with just what ease radiating ribbons of new roads can carry the car-born burglar.

More than nine out of ten of our fellow citizens live in towns and cities now. Urban life at its best is pretty good, particularly if you are in Fulham or Notting Hill, Bath or Wells, Edinburgh

Morningside or Glasgow Hillhead. It is far from idyllic for many. It is certainly much rougher for those marooned in a tower block on the edge of Birmingham and Liverpool, or who have to struggle along the deck-access walkways to their flat in Peckham or Lambeth. It is these people who are some of the most immobile. They are rarely likely to want to travel across four or five miles of London to get a job, let alone fifty miles out of it to have a country walk. But their needs for a decent quality of life are just as reasonable as those of any countryman, and they cry out for even a bit of space in tightly packed inner city areas, or more sprawling edges of town estates. It is good to have somewhere to sit, play ball games without attendant forbidding notices, exercise a much loved family dog. Too often they do not have it, or the 'open space' is unsafe and badly maintained. Surely the planner should do something about it?

But planners planned it – under the direction of politicians, of course – exactly as they planned the deck-access blocks and flats in the sky. 'Planners', like Civil Servants or local government officials, are the easy and often unfair butt for attack or joke. But planners only plan to the remits that they get from council chamber or Palace of Westminster. So it is politicians who must do much better if we are both to undo the mistakes of the post-war years, and not make further new ones in the first years of the twenty-first century. The Tory dilemma, as we ponder how we can undo the worst manifestations of the planning consensus that conspired to produce so much that is environmentally and personally debilitating, is not just how to pay for it but would it be better. Appealing though it might be to go in all over again for wholesale demolition, neither is the money easily to be found nor can we be certain that the replacements would turn out to be acceptable. Not all development, or redevelopment, is bad; it is really the case that large-scale development or redevelopment is fiendishly difficult. Managing what is there will be our major problem. Some people may want to spread out across the countryside so they can labour at their own domestic work station, linked back to base at the end of a fibre-optic cable, but that will not transform the face of our landscape. So the Tory environmental dilemma is found firstly in trying to reshape what the post-1945 era has left us and secondly in attempting to achieve a balance for the new century between convenience and economic necessity on the one hand, and the need to enhance the quality of the country's life and bolster its sometimes flagging community base on the other. We have to break the vicious circle of further environmental pressures without destroying the agreeable conveniences of life on which so many now depend.

Conservatives are ideally suited to this task. We have, or should have, an instinctive attachment to the heritage of our nation. We want to preserve that which has provided the framework for our island's history. We want to keep the attractions of what can often still be a reasonably green and quite pleasant land; we also want to preserve the architecture of centuries that adds so much to our landscape. Conservatives should harbour a natural and healthy scepticism about developments that threaten that heritage. At the same time, many of us, whether Tory or not, are addicted to the utility and recreations that all those roads, shopping malls and leisure centres can give us. Thus we want to conserve and enhance – yet at exactly the same time we want the freedom to drive as quickly as possible to relation or retail park. We do not like planners because planning is done by them; but at the same time we realise that there must be planning. We know it is the way in which, in modern times, we try to halve the difference between the bearable and the unbearable. We want to sustain, not destroy, the fabric of our neighbourhoods and communities and this means the state or local authority sometimes taking some action. Yet, we do not for one moment believe in the perfectibility of the planning process. We want places to be good places in which to live or visit. Yet increasingly we find that, when we get there, 'there' may just not be there.

We also want the country to make money, and people want to shop. Making money often involves development. Making money is also good for the country; this often involves shopping. Shopping will be one of the growing leisure activities of the twenty-first century, and have the impact on our landscape that industry once did. So retail is good for you; it generates cash from the economy from and for an overcrowded country at the same time. All those roads leading to all those sprawling car parks by all those retail temples standing on what only last year was Grade III agricultural land complete with stand pipe, on which stood only a few ponies, are the arteries of the problem. The circle is, if not absolutely vicious, then very troubling. It is difficult to try to reconcile these demands, but that is exactly what we must try to do in the interests of a balanced community in the next century.

Our electors, like Members of Parliament and Members of the House of Lords, are a pretty mixed bunch, with different views of what they wish to conserve, preserve, pull down, or build. Some like to wander as lonely as any cloud over hill or dale. Others rather like to drive from their well-built, ten-year-House-Building-Council warranted house, complete with agreeable Victorian detailing that the late Sir John Betjeman would have approved of, down convenient roads to a well-landscaped shopping mall. There they hope to find discount buying in the hypermarket that can be combined with browsing in those boutiques and eating in cafés which tend to stick to them on concession sites, like limpets to a decent-sized boat. In their oddly British way, the best of these centres are full of movement at the right time of day. Go to the Metrocentre near Gateshead and you will see people moving, browsing, watching, shopping, talking and parading. It and its brethren can be our very own northern and roofed-over versions of the *passeggiata* at dusk which so transfigure and enliven Valencia or Aix-en-Provence or Siena. So just as there are places where a certain modest amount of lonely wandering is still possible, so there are others, too, where good planning has produced the surroundings for those who like a more bustling and urban way of life.

The trouble is, there are lots of other places, which, because of economic change or bad planning in the post-1945 years, have been left desolate to look at and disagreeable in which to live. It is vital to try to understand how this happened. Tories were as active players as anyone else in the process. Only if we have some appreciation of why things went wrong in the last forty years can we then do better in the next half century. It is not easy to admit mistakes. To avoid those that have been made, in future we must start with the community, not with the theory and the master brief (all that theory, all that planning) purported to be designed for people who would live and shop in those schemes, but who were forgotten during the process. That is why all twenty-first-century planning should have community as its focus. Any twenty-first-century planning legislation must have community as its touchstone as well.

What is a community in modern terms, and what does it mean politically? Tangibly, community is no more than a particular group of individuals living in some specific locality or another. But it is exactly that approach which led to so many post-war mistakes. A community was seen simply as an inchoate lump of people, who needed to be accommodated and have shops provided for them. Communities are much more spiritual in reality. They have an intangible quality to them. The key question which needs to be kept perpetually in the foreground when planning is just what is the quality of life for those people in that area? There is little point in giving a community the chance to take power and responsibility from a shrunken state or a vanishing local authority if those new decision-making structures cannot actually have an impact on the environment in which people live. The point of planning is to enhance satisfaction, pleasure and security for individuals. This means that they have the chance, if they wish, to feel part of the community and play a rôle in it. The greater the quality of life, the greater then will be the willingness to become involved in local affairs.

There is little chance of getting that commitment and involvement if people do not feel secure. Security is vital to living a pleasurable life; an 'insecure community' is a straight contradiction in terms. If there is no community safety, then there can be no community, only fearful individuals and families living their own tight lives as little, dislocated civic islands. So as much crime as possible needs to be designed out of twenty-first-century life. Tories must give this their deepest attention. Designing out crime is partly a physical business. It means better locks on doors, electronic tags on shop goods to prevent them being walked out of other doors, toughened glass and isolators to stop car doors being broken into, and then being driven away.

But it is also about attitude and effort. It is about trying to get the community involved, in order to police and protect itself, and based on established community ethics. Men and women are economic animals, they like their comforts – but they generally have an ethical side to them as well. So it is back to basics here, at least as far back as Aristotle. Communities hum because, despite our little failings, people generally carry out the right rather than the wrong actions. So, virtue (a grander way of saying right actions) only gets a look in if there is prominent and coherent social activity. Only in and through communities do we get some sort of shared understanding of what virtue is, and thus what civic virtues can be. We can only have communities if those civic virtues flourish. Different communities flourish in different ways, with different codes of behaviour and backgrounds. But none will flourish where virtues are not valued. So they are learned from and are vital to all communities. Without qualities of honesty, perseverance, humility and courage individuals will always be unable to learn from community tradition or contribute to it. So they have to be encouraged in the new century – and planning must never forget that.

We certainly have the criminal law to protect our communities, as we have locks on their doors to protect the properties within, but it does not exist to make men good, or to bring up citizens unlikely to be bad. The criminal law is simply there to punish that set or style of actions which are defined as being inimicable to the stability of the community. But, like the civil law, it does just that and nothing more. It is there only to lay down and then enforce those minimal requirements that a state thinks are necessary for its stability and that of its citizens.

The criminal law can never deal totally with crime. These days, it is everywhere, but seems to hit communities in particular pockets. We know that the incidence of crime varies markedly. It reaches especial intensity in some small areas where neighbour preys on neighbour, and little crime is actually reported to the authorities. These pockets are at their worst in the inner and outer city estates in which people so hate to live. Bad design does not help, and much design, by oversight, has provided incubators for criminal activity. It is certainly still there in the darkened stairwells of tower blocks, and it is even there in some of the tasteful little closes of modern middle-class estate life. Intruders can easily hide where landscaping allows and prevents eyes on the streets. In such middle-class areas, however, crime normally reaches the ears of the police. Oceans of crimes are not reported by comparison. And they wash over some very small communities.

The opportunities seem greater in some poor areas for three reasons. Firstly, there are those gas and electricity meters behind flimsy doors or windows begging to be burgled. Secondly, 'respectability' is given a low value sometimes, even by those who struggle against temptation. If life seems to have few chances for you, then whether or not you fall foul of police and courts does not matter too much in the eyes of some. Many others amongst the poor in those areas are, by happy comparison, models of civic virtues. These are the people in parts of the country where the honours system never reaches, but who are none the less the gentle knights of the community, full of those little local kindnesses and neighbourliness. Thirdly, the sub- and sometimes subterranean cultures of such areas can be characterised by very weak family structures with not many father or authority figures to look up to. There is a lot of rootlessness, and a high turnover of tenancies. The geography of crime in the late twentieth century seems to be strongly correlated with communities which are not sufficiently settled, and thus able to inculcate the virtues of social norms against crime.

What on earth are these curious-sounding 'social norms'? Well, they should spring from the community. Most of us do not commit crime, either because we think that we should not, or because it does not occur to us. Indeed to turn conventional approaches on their head, one of the most difficult facts to understand about criminal behaviour is why most people most of the time are not at it. A prosperous Britain positively bulges with opportunities to commit crime. There are all those homes and flats stuffed with electronic gadgetry, cars left conveniently unlocked, briefcases strewn carelessly on their back seats. There are those supermarket shelves dripping with consumer goods. The UK is a world laden with excellent criminal opportunities. The chances of being caught when engaged in a bit of casual theft are infinitesimal; once every eight years, Metropolitan police officers pass the scene of a crime actually being committed when they can intervene and stop the thief. So why do people resist crime and not think about it? Because they have been brought up in a community which frowns at the practice. Thus it is essential to underpin safer communities by involving those selfsame communities in promoting those civic values.

No Tory government can impose this, but every future Tory government must use every means possible to encourage it. That is one of the key lessons of the past forty years. Politicians and the planners who serve them forgot what a community means, and failed to provide the security without which it cannot flourish. In fact, we forgot so much and swallowed such copious draughts of theory that communities were destroyed, messy and insanitary though those little terraced rows of houses might have been. They did have the inbuilt civic virtue of having 'eyes on the street'. This meant that crime was less because the community helped police itself. Sometimes welfare was better too. Real care in the community was given by those terraced dwellers, whose kindly eye quickly spotted someone in trouble. It is as wrong to be romantic about the past in towns, as it is in the countryside. But as the post-war tide of technological and economic progress swept on, so people were swept up in a wave of municipal tidiness. Tidiness too often led to community destruction. A sense of community and belonging, that essential belief that you had made the environment a good one in which to raise your family, seemed devalued. The imperative to become a participant in local affairs was all too often undermined as well. Pressure groups have grown enormously in number in recent decades, but usually at some distance from such places. 'Joining' and 'being active' are still too much middle-class pursuits.

Because of this, actual alienation sometimes followed undermining of community spirit. Yet the motives for building those new 'housing units' surrounded by those new ring roads were laudable. Politicians and planners were trying to do good. It is just that the consequences were unintended. It is part of our contemporary folk-lore that the design of the buildings had disastrously unintended consequences. They were by accident purpose built to be the haunt of thug, vandal and drug pusher. It is equally conventional wisdom to compare the graffiti-scarred and urine-soaked lift with the scruffy, run-down, but cheerful old Coronation Street-like area complete with unreliable sewage. The inhabitants – and that is how they still too often feel in those new developments – are threatened and intimidated people. Their doorways are bolted. Some have died in fires because the brigade or neighbours could not get through the bars and barricades that had been erected against the new-style and threatening community in which they have found themselves placed. It is not only the old who are cautious before venturing out in the evenings.

And whatever age, when the inhabitants do venture forth it is quite hard for them to meet neighbours. It is much easier to meet road schemes with congested traffic or find dark and dingy-looking pedestrian underpasses, for all the world looking like contemporary stage sets for the medieval violence of some dark, arcaded Bologna. Once they have got through these uncivil places, they often only lead to other high-rise blocks. It really does not seem quite so blameworthy as it otherwise might for the citizens of such places to start to feel marooned, and thus believe themselves unable to do anything that will affect their community, and its environment. The scale of the problem is vast; the incentive to become involved is tiny. Barriers of the most persistent physical sort have been erected against neighbourliness. These are the road blocks which are strewn across the paths of civic virtue.

The middles of many of our big cities were totally laid waste first by bomb, and then by bulldozer, only to be replaced by out-of-scale and ugly concrete structures. They looked pretty rum when they were completed, but have rapidly aged since to look worse. Who would have predicted in the brave days of the opening of Birmingham's Bullring in the 1960s that it was destined to be demolished only thirty years after the festivities that marked its first inhabitants? It is not too exaggerated to say that where you find concrete you do not find many real communities. Concrete is a very unsuitable material for the outside of buildings in Britain. We are a maritime and northern country, often with rainy skies. All that wear by all that rain makes concrete look quite as unattractive as the structures it supports, and clads provide an unappealing home for the people piled into them. Rarely can any material have been so symbolic both of social as well as aesthetic degradation. Concrete slab housing seems so closely correlated with crime, unemployment, and underclassism.

These problems have been compounded by the fact that many council landlords have shown themselves unable to keep their properties in good repair, or unwilling to involve the community in so doing. There was a great burst of concern about so-called 'inner city' problems characterised by these buildings in the mid-1980s. The concern, once evinced by Bishops and statesmen alike, seems to have ebbed a little in the political mind, but the problem remains. A run of hot summers may help to bring it back to the foreground. The lesson to be drawn from the problems which we have inherited from the concrete age is that it is best to think small rather than large; to relate buildings to the scale of human existence; and to involve the community at all costs. It is the case that we cannot afford to flatten all of these buildings. What can happen is that tenants can be allowed the chance of forming a co-operative; they can be given the opportunity of opting for a different landlord like a housing association; they can buy their own flat or maisonette. If such places are made safe and attractive (even at the cost of some post-modern façadism) then they may be particularly appropriate for the single (young and elderly) and childless couples. Freedom and choice need to be injected into them, for what the tenants themselves decide to do is likely to be much more effective than all the theories of politicians and planners put together.

The same goes for town-centre municipal shopping malls, often providing the only facilities for the car-less members of the local community. Just like the blocks in which some of those tenants live, these shopping centres will never be ideal because of their basic shape and structure. Again, façadism plus better flooring, the introduction of more light, water and greenery all may help.

It seems to be a certain lesson from post-war Britain that the best form of housing is based on brick architecture with pitch roofs arranged in streets. Low-rise housing of this sort with walled or fenced gardens can be protected much more easily than a high-rise block of flats. Pitch roofs deteriorate less quickly than flat roofs. The fewer service areas and common parts there are the better; they normally become rubbish tips or temporary residences for undesirables. And as far as shopping centres are concerned, the more they are on a scale which is in keeping with a typically British market town the better. The traffic needs to be kept out, but not too far away; the shopping environment needs to be familiar in feel, whether galleried or arcaded. It is best if it is not some totally artificial and neon-lit world. There is no escaping the simple conclusion that the big idea of municipal planners and politicians of the 1950s, 1960s and 1970s turned out to be the big cause of the dereliction and decay of so many towns in the 1990s. From this follows an iron rule for the twenty-first century. Do not have big planning ideas; do remember the community.

The children living in such estates now, and who will grow up in the twenty-first century, are certainly no longer underfed compared with their forebears in Victorian England; indeed they may well be suffering from too much food and too little exercise, contemporary couch-potatoes in the making. They have, thanks to our social security system, food, clothes and shoes – but they certainly live in housing often apparently still from hell. Their parents are shipwrecked or adrift in their environment, despite the valiant later efforts of community workers and community architects the Prince of Wales and urban development corporations, and everyone else who have tried to undo the outcomes of all those good intentions and all that high expenditure.

By comparison, the quality of life of the rural dweller is generally nothing like as difficult or as threatened. Many Conservative votes have traditionally come from these parts. Compared to the enormous changes that have been wrought in so many of our towns, there is superficial continuity in the landscape of the countryside. Many a village in the mid-1990s, despite a bit of infilling by the church, some little development in the fields beyond the pub, and of course that row of council houses by the main road thrown up in the 1940s, would often be instantly recognisable today to those who were alive and celebrating Queen Victoria's Jubilee. By comparison, their compatriots who lived in central Birmingham would think that the Bullring was, if they were suddenly landed in the middle of it, something from another planet.

In the countryside, the village shop may have gone, smartly followed by the sub-Post Office. There never was much public transport, even back in the days of coach and carrier's cart. It was a pedestrian world. Most people walked then, often miles, to market or school. It is true there was a glorious epoch of the rural double-decker bus that flourished between the 1930s and the 1960s, but they, like so many of the pre-Beeching railway lines, have vanished. If you do not use your feet these days, it will normally have to be a car. The picture will certainly be thus throughout the next century.

And, as the hedgerows have also vanished, so have most of the farm workers. These days one or two men can do the work that took a couple of dozen only a couple of generations ago. So villages naturally seem emptier and quieter during the day because of changes in the farming economy. They are generally pretty well kempt. All that listing of all those grade II cottages, all those weekenders moving in with their Land Rover Discoveries and Renault Espaces mean that the picture-postcard view of the village is a well-kempt one. The village shop and village school have gone like much of rural real life because so much employment has migrated to the towns. All of these changes, in both city and village, have been made possible by the great transport transformation. Yet the umbilical motorways have helped to bring about what Stanley Johnson referred to over twenty years ago as the 'twentieth century's witches' brew', changing both the physical shape and sometimes the spiritual nature of our local communities.*

It is never going to be possible to stop the brew simmering. The effort to stop it bubbling over intolerably has to start with our town life. The greater impact that communities have upon decision makers, then the more people will see their quality of life in town is improving, that they really can have some effect on outcomes, on what happens next in their lives. Yet if Conservatives should not believe in the perfectibility of the planning process, they do need to have policies for land-use patterns which will help communities reform, knit together and flourish. All

*Stanley P. Johnson, *The Politics of the Environment*, London, 1973, p. 55.

proposals for urban renewal and refurbishment, let alone new development, are very expensive. They do in the future need to be guided quite explicitly by a desire to get a 'community gain' just as much as the 'planning gain' of traditional policy. All development on any scale in the future must contain space specifically dedicated for communities to grow in. They need green, or at least greenish space, for recreation, for walking the dog, for their young to expend their energy in. All too often in the inner city in particular there is none of that space for those young people and we can see how those energies end up being misdirected in other ways.

There also need to be buildings containing somewhere for the community to go to. There must be rooms for residents associations, spaces for all sorts of clubs from aerobics to Zen Buddhism and back again, as well as halls in which Bingo can be played. It certainly is a grand illusion on behalf of both politicians and planners that they can make communities happen. If they try to turn that delusion into reality they would be likely in the twenty-first century to make the same *dirigiste* mistakes as they did when plotting those 'villages in the sky' in the 1960s. But Tories can and should make a quite conscious effort to provide the stages on which people can erect the necessary scenery and act out community life, if they wish.

Since the last war, there has been much talk of 'development gains'. These can be anything from a new access road or a contribution to car parking provided by the developer in the town in return for that profitable permission to build houses or shopping centres. Many developers strive hard and well. They succeed in building to a high standard, and offer good planning gains to the local council. But now specific community gain needs to be put into quite as much focus. A lot of local government and planning law already contains in it the ways to take into account the community, and community development needs – that is, if politician, planner and developer alike are so minded. Tories believe in light-touch planning, and indeed in planning deregulation where possible. None the less, it seems vital that in the new century the idea of community is pushed to the forefront in such planning as there is. Every development planning application, as opposed to one affecting the sign on the front of a shop or the conversion of a loft, should have attached to it a statement of community impact. This is not to wish to load unnecessary costs on developers. Some of them realise that this makes as much economic as environmental sense. This is because well-built schemes in good settings sell better; people are expecting higher and higher standards and will pay more for them, if they can. However, not all developments are like that, and not all planners and developers think consciously about the community. If in the post-war years planners and politicians had thought more clearly about these things and less about irritating and petty rules over elevations and colours, then post-war life might not have been quite so constricted and difficult for so many.

If planning had started from the bottom up, then the prime question should have been asked about whether people would really like to live in a flat that was thirty or forty storeys high. People would have pondered what it would actually be like to travel daily with a pram in a lift up and down those thirty storeys, every time they wanted to stretch their family's legs and get a breath of air. How long would it take? How would they meet their neighbours? Was a liftshaft really the same as a village street? Was the green space on those architectural drawings around the base of that high-rise block really going to be well kempt? Could it really be maintained like someone's back garden, were there the staff to do it? And, would the proposed inhabitants of that tower block really feel happy with no privacy in the open spaces? Would they actually take a deck chair down those twenty or thirty storeys and sit out in the middle of that green patch of land? What would it be like for children to be brought up in such a flat, where it was not safe for them to go out on to the balconies, and even more dangerous if they went by themselves down that liftshaft via those strangely threatening common areas and lifts? And once the young, families, or the elderly, actually made the ground floor, where were they going to shop, how were they going to get there, how were they going to cross that road? What is the meeting place, where are the meeting rooms?

If architects had been forced to consider community gains and the community aspect, many would have been forced to recognise that it is nigh impossible to think of a community being easily made out of a tower block. But if the same densities can be achieved, and they can, by low-rise building, then there is at least a chance of community life taking off. Life might have been very different for a very large number of our people if these sorts of questions had been asked. As a result, eyes might have remained focused on the street or the close, rather than being left staring hopelessly out into mid-air, or at the stained concrete-clad façade of the next-door tower block.

It is not only the tower block that has suffered thus. There are dozens of 1960s and 1970s estate developments, privately and densely built houses grouped around ubiquitous closes, ten or twelve to the acre, which had not much focus either. Very often they were built without a shop let alone a community centre. The social problems that were once again at least partly caused by this lack of attention to the basic community necessities of life are attested to by many a local beat constable or probation officer in what appear at first glance much more privileged and middle-class environments, than the inner or outer city estates. These community considerations are vital as the massive national task of rebuilding and refurbishing our estates, and the communities that they contain, rolls on. This will take two or three decades. It will also demand an enormous amount of money and planning effort. The opportunities for further mistakes are legion, and that is why we must learn from the immediate and still living past all around us, and put the community first in all future planning considerations.

Just as we know that most of our population for the next few decades is already living, we can also be pretty secure in the knowledge that most of our homes for people who are going to be there in 2020 are already built in 1995. In an era when homelessness periodically attracts the headlines, to most people's great surprise, there are more vacant homes and flats in the UK than there are homeless people to fill them. Some of these are owned by local councils with too little zip and vim, unable to tackle the task of refurbishing and refilling them. Far more are in private hands. They are part of what is by any European standard a hopelessly antiquated private rented sector; bringing some freedom, to match security, back into the private rented sector along continental lines is the one piece of European harmonisation that I think every Tory could countenance. Things went badly for the private landlord early in the present century and thus homelessness has been caused. The noose began to be tightened around its neck in the years following the First World War, and has grown progressively tighter and tighter still. Conservative governments have taken the first steps to loosen the regulatory grip since the mid-1980s. There have been a number of Acts to this end. Ways of matching tenant's and landlord's security have been found in measures like shorthold tenancies.

The big leap forward into a much less regulated form of landlord and tenant legislation, helping to end homelessness, will however only come if Labour and Liberal alike can be brought to support it. If these Parties are serious in their concern about homelessness, and about mobility for those seeking work, then this is one of the next frontiers for their modernisers to contemplate crossing. In a low inflationary age, renting will come to be seen by more as a reasonable and proper alternative to buying. It will take a few more years before attitudes change, and people realise that property prices are no longer the great store of potential value nor hedge against inflation that they once were. The Right to Rent should become as telling an idea as the Right to Buy. It is vital to give people the opportunity to rent, the chance to get a roof over their head, or to move easily in search of work. And in future decades, those seeking new employment opportunities will not always be the Geordie or Scouser or Scottish blue-collar wearer moving south on their legendary bike. It is as likely that some of those migratory movements will be in the reverse direction, as not only white-collared but sometimes surprisingly young ex-financial service workers from some South-Eastern or Midland town move ahead of their families looking for a new job. The political problems caused for twenty-first-century government by the insecurity of these new white-collar unemployed will only be compounded if there is not the opportunity to let them move easily to a new home.

Economic growth will always demand new housing development. Some of these developments should be on 'grey' already part-used land in or about our cities. Derelict land is sometimes both inconvenient of access and expensive to develop. It presents a challenge for planners and builder alike. But our cities still contain far too much of it. Bodies like Railtrack and its successors have some interesting challenges in land disposal. It is always undoubtedly easier to build on green land. Some edge-of-town sites as well as set-aside agricultural land and other fields will continue to go under bricks and mortar. The competition for them is fierce. Much of our apparent housing needs could be realised, however, through building on urban and other derelict land, as well as by Rent Act reform. As we enter the new century, just as we must ensure that the community is put first in planning, then we should view the major built-up areas of our country as already firmly established.

It is the same with roads. Possible road lines are there in the mind's eye not just of planners, and the suppliers of the black top which will cover those carriageways, but also in those of the fiercely competitive industrialists and retailers who want to move goods at home or to Europe more easily. They are joined by the infuriated motorist on his or her way to workplace or relative who profoundly wishes for a by-pass around some town to relieve its intolerable and seemingly historic bottleneck. Anyone who has tried to get through Newbury in Berkshire on a summer Saturday afternoon when the races are on, or get near it during the peak hours on a weekday when the dash to work is on, must have felt these emotions. Sometimes they are relieved by the magic of by-elections. This happened after all in the 1960s when the Humber Bridge was magicked out of thin air to help Harold Wilson's government dig itself out of a by-election hole. It was the same in the 1990s, during the Newbury by-election. By-passes were fiercely debated, but all parties seemed to vie with each other in calling for one, and thus catch the votes of those infuriated motorists.

It was duly offered. Immediately every environmentalist in this part of South-Central England rose up in arms. Sites of special scientific interest and civil war battlefields are prayed in aid of the campaign against this once universally 'much needed by-pass'. Interesting new arguments have been produced as a result.

Some self-styled environmentalists now argue, 'It is a good thing to have bottlenecks,' because traffic is slowed down and therefore at least some of those who may wish to travel through the area on the long journey between and betwixt the Midlands and the South Coast ports might be deterred completely from doing so. Thus road use will be diminished. It is worth pausing a moment on this sort of argument, for those sorts of environmentalists are generally also against air pollution, noise and the general upsetting of residents. What about all that delay for Newbury residents, all that persistent noise for those whose homes lie along part of the route around the town now besieged by the car, as it once might have been by civil war soldiers. Surely all those fumes and that noise from all those cars causing all those respiratory illnesses – and all that asthma amongst the children – are exactly what caused some of the environmental uproar in favour of the by-pass in the first place. Yes indeed, it was. So the circle of protest goes on, and the environmental/economic arguments become more and more fantastical. All that we can be certain of is that in the twenty-first century the witches' brew exemplified by the saga of Newbury by-pass will bubble more fiercely, as more and more environmentally irreconcilable ingredients are tossed in.

Another incendiary ingredient is the development of shopping as a national pastime. Sometimes this is the nearest to actual physical exercise that some video-watching contemporary couch potato seems to get. 'I shop, therefore I am', is already the motto of many. When not working, then shopping – late, or all over the weekend including Sundays – has become just as much a ritual as going to the pub, or going to church, used to be. Sometimes it is in some agreeable inner city area. The refurbished shops around Camden Lock or the refettled canal and river front in Gloucester or the rebuilt Grade I magnificence of dockside Liverpool provide a setting for that which was once a simple necessity of life but is now a major leisure activity. Quite as often, though, it is to the out-of-town superstore that they go. Sometimes leisure facilities are hard by. These new developments gobble up land, affect the view for miles, yet give miles and miles of pleasure for lots and lots of people as well. These developments also, it is alleged,

destroy the fabric of inner-city shopping and lead to the dereliction at worst of many a market town's traditional shops. At best,
some would say that all that are left in such places are a lot of
gift shops, boutiques, souvenir halls, coffee stalls, and emporia
selling the mysterious pot-pourri of fond Edwardian country-lady
memory.

Take Burford, in west Oxfordshire. It has gone exactly down
that route. It is full of pretty stone buildings of great architectural
quality, strung down either side of an equally pretty steep-sloped
High Street. As late as the late 1980s it was possible to get nails
counted out by the dozen into paper bags, hazardous though they
were to hold, in the ironmonger at the top of the High Street.
Like most of the 'old' shops, it is gone. Now the shop fronts display sheepskin coats, pottery, or wood-burning stoves. Fine pic-
tures and antiques are also there, vying for the passing carriage
trade and the Cotswold weekenders. A 'Ministry of Taste' official
might think all this deplorable. A 'Ministry of Community
Affairs' Civil Servant might regret the car-borne journeys to the
supermarkets of Witney or Oxford which have replaced the food
shopping, in and out of greengrocer, butcher and baker in turn
down the High Street. The simple reality is that people have
chosen to shop in this way. They like to bulk-buy here and do
some specialist shopping there. Thus they have created a new
retail world.

Commentators, planners, politicians and social historians may
all in their different ways deplore what has happened, but they
have no right to despise it. The new reality is often that out-of-
town shopping centres offer what people want, a bit of fun and
something to eat all under one roof. Video shopping, followed by
video-interactive-superhighway shopping, is sure to come along,
but it will not destroy either superstore or corner shops, rather
mail-order buying. Looking, feeling, touching, browsing and
sluicing all the while when doing it are much part of the British
way of shopping. 'Cable shopping' will not disturb this pattern;
rather, eventually it will replace mail-order buying from cata-
logues. What individuals and communities want are the dynamic
motors of change. It is the sometimes dismal but always democratic job of politician and planner alike to accommodate what is

happening, not row against it.

Just what are the limits? Certainly not automatic presumption against any more out-of-town developments. Those who think that drawing a line under 'superstoreland', with its architecture quite as distinctive as any that Underground line-linked Metrolands of the 1920s and 1930s ever produced, will lead to the rebuilding of city centres and market town squares, are crying for the moon. Shoppers do not generally wish to pick up the tab for rescuing declining town centres. They go out-of-town to shop and eat because many town centres do not offer the facilities they want. A lot want to shop until they drop from dawn till late under cover with cheap and easy parking. While there are a good number of such out-of-town retail palaces now, that is not to say there should never be another.

They have come to dominate the leisure as well as shopping lives of so many in an amazingly short time. The British, unwisely derided once for a nation of shopkeepers, happen to be brilliant retailers. We are exceptionally good at selling fashion, furnishings, and food. That is why British stores are such a rip-roaring success in Paris, where now not just English chic but English sandwiches are sent on a daily basis. Retailers are also vital to our manufacturing industry. Solemn condemnations of those who run shops for not making things are just silly. If there are no shops, then agriculture and manufacturing have no outlets. Britain has seen greater changes in retailing over the last fifteen years than at any time since the sixteenth century. Then shopping moved from the drama of the market square, goods for sale huddled under butter cross or dispensed from the back of a carrier's cart, into the open-fronted and then covered shops. These dominated British shopping from the 1550s to the 1950s.

Then came the supermarkets. Eventually some moved out-of-town. The very cramming of so many small shops into so many narrow and congested streets, once a great convenience for the pedestrian and bus- or rail-borne out-of-town traveller, suddenly became a great inconvenience to the new car-owning classes. They wanted something else and have got it. The transformation has been extraordinary. While in 1980 only about five per cent of retail sales took place in purpose-built out-of-town developments, it is now about twenty per cent, and by 2020 it will be above a third. While these developments have brought great convenience to those with a car, for people without one, in particular in rural areas, their growth has been more than inconvenient. Sometimes they have sucked the life away from the small village shop, and left village people marooned on the old retail shoreline.

There are three big trends which politicians have to understand about modern shopping. There is the once-a-week big food-shopping trip. Then there is the less regular but still important visit to get some electrical gadget, carpet, furniture, or Do-It-Yourself materials. Both of these are most easily satisfied in many places out-of-town. Thirdly, there is the 'comparison' shopping for smaller, often higher-value goods like accessories, clothing or footwear. Such is usually still the monopoly of a town centre. Added to this, distance is no longer the disadvantage it once was. People sometimes seem quite to relish the trip to the superstore as much as they once relished the trip to the seaside. Retailing is one of Britain's most dynamic industries and it will play a critically important part in shaping how our electors live in the twenty-first century.

Future out-of-town development, where and when it happens, should probably often be in regional centres on a very large scale indeed. These could be lost in grey land of little landscape value with convenient access off some motorway or link road. And then there is a possibility that some very big stores could take another look at city or town centre, where there may be some marshalling yard or derelict land which could be used. But to think, as some do, that this is therefore going to save the traditional city centre is a mistake indeed. There is no clear evidence that the stuffing is automatically put back into the town centre this way.

There is a market town, of which I am fond, which demonstrates this. Fifteen years ago, one of those mega-stores appeared on its very edge. It was just out-of-town, but within walking distance for some. It also provided a country-wide shopping focus for people coming in for miles around. The result is that many of the town centre shops suffered badly exactly as locals predicted. Some of them were not very good or very attractive or particularly cheap. Some whole streets suffered. Steadily their shop fronts closed, slumbered, turned over in ownership on an annual basis, and were let by land agents to be used for charity Christmas cards or by Oxfam shops when empty. Then, little by little, a certain amount of life moved hesitantly back into them. Some people provided exactly that small, specialised, 'comparison shopping' which planning theorists hope will appear in such semi-devastated town centres, providing a perfect foil for the out-of-town shopping centre. One of those new places was a brilliant, specialised cheese shop. It began to flourish. Then, only a year or so ago, just as many have been calling for, another superstore moved bang into the middle of the town. Exactly as planners and politicians of all sorts, shapes and sizes want, it used a piece of old railway land that was derelict, turned neat planning theory into reality. The result? What could be the beginnings of another cycle of decline for some of those specialist shops. The cheese shop has not had quite such a good time since, for the new town centre supermarket does those specialist cheeses too. Brie may not be in quite such a state of grace, slumbering cling-filmed in a cold cabinet rather than being carved on the marble countertop, but if shoppers are in a hurry, and in the supermarket, then it is to hand. So the cheese shop now sells in a semi-wholesale fashion as well as to bigger buyers, restaurants and colleges miles away. This interesting little retail parable is a telling example of how difficult it is to predict – and therefore to plan.

For the twenty-first century, a twin-track approach to planning is the right one. One track is that of guiding new developments where needed or promoted by imaginative retailers to appropriate locations. These are but larger regional places consistent with the motorway and road pattern that is already there. The other track is not to forget both the environmental impact of these new developments as well as the promotion of existing centres. This means making them more attractive to shopping, and that means being safer, cleaner and with some life after dark. To this end, no sensible council should be without its city manager or town manager to think all this through in co-operation with the retailers and restaurateurs so that town life can be supported. A myriad of minor measures are what work here, everything from promoting the use of public buildings in the evening through to a concerted effort to get people to live in the often vacant areas above shops that are such a national waste. It is exceptionally important politically for Tories in the twenty-first century to realise that policy towards the simple shopper is of critical importance to the future viability of our towns and their environment.

In doing this, we must not carry on getting the worst of both worlds, fully satisfying neither conservation nor commerce. Bang in the centre of Rome or Siena absolutely no building is allowed. In any event there people seem, with instinctive taste, to realise that they should not modernise their façades either. None the less, there are planning laws to stop it. In the centre of some mid-west US town by comparison – if you can find that centre – absolutely everything goes. In the twenty-first century it will be necessary to take a much more radical approach to town planning for two reasons. Firstly, to conserve what beauty is there; secondly, to open up the opportunity for the regeneration of many of our towns which, though often containing individual decent buildings, are not historic gems. Look at Somerset for how to get the worst of two worlds. There are Bath and Shepton Mallet. We have been much too timid in Bath. Too much inappropriate development has been allowed there in post-war years, and there is still some going on, chipping away at the fabric and context of a world marvel. It should become a total no-go area.

We have been equally timid with Shepton Mallet, too. There restrictions have been much too tight and there could be much more life if anything were allowed to go. Similar planning regimes are inappropriate for dissimilar places. Lots of people in both places have been allowed to do only half or less of what they wanted to do. It would have been better to have been able to do nothing in Bath and to have gone the whole hog in Shepton. There are in Great Britain and Northern Ireland a number of manifestly heritage cities and towns, the sorts of places that Goering ensured were not bombed. It is time that a national approach was taken to the designation of such places and absolutely no further building allowed in them. People flock to central Rome or central Siena to look, but also to shop, to eat, and to spend money in enormous numbers under exactly such a tight regime. By the same token, in other less architecturally blessed places many more people could be induced back into their slumbering or decaying centres if planning controls were much lighter.

We need to look as hard, also, at the roads that criss-cross our country, and the countryside through which they have been driven. Roads first. We should not have any more motorways. Just as it is true to say that Britain is pretty full, then it is equally true to say that roads create a large amount of new traffic. We should regard our major road network as largely complete. It needs to be well kempt, for endless minor roadworks cause endless delays. Here and there, an additional lane on an overcrowded motorway can be an effective use of land. For example, there is no good reason why the otherwise three-lane M40 from West London to Birmingham should narrow to two lanes at High Wycombe with all the delay and cost that ensues. By and large, however, most new building in the early twenty-first century should be of by-passes around the most congested small towns and long bottlenecks. By-passes can make a significant contribution to environmental matters in two main ways. Less exhaust pollution is created by vehicles travelling at fifty or sixty miles per hour on a by-pass than when barely moving in a village or town jam. Secondly, the quality of life for the residents of those by-passed places shoots up – there is less noise, less pollution, fewer accidents. Steadily and carefully improving trunk roads can have exactly the same effect.

Could a Tory road policy which was restricted like this take all the future environmental and economic strain? The answer is probably not. After all, combined car and freight road traffic is slated to double by 2020, even though vehicle emissions will fall by nearly the same amount. A 1995-built car sends out only about ten per cent of the emissions that its mid-1970s forerunner produced. Thanks to everything from better engine design to well-formulated additives for petrol and diesel, lorries and cars may be cleaner and less noisy now, but there are going to be more and more of them. It is searching for the end of the environmental rainbow to think that railway tracks can ever make all

the difference to dealing with the dilemma that faces us politically. The railways carry about ten per cent of the nation's traffic at
present. Even at their mid-twentieth-century peak, however, they
never got within whistling distance of carrying the people and
goods that roads have done.

Roads have been Britain's main arteries for pedestrian, rider,
horse and cart and now car and lorry. It is easy to say 'put it all
back on the railways', as many a self-styled environmentalist of
the less thoughtful persuasion is inclined to do. If they were right,
then we should do it. The case, alas, does not stand up to examination. Making the case in this less than thoughtful way indeed
damages the very cause it sets out to promote. It is a good thing
that there should be new metro-lines here and there to bring real
rapid-transit comfort to short-distance commuters into, for
example, Manchester or Newcastle. In exactly the same way
new-style trams can transform a lot of inner-city transport. Effective bulk-freight methods can bring business back to the railways
in a variety of ways. There is even something to be said for looking hard at trying to attract more bulk traffic back on to the
limpid waters of some of our canals too, undisturbed as they are
today by much more than the occasional hopeful angler's float.

Being able to put bicycles on trains is a good thing for those
people who like pedal power. High-quality cycling facilities are
already provided in many of our towns. More cycle tracks
between places need to be promoted. (But cyclists need to
remember good manners and consideration for others, just as
much as do the arrogant motorists they often criticise. Their careless car-borne behaviour is neatly matched by the worst of the
pedal-fascists who hurtle through red lights, or across pavements
crowded with walkers – for what else is a pavement but a
'pedestrian track'.) We should take a more integrated approach
to the complex problems of dealing with endemic overcrowding
and delay. But we must also recognise that there are no magic
solutions. The big political challenge for the twenty-first century
is to be found in the management of car-borne and lorry-carried
traffic.

Political and environmental realism means looking at the
almost transcendental influence of the car and truck on late-

twentieth-century society. The face of modern industry has been transformed through the adoption of the 'just-in-time' techniques sensibly copied from the best of Japanese and US manufacturing methods. By exactly the same token, the face of most food retailing has been transformed by just-in-time delivery techniques. This ensures not only that a Waitrose or a Tesco or an Asda get their bags of salad artfully composed from the now commonplace lollo rosso or lamb's lettuce that were only memories of a French or Italian holiday back in the 1970s, but that chilled supermarket food crosses the Channel to the Marks and Spencers stores of Paris on a daily basis. In exactly the same way, being or delivering 'just-in-time' has moulded our personal lives as well, and will do so more and more in the twenty-first century. Lifestyles, recreation, shopping and employment will be ever more moulded by ease of access. Only the car, van and lorry offer this personal and flexible mobility. Most motorists aspire to getting in their cars, not getting out their train timetables, except for commuters or for those longer journeys on business or pleasure, where it is indeed best to let excellent Inter City trains take the strain.

Why should not people enjoy this sort of personal mobility? It is a vital blessing to those like women returners-to-work, full or part time, for example. They can, because they have a car, handle not only family life, the school run and shopping trip, but get to work too – performing each task 'just-in-time'. No car, for many, means no job. The increase in female employment is not just due to changing attitudes and aspirations, education and encouragement by enlightened employees, it has been made possible by mobility. Juggling all those personal pressures is only possible if every domestic and business task can be done just in time too. It may be a little romantic to say that the car is a major engine of female emancipation – but it certainly plays its part.

Social changes like these will greatly influence the politics of the car in the new century. The petrol and diesel which go into them are the lifeblood of personal mobility. They raise good revenue for governments. Big price rises will not necessarily deter the growth in car usage. Price rises caused by governments are never popular as far as fuel is concerned. They do not work either. Look at past oil-price explosions. There was rationing at the time of Suez; but there was not at the time of the later oil-price shock, in the 1970s. Then, petrol went up between a quarter and a third in price. But traffic fell by just two per cent. This is the sort of reduction that might have occurred on the first night of the National Lottery, and nothing like as much as the drop of traffic on the roads that occurs during somnolent Christmas afternoons. Such a price rise for such a small gain would not only be next to useless in practical terms, it would have a devastating effect on people who are totally dependent on their car in a sparsely populated lowland Dorset, or upland Northumberland. There are twenty-two million car owners in voter land. Their reactions to massive petrol-price rises would make the protests about the increases in the VAT on domestic fuel of 1993 and 1994 seem a tea party by comparison. So, if it is hard to imagine another massive increase in motorway building or a huge rise in fuel prices what is to happen next?

It must be the introduction of 'road-pricing'. This is a slightly less lethal but none the less politically very painful nettle which will have to be grasped. Better public transport, however enormously subsidised, will not take away the pain. Good public transport is properly the favoured mode of movement for commuters or those who want to cross cities. For all other journeys the car will always remain the most practical choice for those who can afford it and its fuel. More competition amongst those who want to provide bus or other rapid public transport systems will help. Those living without cars in rural areas need to be helped as well. But for any politician to suggest that public transport can deal with all the problems caused by increased personal mobility in the twenty-first century is again to throw environmental dust into the eyes of our people. The only way to deal with our most congested motorways and trunk roads, and the congestion of our overcrowded city and town centre streets, is to charge for their use. This should be done cautiously and only where necessary. We do not know yet what works; political prudence demands such an approach. It will not be appropriate everywhere. For some jammed small town the answer may lie in anything from a small and well-screened by-pass with a quiet road surface, to banning cars totally over quite an area in their centre. Where this happens, however, residents in such places with cars have their rights like any ancient lights. Their needs must never be forgotten. If it is more difficult to get into a place, there can be multiple benefits. Limiting access into the City of London as an anti-terrorist measure has cut pollution and accidents there. But the traffic thus denied, reduced by a third, now flows through the surrounding boroughs to their frustration.

Pricing for using roads seems, with all its fiendish difficulties, to be the only answer for other areas. Technology is certainly not a problem. Old-fashioned toll booths collecting cash are no part of the solution, and where they exist they are usually part of the problem, causing aggravating delays through queuing for payment or to collect a ticket. Better technology is already there, from smart cards to satellites, which will soon help to control some of London's computerised black cabs from above as they are summoned to a house or office for their next fare.

In asking people to pay to use roads, happily a bit of principle can be conjured up to match the environmental imperative and political expedience of it all. This is because, while it is both wrong and politically impossible to try to take away the freedom of movement that most people now take for granted, it is certainly right to moderate that freedom. In other words, there is something now virtuous in paying for what you once enjoyed more or less free. At a particular time freedom to do something occasionally runs up against the buffers of the problems that you cause for other people while doing it. Yes, you have paid for your car, its fuel, and contributed handsomely to the costs of the roads you use via the tax disc. So, you have earned that freedom, consistent with fine old Tory principle. But the enjoyment of the freedom already carries with it certain responsibilities. These include trying to drive safely, not speeding, avoiding accidents, doing your best not to kill or maim. The responsibility not to damage the lives of others has grown progressively bigger in post-war Britain. In the next century, it will be clear that if you want to travel down this particular motorway or bang into the middle of that particular town you will have to pay for the business opportunity or pleasure trip you are taking. This is in order to share the responsibility of preserving a reasonable lifestyle for an over-crowded country. Having to pay will make most people think twice about going at all, or at least once about going on public transport or perhaps sharing a car.

A good start has been made in this respect in the USA, using their land-gobbling multiple-lane highways. On some of these, one or more of their lanes is reserved for cars for multiple occu-pants. These are just like the familiar bus and taxi lanes of some central London street. A partly widened M25 might do this, for example. But in the USA, and in Hong Kong as well, road pricing is already working well. It certainly is not some neo-liberal eco-nomic template, but rather an essential means of realising the major environmental goal of moderating the motor car. It is gen-erally cheaper, as well as more convenient, to travel by road than by rail. But surprisingly few drivers, even business travellers, take account of the value of their own time in all this. Surprisingly large numbers regard the costs of their car as being fixed, leading to the sometimes irrational decision 'I have a car, therefore I must use it.' So the marginal use of roads must be reduced on environmental and economic grounds. For the costs of conges-tion imposed by any one individual car driver on other road users, from businesses to emergency services, are not borne by them. They should be encouraged to use alternatives if they are available. If they choose not to, then they should pay some con-tribution towards those costs.

Once the decision in principle has been taken, the automatic vehicle technology to collect tolls is easily available today, even before satellite monitoring is fully developed. The car or truck has its own tag. These tags are logged by roadside reader units, fed into a computer system for billing, or as a charge on a pre-paid amount. Such schemes are infinitely flexible, need not apply at weekends, and can be turned on and off at will. For example, they can be used to take account of the need for lively streets at night in our town and city centres. Traffic that is generally rightly dis-couraged from going into town centres in the day, at night is des-perately needed not only for the club, pub and restaurant trade, but to bring some life into streets that suddenly go dead. The car can be a daytime enemy to towns because of its economic and social costs; but it can be a night-time ally of civic life.

Charging takes away freedom, but does leave some choice – albeit costly – to pay the congestion charge if you wish. This is part of an approach to mobility and transport which recognises specifically that as a country we are full to bursting point, that freedom has its limits (you may not enter that part of town by car unless you are a resident) and that it may cost more (if you want to go to that part of town you must pay a congestion charge). There are no magic solutions; only that half solution which tries to manage the traffic to fit the roads, not extend the roads further to take the traffic. What is the point of the freedom of the road if exercising that freedom just takes you into one of the country's neo-perpetual traffic jams? What is the point if you end up with a bit-part on the slow-moving ballet that is the M25, a road which created forty per cent more traffic in the first five years after it was built?

People will not like this new approach to further pricing for travel. But they will bear it in a grumbling and British sort of way. They will endure it best of all if it is introduced little by little, here and there, and if it is made acceptable by some of the 'profit' from the motorist going back into improving roads, and to improving the local environment as well. Motorists who are determined to press on, activate their payment chip as it crosses a motorway entrance road or a city boundary, will be mollified a bit by knowing that some of the 'deterrence money' will go to improving road repairs and conditions. Local residents would be made happier that a tree-topped bank was built next to their by-pass, or the next time that a nearby and noisy motorway was resurfaced, it was done in state-of-the-art, sound-deadening black top (incidentally, in this environmentally concerned age, why cannot this surface be brown top or green top?). Other residents might get contributions to double glazing. Thus motorists will have to be weaned on to schemes they will never love, but may tolerate.

And of course, just because people use cars it does not mean they hate 'the environment'. Many of those car users also want to live in decent surroundings, and that irritation with road pricing may be mitigated by a bit of understanding of why it is being done in the first place. The simple political lesson of this is that if you want to get people to change their behaviour, you had best proceed fairly slowly, and give them something recognisable in return. Then grumbling acceptance is the more likely.

There is much grumbling too in the countryside, though from far fewer throats than townsfolk and the motorists who come from cities. Only a tiny number of our fellow countrymen and countrywomen now live off the land in the countryside. The countryside will never again be where most people live or get their livings. The countryside should, above all else, be the repository of truly Conservative values. Conserving everything from a rural way of life, even some furred or feathered game, should be quintessentially a Tory tenet. The countryside also has always been the place to go in order to collect Tory voters by the trailer load, from country village and market town alike.

The country has, however, suffered a lot of attack. Its real rather than weekending denizens often feel resentful as a result. Rebuilding some of the broken bridges with the countryside, by good policy towards it, may well save a good many Tory seats in future decades. The Conservative Party must not drift too far from its roots. We have long ago lost metropolitan votes by the bucketload, from the days when we used to dominate the politics of a Liverpool or a Manchester. It seems fanciful now to imagine that we would easily re-establish a twenty-first-century hegemony in places like that. By comparison, our grip on the suburb – where most of our people live – seems secure. In the countryside, however, the Liberal Party has proved surprisingly adept in the last twenty years at moving in to organise the brand-new communities that have been tacked on to the edge of many market towns in the shape of new housing estates. They have often deserved the votes they get there in local elections. Tory organisations have not always been as alert to the social and political implications of this rush to the countryside. And the increasing suburbanisation of much of the Conservative Party apparatus has meant that sometimes it has seemed surprisingly divorced from its natural heartland. The countryside could be a surprisingly difficult political battleground in the twenty-first century for the Conservatives, for the first time for a quarter of a millennium.

Why? Because the countryside feels deprived, first of all by losing one by one the facilities which were usually there until the
1960s. Then began to vanish the branch railways, which once
(very expensively) carried not only people but little loads in
guards' vans to be dropped off here and there at rural halts.
Buses took their place for a while, but they became rarer and
rarer, too. This was not just because of the subsidies they needed
but because more and more people used cars instead. Supermarkets with their undoubtedly more convenient and cheaper goods
hoovered up the trade that once went to the village shop. Sub-
Post Offices went the same way in some places because of that
selfsame lack of demand that social change and the motor car
have created. And then there is the two-up-and-two-down cot-
tage where affluent weekenders have squeezed out local youth.

Some of the attacks on rural life are very striking. A motorway
or trunk road crashes through the countryside for the greater
convenience of its users, farming life is disturbed and the very
appearance of the landscape changes. People have been buying
up the countryside, changing it and managing it in a way which
seems particularly 'towny'. More and more of the countryside is
thought of as a museum, designed by and for the convenience
and amusement of town dwellers. Entertainment complexes
squat where once more lordly pursuits held sway. A totally ersatz
landscape of 'visitor centres' and 'experiences' of this or that is
evolving. The countryside, as well as being a bit noisy, always
has been mucky, too. So the whole place is tidied up; people now
go to play golf there in increasing numbers. These new golf
courses bring some money to farmers who have been forced out
of the farming of their poorer-quality land. National Trust green
now covers many of the gates and railings of a once more varie-
gated rurality. Hugh Dalton, the Labour Chancellor, saw the
National Trust then as 'practical socialism in action'. Both
extreme and extremely patronising though this view may have
been, the National Trust is the greatest land owner in our country. It has more members than those who go to an Anglican and
Church of Wales church on a Sunday. It is a sprawling and sometimes nannying institution, self-conceived to the national good,
self-consciously trying to be to the countryside's good, but alas

covering it on occasions with a sort of plastic rurality. As a result of this sort of well-meant bossiness and tidying, some counties can seem now more theme park than countryside.

The people who live there not only feel sometimes deprived and attacked, they also are coming to the view that people no longer understand them. Hunting is a good case in point. Most farmers love the countryside. They understand nature, and appreciate it, even if as always they have a necessarily utilitarian attitude to the land and to the animals that they rear on it. Happy animals produce more milk, better meat. Most countryfolk like wild life, are often naturally conservation minded as well. Far from all farmers or farm workers shoot, fish, pursue the hare on foot or on horseback, or hunt the fox and deer. Yet for field sportsmen and non-field sportsmen alike in the countryside, the threat to hunting is a potent issue. Set aside the double standards that are apparently there amongst those people who eat meat with relish, yet criticise those who pursue meat on the wing or four legs. Forget as well the double standards of those, like the Labour Party, who love to have it both ways. They want the votes of the nation's six million fishermen yet are in full cry after the hare courser, or the huntsmen of deer and fox. The reality is that many of the unhunting countryfolk rather fear that all of this is symbolic of the fact that 'they' do not understand, want to interfere, are the thin end of the wedge about to be driven deeper into rural life.

Now, in the House of Commons, whether or not an MP is for or against field sports is treated reverently as one of those 'issues of conscience', just like whether or not to take life at the end of a hangman's noose, or at the point of an abortionist's instrument. No whip interferes, though you have to be brave to vote for field sports in the Labour Party or independent minded if you are a member of the Liberal Party. But there are quite a number of Conservatives who are opposed to hunting as well, representing usually urban or suburban constituencies. The issue will come back to challenge them again and again. They must vote as they will, but they must also realise that to vote against country sports is seen by countrymen and countrywomen as a vote against their way of life. The cumulative electoral consequences could be severe. Country people suspect that if the anti-hunting wedge is driven in, then thereafter the anti-country feeling will grow deeper still. Soon there will be animal welfare officers or whatever on every farm, they fear, and there will be more and more incomprehending urban interference.

In 1995, animal welfare remains at the front of the catwalk of fashionable concerns. There is much agitation over calves raised for veal. It is hard for calves bound for veal production in Holland to be sent on the hoof any more by ship. As a result they sometimes travel by air. Over there they are popped into crates, fed up, and soon slaughtered (they would not have lived at all if there was not a demand for their meat). Swiftly back come the choicest bits of many of their young carcasses bound for Britain's restaurants (often by the very ships which were judged unsuitable for them in their short lives). Decent conditions for animals on the farm – and while being moved – are important. But demonstration politics, however well motivated, as over the issue of how veal calves are moved, seem to be part of the late-twentieth-century disease of self-deception. The essence of the matter is that we kill vast numbers of animals for the pleasure of eating them, sometimes by hunting, but usually in the abattoir. Any meat eater who does not like the idea of 'chasing animals for pleasure', but who tucks into a beef steak or a lamb chop with relish, really should pop along to an abattoir and see what it is like. Despite the substantial and rightful increases in animal welfare this century, look into the eyes of the beasts queuing there and you will see that they know that something rather unusual is about to happen. It is a self-serving sham to pretend that things are otherwise.

So, to think if we had the countryside patrolled by a lot of supernannies that compassion would thus be better served is totally wrong. Artificially induced compassion like this is one of the more disturbing of urban human failings. If applied in the countryside, it will damage what urbankind want to go to see. And if too many Tories conspire with that process – too easily driven by the piles of campaigning postcards and faxes on their desks – not only will we lose votes, but some of our deepest roots will be permanently damaged. Despite the valiant attempts of local Tories, we have been driven from or evacuated vast tracts of Scotland, Wales and Northern England. We have lost our inner city bases completely. However well we are dug into the suburbs, we should not gratuitously offend our rural heartlands as well. Conservatives should never give in to moral terrorism that characterises single-issue campaigns to ban things. They should rather strive to protect the ancient interests of minorities, and not needlessly intervene in moral disagreements between different groups of citizens on this or any other issue.

One of the most pressing imperatives for the new century is to protect, but not mummify the living countryside and those that make their living from it. The countryside needs Tory advocacy as well as understanding by urban and suburban Tories as to what makes it tick. There seems, alas, no other way of doing this except by creating a Ministry of the Countryside. Why use the word 'alas'? Because usually the cry for a new Ministry especially for this or that is a despairing one and can have desperate results. It is extraordinary to recall that for a while in the 1980s there was in the Department of the Environment a Junior Minister charged with being, *inter alia*, the Minister for children's play. Such agitation for new Ministers is usually the mark of a brain-dead politician who can think of nothing else, or of one who seeks a soon-to-be-forgotten media sound-bite of the 'Mr X calls for' variety. We should abolish the numbers of Ministries, not add to them. But the need to have a (small) Ministry to be the advocate for the rural world that we are in danger of first ossifying and then destroying, is pressing.

Consistent with the desirable style of a thoroughly modern Ministry, it should be concerned with two things only. First policy; and then oversight of the agencies that already exist and will be brought together under one roof, to ensure that they are as benevolent to the countryside and its economy as possible. Happily, the overall number of Ministries would not be added to, as a renamed Ministry including responsibility for agriculture, fishers and food should be joined by the relevant bits extracted from a rather tubby Department of the Environment, under one Ministerial head. The chance should be taken en route to suppress a junior Minister or two. But the real opportunity would be to bring those looking after rural and coastal interests under the same roof as those who have the job of conserving countryside and seashore. The view from the Whitehall village these days is through urban-tinted glasses. The countryside needs at least one voice to try to keep the balance. From time to time jibes of 'producer capture' have been hurled in the direction of the Ministry of Agriculture, Fisheries and Food by those who see that Ministry taken over by farmers and fishermen. That has been a fair charge in the past. If that is the case it is equally fair to point to the 'invader capture' by those who wish not just to come out from town into the countryside, but to imbue it with urban values as well.

How we live by 2020 is going to remain very varied, despite the social levelling brought about by mass communication and mass entertainment. The Tory view of this must be realistic, balancing the pressures on space with the realism that these pressures are there precisely because people have created them by the way that they want to live, make money, and enjoy themselves. So planning will always have to be there. It should be as indicative and light-touch as possible. But the dreams with which Tories have sometimes flirted, of letting most things rip, face not only the electoral wrath of Nimbyists, they fly in the face of the crowded reality of life. It certainly is possible to have much lighter-touch planning in our less beautiful city and town centres to keep them ticking over, yet by comparison it may be necessary to have stricter controls accompanying a deeper understanding of some of our most beautiful countryside. There can be, and should be, no master plan, however. None the less, to make life better will call for huge national effort. There will be four or possibly five general elections held by 2020. As always, during those general election campaigns, the wealth of the nation, and the protection of its citizens, the health of its people, the education of its children and the rest will be to the forefront. But in addition to these eternal political preoccupations – and running throughout the next twenty-five years – must be two consistent threads for the Tories. The first is the betterment of the living conditions of our people in deprived urban areas. The second is to resist the potential and final swamping of the countryside. In the case of urban deprivation, it is a matter of finding the will, the ways, and the cash, for renewal. In the case of countryside it is rather to try to fend off pressures to develop or, sometimes worse, the pressures to impose the views of the urban majority on the rural minority. These ends will only be half met if they are left half specific. And they will never be achieved at all if the focus for renewal or of conservation leaves the community out of the equation as it did through most of the latter half of the twentieth century. If we wish to dominate the politics of the twenty-first century, then Tories must think deep and long about political things to come on these further horizons.

Yet all the time, crowding in daily on government, are events, while looming over rather nearer horizons are the clouds and challenges of the next general election. Equally inevitable is the traditional British preoccupation, when that election is called, with the record of the party in power. This cruel but proper concern with things that have been done will be all the more testing when it is concentrated through the prism of experience of more than sixteen continuous years of Tory governance. This may, however, be more frightening to contemplate in prospect than it need be in reality. There is no iron political law which can guarantee perpetual office and power for any one party, however fresh and thoughtful it may suddenly manage to be. But equally neither is there some parallel law that says just because a party has ruled for a record span of years, then either ennui on behalf of the electors, or a failure of will on behalf of the elected, will lead to decimation.

It is always right to be fearful of the effects of division leading to political meltdown, the chance of being out of power for a generation, and so on. But these things are not all written in the political runes. The challenge simply gets bigger as each election comes round. Opposition must be duly challenged too. This book has concentrated on the Tories, but, in looking at how to meet the challenges of some of the key issues at general elections, it is necessary to bring the alternatives into just as sharp focus.

For Labour, least said, soonest elected is undoubtedly the best strategy or tactic. It is exactly what I would be advising the

Tories to do for as long as possible in the run-up to a general election, if the tables were turned, and we had been the natural party of opposition since 1979.

To steal the most wearable or fashionable political clothes offered by the Tories, and hum Tory-derived and cosy-sounding tunes about the family or security in the streets or the need for high educational standards, may be flattering for us as a Party as it is logical for Labour. But as always in election campaigns the properly sharp questioning of an opposition about exactly what does that mean, how much does this cost, and how will the other be paid for, will blow away much of the insubstantial presentational cover from Labour, just as much as it will focus on what we have done.

There are, however, a trio of tasks which have to be successfully completed in order to persuade a late-twentieth-century electorate to give the Tories a fifth term, and carry us over the watershed while in power, into the next millennium. Firstly, we need to explain where we wish to be on the further horizons, giving a clear sense of strategy over a long period. Secondly, as always, the responses to the more immediate challenges of the actual general election campaign must be appealing. Thirdly, we must also lay out clearly what we have done to the good of the country and to improve the condition of its people.

Electors are not as stupid as many political commentators and public opinion survey companies treat them. Most may be worried about the now, many about the next year, a few about the next century. 'What have you done for me recently?' and 'What are you going to do for me next?' may be immemorial electoral ripostes to the request 'Please vote for me'. But the record does mean something. Their condition, and that of the country in which they live, are greatly improved from sixteen years ago. The benchmark represented by how we were in 1979 is very different from the new benchmark which the Tories have set in 1995. The most thoughtful of voters with long memories will reflect on whether or not continuation of the then Labour government's policies current in 1979 would have produced such beneficial results. Few, however un-Tory they feel now, are likely to say yes. So the reiteration of the Tory record should not be found just in a litany of little lists of the perceived successes of this or that Department. Rather it should be in the setting of new benchmarks for the electorate – how we were then, how we are now – to act as a touchstone from which to express the continuity of Conservatism. If change is often our political friend then continuity should always be our firmest foundation in fighting elections.

If a minority of our thoughtful voters reflect on the past, the majority also ponder their feelings about the present. Too many politicians believe that these days the electors just wish to 'feel good'. The chances of electoral success for the Tories will be closely calibrated to the intensity of that feeling, the argument runs. In other words, that the fructification of the pound sterling in each person's pocket is the sole determining factor that will decide who controls the Houses of Parliament. People are not so easily bought, however. 'Feeling secure' and 'feeling right' are suddenly now just as important as feeling well-off or, for that matter, feeling fearful about what the opposition might do if they got the chance.

The record shows this to be true. The last sixteen years have seen successive Tory administrations asking electors to be realistic and responsible about the problems that have to be dealt with – and these were very often very uncomfortable; they have not just given people the chance to feel good. Of course, electors have liked their generally rising disposable incomes, newly purchased council houses or shares, that second car in the drive where thirty years ago there was none. But they have also, when asked and after much earnest debate, accepted some very difficult policies which were not about making them feel good, but rather doing the right thing.

At home, the record shows that in tackling trades union reform, which was vital to restoring our economic competitiveness, the public did not support us because it made them feel good. They often had mixed feelings, and more than a little sympathy with the miners, for example during the long haul of that historic strike, but they thought that these policies were responsible and right. With defence, the story is the same. The great battles over whether or not to have Cruise land-based nuclear strike weapons in Europe, the dockside sit-ins at the Trident nuclear bases in Scotland, the protests of the Greenham Common female peace corps, are fading into folk memory, as a result of the electors thinking that an uncomfortable defence policy was also the right defence policy. It has indeed brought peace. Tory policy on defence at home and abroad was successful not because it was about making people feel good, but because it persuaded people that it was best for the country to act responsibly.

The same is true in the case of the economy, with the steady early-1980s withdrawal of subsidies from loss-making utilities or manufacturing industries like British Steel or British Leyland. It was never a comfortable policy, to promote long-overdue structural change in these and other industries, thus seeing men and women lose their jobs with all the pain that no euphemisms about 'down-sizing' or 'de-layering' can ever ease. The policy was eventually accepted as responsible and right in the longer-term interests of the efficient economic workings of our country in a fiercely competitive world. Concentration on persuading people to feel right about proposed policies, as well as feeling good, should now be a central strategy in an era of emerging post-material politics.

There are few outside of monastery or nunnery walls who would not like to be better off next year than this year. But there can be equally few who wish to see a return to the cycles of boom and bust that have been endemic in economic management in the United Kingdom since the late 1950s. Tories contributed a spectacular example of this in the mid-1980s, as the record uncomfortably shows. So the engineering of pre-election booms, as opposed to responsible tax cuts when economic circumstances allow (which are a proper part of our long-term aims), would be greeted entirely understandably with a 'feel cynical' response by the electorate now. Instead, they would think that they were responsible and right if they are successfully persuaded that this time around inflation is under permanent control, that steady growth is there to bestow improving incomes and improving social and environmental spending. They have to be persuaded that the aspiration to break out of the cycle of unsustainable (and deeply immoral) boom followed by counter-inflationary bust really is deliverable and that it is right to continue present policy.

Electors will feel responsible and right if they are persuaded of this by our record and our rhetoric. At the same time, they will of course test hard the likelihood of Labour being able to deliver the same end-of-century economic stability. They will ask if Labour will take the right or responsible decisions about inflation, ponder whether they can meet the costly election pledges that are bound to come along without unsustainable increases in public expenditure, reflect on how much they will be forced to give in to the demands of the unions. In the 1980s, blue collar workers were like gorillas in the forest, suffering from a shrinking habitat. In the mid-1990s, unlike the mid-1970s, the most powerful of those that remain are now no longer the miners or the car workers, but the publicly paid salariat of nurses and social workers and lecturers and teachers to whom Labour look for support. That is why it is as important for Tories to be honest about the right approach in the next sixteen years as we were so straightforward about the necessity of keeping nuclear weapons or breaking the unholy hold of some of the manual trade unions in the sixteen years after 1979.

At the same time, there is a more difficult message to promote for many in an ever-widening 'middle class'. A substantial number of these electors are natural Tories. For them, as for government, the uncomfortable message is that insecurity over unemployment is going to be a fact of life for many over the coming decades, let alone the coming years. Changes in white-collar employment patterns, the extraction of layer upon layer of middle management – driven by the need for ever greater competitiveness – will mean that many have to get used to the endemic job insecurity that is part and parcel of, for example, the life of a Member of Parliament or Minister. No government on earth can fly in the face of these structural changes. What a Tory government must do is to be honest about the limits of its room for action, while ensuring that the social security benefits are adequate and the re-education opportunities readily available for all of those who want them, as they search for new work.

This difficult message must be conveyed amidst equally endemic and politically exhausting debate about Europe, and especially its size, nature and direction. That discussion will rage and blaze right on through the next election until after the turn of the millennium. What is clear now is that the Labour Party is deeply 'Europhile', not so much from belief in some European vision as from its inherent instinct as the Party of bureaucracy and regulation to be drawn to the bigger and better bureaucrats and regulators of Brussels, as inevitably as a moth to a flame. Labour are not prepared to argue Britain's case in Britain. In Brussels they would become as centralist as the Belgians. As the reformed fine-print men and women of the European Union, the Tory view should continue to be informed by the national interest, sovereignty, and making what is already there amongst the twelve countries work a great deal better before anything else ever happens. Above all else, the British view should seek always to persuade the European Union to do economic things for purely economic reasons, political things for purely political reasons. If there are to be advances on defence, then those advances should be driven by security and nothing else.

Given these clear economic and European imperatives, on the home front, much of the battle will be joined on the basics; on the community; and on the environment. Firstly, 'backing the basics' means continuing as we have with some success to respond to the concerns of electors about their homes, their children's education or health, their worry about going out at night to find their possessions stolen or cars vandalised when they return. Labour is likely to do nothing further to extend home ownership. It is certain to fudge the drive for higher educational standards at all levels, either by suppressing the information that makes it possible to judge improvements or else by 'adjusting' examination results for 'socio-economic-ethnic' reasons until they are reduced to meaningless tables. Professional trade union pressures would drive education and health policy again, with disastrous effects on the health service reforms and the greater efficiencies which are shortening both waiting lists and waiting times. And of course Labour criminal justice policy is likely to be Scandinavian in its style and dimensions.

For the Tories, it is critical to continue the drive to make home ownership available for more and more people. It has been clearly recognisable as a cornerstone of Tory social policy since 1951.

We have held power for thirty-four of the last forty-four years since then, partly because of the appeal of owning your own home. Since 1979, we have extended the numbers of people who own their own flat or house from just over half to over two thirds of the population. This has been of immense social benefit to families. It has provided them with security and a repository of wealth to pass on to their children. Wider home ownership has been of immense help to the Treasury, too, in saving the cost of the provision of rented housing. Above all we have helped people to get what they want, which is always a good thing. At the same time it has had the moral benefit of also giving them a stake in the community, when social bonds have never been looser. We forget our successes on the home front like this at our electoral peril.

We must also continue to raise the sights of parents and young people, giving them the best educational start in life so they can have anchors for it in future. Educational standards are going up. After the turmoil which always accompanies major changes, all the evidence is that regular testing and the publication of the results of examinations is increasingly popular with parents as it always has been with employers. 'No new educational policies for five years' has been promised in response to the sometimes understandable complaints about pace and implementation of educational change. That makes the effective completion of existing policies all the more vital for our international economic, and domestic political, success. Explanation of the fruits of the health reforms, which are becoming clearer by the year, will produce the same beneficial results.

Most testing of all to handle is the sense of personal insecurity people develop in the face of perceived threats of crime that parallels the insecurity many feel about their jobs. In this, as with the difficult political issue of employment, honesty about how to deal with crime is the best policy. There is indeed a lot of crime about, despite a recent and welcome dip in its recorded levels. It is vital to recognise that in the long term anti-crime policies must begin with the young, and that criminal prevention must move centre stage now in order to join the other important recent initiatives. But, the electors may cynically say, while we wait for the long term to turn up, they may be burgled or beaten up. So in the short term the concentration must be on ensuring that detection is more likely, that punishments are tougher. 'Tough on crime, tough on the causes of crime' has been Labour's uninterrupted mood music for too long. During the hard-edged arguments of a general election campaign, it will be seen to have been sung to an empty score.

As with the basics, so also with the community. This is a cosy phrase which resonates with many. It is political booty which Labour would like to capture and ride off with rapidly over the electoral horizon. Just like their meaningless mantra over crime, that cosy feeling given by Labour to the essentially nice word community would turn out in practice to mean the reinvention of big, over-bureaucratic government leading to a new if more softly packaged totalitarianism. Seeking socialism without the loony left, Civic Labourism would certainly mean a return to bureaucratic statism, bent on a renewed late-twentieth-century attempt to promote a socially ordered world, exactly as was tried after the Second World War. This time around, 'regulationism', with which Tories have to struggle hard enough when in government, would be unbound. The new Labour world would be perfectly harmonised, hygienic, safe, every element neatly labelled and run by a new-style burgeoning salariat, political correctness made flesh. It would also be perfectly dreadful, a 'Nurseryland' Britain.

Civic Conservatism by comparison is an appealing and potent alternative, much more in tune with the times, matching ownership with duty. Rights and opportunities to run local communities, in the Conservative vision, should be given more and more to local people not to more and more officials. Personal sovereignty means as much as national sovereignty to most of our citizens. To them, the seminar room phrase 'smaller government' signifies getting government off your back, and government letting you keep more of your own money.

Thirdly, in an age when electors wish to feel right as well as to feel good, environmentalism, having caught its breath during the recent recessionary years, will roar back on to the political agenda. There are already clear signs of a second wave of post-materialist concern for the environment which quite matches that of the prosperous mid-1980s. Electors rightly care much more about the state of their surroundings. They are concerned as much about tackling urban dereliction as they are about protecting the countryside or over getting control of the traffic problems that so blight the most crowded and prosperous islands on earth that are the United Kingdom.

The Tory years have done an enormous amount to improve the environment of our people and their surroundings as broadly understood, everything from promoting animal welfare and the performing arts to preserving the sites of special scientific interest and back. At the same time, we have resisted the worst and most intrusive fetters on personal freedom that a cellophane and shrink-wrapped Labour approach to environmental, let alone personal and community, issues would produce. For it is not just in the single-minded promotion of 'feeling good' that success is to be found. It is also there in a clear statement of a broadly successful record when married to an equally clear new agenda for the years ahead that recognises the importance of our cultural identity – all underwritten by a steely determination to do right. This is the only approach to the next election to come. It is vital, as well, in order to meet the rapidly changing politics of the new century.